D1601489

EQUALITY

The Impossible Quest

CASTALIA HOUSE

NON-FICTION

SJWs Always Lie: Taking Down the Thought Police by Vox Day
Cuckservative: How "Conservatives" Betrayed America
     by John Red Eagle and Vox Day
On the Existence of Gods by Dominic Saltarelli and Vox Day
Equality: The Impossible Quest by Martin van Creveld
A History of Strategy by Martin van Creveld
4th Generation Warfare Handbook
     by William S. Lind and LtCol Gregory A. Thiele, USMC
Four Generations of Modern War by William S. Lind
On War: The Collected Columns of William S. Lind 2003-2009
Transhuman and Subhuman by John C. Wright
Between Light and Shadow: The Fiction of Gene Wolfe, 1951 to 1986
     by Marc Aramini
Compost Everything by David the Good
Grow or Die by David the Good
Astronomy and Astrophysics by Dr. Sarah Salviander

MILITARY SCIENCE FICTION

There Will Be War Vol. X ed. Jerry Pournelle
There Will Be War Vol. IX ed. Jerry Pournelle
Riding the Red Horse Vol. 1 ed. Tom Kratman and Vox Day

SCIENCE FICTION

Somewhither by John C. Wright
Awake in the Night Land by John C. Wright
City Beyond Time: Tales of the Fall of Metachronopolis by John C. Wright
Back From the Dead by Rolf Nelson
QUANTUM MORTIS A Man Disrupted by Steve Rzasa and Vox Day
QUANTUM MORTIS A Mind Programmed
     by Jeff Sutton, Jean Sutton, and Vox Day
Victoria: A Novel of Fourth Generation War by Thomas Hobbes

FANTASY

Iron Chamber of Memory by John C. Wright
The Book of Feasts & Seasons by John C. Wright
A Throne of Bones by Vox Day
Summa Elvetica: A Casuistry of the Elvish Controversy by Vox Day
The Altar of Hate by Vox Day

AUDIOBOOKS

A History of Strategy, narrated by Jon Mollison
Cuckservative, narrated by Thomas Landon
Four Generations of Modern War, narrated by William S. Lind
Grow or Die, narrated by David the Good
Extreme Composting, narrated by David the Good
A Magic Broken, narrated by Nick Afka Thomas

EQUALITY

The Impossible Quest

MARTIN VAN CREVELD

Equality

Martin van Creveld

Published by Castalia House
Kouvola, Finland
www.castaliahouse.com

Cover Design: Christopher Kallini
Cover Image: *The Danaides*, John William Waterhouse (1903)

ISBN: 978-952-7065-52-5

Contents

Introduction

The histories of justice and liberty have often been written. Not so that of equality, which, so far has failed to find its proper biographer. There seems to be no equivalent to Plato's *On Justice* (better known as *The Republic*) or to John Stuart Mill's *On Liberty*. That is strange, for equality is quite as important as the other two. Never has this been more true than in our own day. On one hand, we are inundated by volumes that warn us of the dangers of growing socio-economic gaps and by movements that protest against those gaps.[1] On the other, equality's opposite, discrimination, has not only become taboo but is being used as a lever for all kinds of social reforms, credible and incredible alike.

In fact, so closely linked are the three concepts as to be inseparable. Where there is no equality there can be neither justice nor liberty. On the other hand, equality itself is not without its dangers. Should it be pushed too far, it can easily reach the point where it limits, or even eliminates, both liberty *and* justice. Most people will agree that, for both individuals and communities to be able to lead "the good life," a proper mixture of all three qualities is needed. Yet submitting a comprehensive plan as to precisely what the mixture should be like is beyond the powers of the present author. Instead, while keeping the other members of the trio in mind, this volume will trace the history of equality from the earliest times. This includes its origins, its development, the various forms it has taken, its benefits and its costs.

On the face of it equality is a simple concept—what could be simpler? In reality, nothing is further from the truth. To realize this fact, all one has to do is to follow the tortuous phraseology of Sun Yat Sen, the great early twentieth-century Chinese revolutionary and reformer. Sun Yat Sen received parts of his education in Hawaii and British Hong Kong and he traveled widely. Returning home, he realized that the idea went too far for his people. Especially problematic were the members of the urban, better-educated, classes who formed his principal audience. While they were the only ones who might understand what he was talking about, he well realized that they would almost certainly feel threatened by it. Hence he did what he could to reassure them. Adopting democracy, he said, would lead to political equality. Everyone would have the right to elect and to be elected. But that was as far as things would go. The traditional Chinese system of "true equality," meaning the kind that placed the "sage" on top of the social ladder and the "dullard" and "inferior man" at the very bottom would remain intact.[2] In Sen's more popular work, *Three Principles for the Chinese People*, equality is hardly mentioned at all.

There is equality before God and there is equality here on earth. There is natural equality and there is the kind of equality that human society creates. Some people even want to extend equality to animals and plants as well. There is equality of body and there is equality of mind. There is economic equality and there is equality before the law. There is civic equality and there is political equality and there is equality of opportunity and there is equality in death. There is equality among individuals and there is equality among groups, nations, and races. In Aldous Huxley's *Brave New World* this truth is held to be self-evident that men (and women, though Huxley does not say so) are equal in respect to their bodies' physico-chemical makeup but in no other way.[3] The list goes on and on. That is why equality is impossible to define—and also why, instead of engaging on a hopeless attempt to do so, I have chosen to write its history instead.

To begin at the beginning, is there any sense in which equality is "natural?" If not, how when, where, and why did the idea develop? What forms has it assumed? What role has it played in human history? How did theory and practice interact? Are we getting closer to it? What is the promise? What is the threat? To answer these questions, we shall start in the animal kingdom. However, we shall not take on the whole field of zoology. Does it really make sense to compare ourselves to scorpions or goldfish? Instead we shall limit the discussion to mammalians and our closest relatives, the primates. Next, something must be said about the simplest known human communities, commonly called band societies or, referring to others with a slightly stronger form of organization, tribes without rulers. It will be shown that, even among them, both in and out of the family, equality is far from absolute. As the name implies, chiefdoms, which until not so long ago represented the most common form of political organization on earth, were much less egalitarian than tribes without rulers. Indeed there is good reason to believe that, both before and long after modern imperialists introduced them to the concept, the populations of most chiefdoms could not even grasp the meaning of the term.

The earliest known people who consciously set out to build polities based on some kind of equality were the ancient Greeks from about 650 BC. Why, when, and how they came up with the idea remains obscure. The experiment, which took several different forms, was made on a relatively small scale. In all, it lasted for about three centuries. For almost two thousand years it remained almost the only one of its kind. Yet it has never been forgotten, and its impact on the modern world has been enormous beyond measure. Hardly a month goes by without a book being published on the way it was reached and how it worked. That is why it will be treated in some detail. Both the system's advantages and its disadvantages, as presented by contemporary and subsequent critics, will be discussed.

As the onset of the Hellenistic Age ended the independence of the Greek city-states, the curtain closed again. Starting with Republican Rome, in most polities, indeed, before the second half of the seventeenth century equality was not even present as an ideal, let alone as a reality. To the extent that it dared raise its head it was regarded as a threat, a mortal threat even, to the foundations of the social order. Any attempts to bring it about had to be, and often were, stamped out by the most brutal available means. This was true both in centralized polities, i.e empires of every kind, and in decentralized feudal ones. Indeed it could be argued that, whatever the difference between the two systems, inequality was precisely what they had in common.

Such being the case, wherever these organizations existed, and as long as they lasted, equality's appearances could only be isolated, temporary, and/or imaginary. Especially in Europe, there were quite some uprisings, revolts and wars whose declared objective was to establish some sort of equality or at least to decrease inequality. Practically all of these experiments were defeated within a matter of days, weeks, or months. However, as in George Orwell's *Animal Farm*, even the few that held out for a while tended to fail in their purpose. Often the leaders, having seized power, lost no time in making themselves much more equal than their followers. Even when they did not, they usually found themselves constrained to resort to force, meaning unequal power, so as to maintain the equality they themselves had created. As a result, something approaching equality could be found mainly in the monasteries—not only European ones—on one hand and utopias on the other. Both will be explored here, albeit only fairly briefly.

The honor, and a great one it is, of making the first attempt to devise a political order based on the assumption that everyone is born equal and that no one has any more rights than anyone else belongs to Thomas Hobbes in *Leviathan* (1651). From him it passed to various Enlightenment thinkers who fervently hoped to establish equality inside their own polities. But there is a difference. Hobbes' citizens were equal in the sense that none of them had any rights at all, a situation he saw as essential on the way to achieving his overriding goal, i.e. the maintenance of law and order. His successors, to the contrary, saw equality as a prerequisite to liberty and justice. They wanted upper-class privileges to be abolished so middle-class people like themselves could forge ahead as fast, and as far, as possible. That is why their version of it has often been called liberal equality. One and all, they would have approved of what the well-known late nineteenth-century Cambridge historian, Lord Acton, had to say: "power [meaning, a situation where some people exercise unequal power over others] tends to corrupt, and absolute power corrupts absolutely."[4]

At this point, some might argue that the plan of the book is too Euro-centric. It is true that one may also find occasional dreams of equality in other parts of the world. Some of them will be briefly dealt with. To repeat, however, before 1776, and putting aside the monasteries and the revolts, the only place where they led to the establishment of real polities, even such as were relatively small scale and only lasted for about three centuries, was ancient Greece. Hobbes himself was a European (never mind that the British remain reluctant to admit that fact). So were the remaining prophets of liberal equality. Thanks to colonialism, which paradoxically created as much inequality as has ever existed at any time and place, that kind of equality spread from Europe and European-settled North America to other parts of the world. As one of my teachers used to say, for centuries past people in the so-called "developing world" did not know they were equal. But by the 1960s, and thanks above all to the invention of the little transistor radio, the message had reached them—with a vengeance.

It is also necessary to discuss equality as understood by various kinds of socialists and communists. Having originated in the nineteenth century, those twin movements played a huge role in the twentieth. Though communism has all but disappeared, some forms of socialism continues to make its influence felt in many countries and may even be on the rise. Nor can we leave out the question of race. As the title of one of the first important works devoted to the purpose, Arthur de Gobineau's *Essay on the Inequality of the Human Races* (1853–1855) indicates, racism was specifically meant to prove that some people were superior to others. That the attempt was unsuccessful, scientifically speaking, is hardly worth saying. Yet paradoxically the movement that adopted racial doctrine and used it as the theoretical basis to perpetrate perhaps the most horrible crimes in history had a lot to say about equality, too. To ignore that fact is to miss both the nature of National-Socialism and some of the reasons that made it as popular as, for a while, it was. It also means passing over some of the most important developments in the post-1945 world.

A separate chapter must examine the equality of women as well as that of other minorities such as the sexually different and the disabled. Here it is undeniable that some progress has been made. The trouble is that these "minorities" have now grown into a majority. Increasingly, society is treating the minority, which in developed Western countries consists of able-bodied heterosexual white males, as if they were less than equal. As so often in history, equality for some can only be achieved by discriminating against all the rest. We must also explore the way advancing science and technology may impact the future of equality. Finally, there must be a chapter about equality in the face of the greatest equalizer of all: namely, death and its aftermath.

Planning to write a history of liberty, the aforementioned Lord Acton had to give up because the subject, at any rate in the way he proposed to treat it, was simply too large. Surely equality is no less so. Reading everything that has been written about the subject is far beyond the ability of any individual, however industrious and however long his or her life-expectancy. Yet once the idea had come to me, I simply *wanted* to write this book. In fact it almost started writing itself. Following the example of Thucydides in his *History of the Peloponnesian War* and of most historians, Lord Acton included, until the second half of the nineteenth century, I could have chosen not to provide extensive documentation. I might also have decided to do the opposite, which presumably would have led to twenty-five pages of footnotes for each sentence. In the end I compromised. I tried to read as much as I thought was needed to understand the material sufficiently well for the purpose at hand and to present my main sources in the approved scholarly manner. I can only hope I have succeeded.

Chapter 1

Whence Inequality?

However much some people may resent the fact, in nature inequality and not equality seems to be the rule. Sticking to mammals, two great groups must be distinguished. Some live in prides, meaning some females, their young, and one or more males. That, for example, is the case among lions. Prides lead separate lives and do not often come into contact with each other. Inside each pride, it is the males that dominate. However, since the males of each pride must compete with outsiders who try to take their place, inside each of them there is considerable turnover. As a result, a regular hierarchy and dominance are not established among them. Dominance is even less important in species whose male members spend most of their time on their own, as orangutans do.[1]

Many other species live in groups or herds that include a fair number of individuals of both sexes. They are, to misuse Aristotle's saying, "social animals." Here the situation is very different. Dominance and its opposite, subordination, are ubiquitous. Species whose life is based on inequality include Old World monkeys, wolves, red deer, baboons, marmosets, macaques, vervet mon-

keys, bison, and rats. Both six-ton elephants and tiny mice are on
the list. To the extent that the living arrangements man has created
for them allow, so are domesticated animals such as cattle. Furthermore, horned cattle tend to dominate dehorned members of
the same species.[2] They thus provide experimental proof of the role
played by physical force and the ability to inflict damage as well as
the animals' ability to understand these things and act accordingly.

Some veterinarians believe that neutering a horse or a dog, or de-
clawing a cat, will cause the animal to suffer through loss of status.[3]
Within every species dominance translates itself into better access to
food as well as sexual partners. In other words, the needs and claims
of some receive priority over those of others. Last, but not least, the
laws of heredity mean that animals are likely to have offspring similar
to themselves. While individuals change, inequality as such tends
to be self-perpetuating. It prevails not only at any one moment but
over time as well. Seen from an evolutionary perspective, that is
probably why it has come into the world.

As we shall see, among humans inequality probably had its origin when some people convinced themselves, and succeeded in con-
vincing others, that they were closer to the spirits, or gods. Other
factors involved are descent from some particularly prominent an-
cestor(s); special rights allegedly conferred some time ago (often,
the older the better); and wealth. Differences in physical force, intelligence, aggression, courage, health, age and sex can also make
themselves felt. Animals are simpler in this respect. As far as we are
able to judge they do not have gods. They do not treasure the memory of ancestors, or acquire formal "rights," or own property that
can be kept or given away. Even if they did, they would be unable
to leave any of those things to their offspring. Still, within any given
species—here I shall not deal with interspecies relations—some in-

dividuals are male, others female. Some are in the prime of life, big, strong, healthy, and lusty. Others are old, or young, or small and/or weak, or suffer from injuries or from sickness. Some are courageous, aggressive, and intelligent, others less so. These differences translate themselves into dominance or, if one wishes, inequality.

Inside each group competition for the top positions, and thus for the advantages that inequality confers, is keen. Individuals who try to upset the existing pecking order may, should they fail, suffer severely. Nevertheless, barring extreme shortages of food and/or sexual partners as well as overcrowding, the fact that some animals dominate and that others acknowledge that dominance does not prevent the members of most groups from living together in reasonable harmony. To the contrary, it is perhaps the most important reason why they can do so without tearing one another to pieces all of the time. It provides a shortcut to deciding who gets how much of what, and when. Inequality, in other words, is precisely the principle upon which their social life is based and is made possible.

Sir Solly Zuckerman (1904–1993) is often seen as the father of modern primatology and the person who did more than anyone else to put it on a scientific basis. As he wrote, "every ape or monkey enjoys a position within a social group that is determined by the interrelation of its own dominant characteristics and those of its fellows. The degree of its dominance determines how far its bodily appetites will be satisfied."[4] Social relationships based on dominance prevail both inside the "family" and outside it. Such relationships, Zuckerman continues, "may be regarded as a series of adapted responses conditioned through pain and fear. The scope of an animal's activities within a group will be limited by the possibility of danger arising from its desires overlapping those of a more dominant animal. The only equality within a social group is an equality of dominant characteristics. A state of balance is only temporary, and at any moment may be disturbed to a greater or lesser extent, the members of the group readjusting their mutual relationships. The group then settles down in a new equilibrium. Within the group each animal seems to live in potential fear lest another animal stronger than itself will inhibit its activities." He supported his views by conducting experiments with caged animals in zoos. For example by offering food to a subordinate monkey in the presence of a dominant one and observing the results. Not, it goes without saying, that predicting those results was very hard.

Another great primatologist, Jane Goodall (1934-), has spent many years observing chimpanzees in the wild. She, too, found that chimpanzees, male ones in particular, engage in a struggle for dominance. Presumably because her subjects were neither overcrowded nor bored, she witnessed less violence and more peaceful forms of interaction. Dominant animals threatened, hit and occasionally fought subordinate ones as well as each other. However, life did not consist entirely of struggle. On occasion, a dominant animal might reassure a subordinate one and conciliate it. The usual method of doing so was to touch its face and back as well as its groin. Conversely, subordinate individuals often went out of their way to appease superiors. They did so by making special noises, approaching them as gingerly as possible, and grooming them.[5] Making inequality work was a two-sided activity. At a minimum, both the equal animal and the less equal one had to signal their intentions and to understand the signals produced by the other. To do so they made use of all five senses. Other researchers found that where neither dominance nor subordination existed, as between males belonging to different groups, the outcome could well be deadly fights.[6]

Today's most celebrated primatologist is probably Frans de

Waal, a Dutch-American. The way he sees it, within every group of primates a constant struggle for dominance is taking place. Once established, it manifests itself mainly in the form of privileged, meaning unequal, access to sexual partners and, under some circumstances, food. The precise form of the struggle varies considerably from one species to the next. Particularly interesting in this respect are bonobos on one hand and chimpanzees on the other. Genetically speaking, both are our closest relatives. Neither is closer to us than the other. Bonobos, also known as dwarf or pygmy chimpanzees, are relatively peaceful. Perhaps this has something to do with the fact that, unusually, among them it is females that dominate the group. Fights, involving both males and females, do take place on occasion and can be quite vicious. On the whole, though, achieving dominance is mainly a question of building coalitions with other animals. Often this is done by using sex in which bonobos seem to engage almost all the time.

Even so, in the final analysis "[bonobos] are better described as tolerant than egalitarian."[7] Chimpanzees are quite different. Groups are invariably headed by males. Inside each group, all adult males dominate all females. The struggle for power is what makes them tick.[8] Much of it is waged by political methods, meaning manipulation and the formation of alliances. Displays of power, visible, auditory, or both, also play a very important role. However, chimps are very aggressive animals. Competition can easily explode into violence—which may or may not be followed by reconciliation. Fights to the death, including the squeezing out of testicles, have been recorded.[9] Among both species of apes dominance would be meaningless if it had not been accompanied by its opposite, subordination, and the behavior that is appropriate to it. For every animal that is more than equal there must be at least one that is less so. Some chimpanzees literally grovel in the dust in front of others. Such behavior can be understood as a kind of ritualized confirmation of the dominance relationship.[10]

At any one moment, the position of each individual in the hierarchy reflects his or her personality, age, experience, and ability to form connections with others. As among humans, dominant individuals tend to be surrounded by others of both sexes. Subordinate ones are isolated and may even deliberately isolate themselves further still. But why follow Dame Goodall all the way to the jungles of Tanzania and Prof. de Waal, to the city zoos of Arnhem and San Diego? As any dog owner knows, an animal that wishes to threaten another will pull its ears back, have its fur stand on end, growl, and bare its teeth. One that wants to appease will turn over on its back, expose its throat and belly, and roll about. Excepting psychopathic dogs—there are such creatures, although the percentage is said to be much lower than among humans—both signals are understood perfectly well. Both dominance and subordination are quickly and, in terms of lost fur and injuries, cheaply established. Only occasionally does a fight follow.

Countless similar studies of other primates have shown that, among them too, dominance and subordination are pretty much universal.[11] The position of each individual in relation to all the rest is determined very precisely by its qualities, physical and mental. In this sense it is even possible to speak of "justice" or, at any rate, equity. Some monkeys seem to understand that equity consists of each individual obtaining what he deserves according to his qualities. They react angrily when it is disturbed.[12] Whether the 1.5 percent of genetic material that separates us from both chimpanzees and bonobos represents "a giant leap" or "a small step," I shall leave for the philosophers to decide. Certainly they are closer to us than any other living beings on this planet.

*

In view of this, it is not surprising that equality is not popular among what, in an age less politically-correct than our own, the Germans used to call *Naturvoelker* ("nature-people"). Take the so-called band societies, the simplest known human ones of all. Until 1860 or so one of them, that of the Andaman Islanders in southern India, represented one of the most isolated populations on earth. Probably no group of contemporary people so much resembled our Stone Age ancestors. The Andamanese seem to have originated in present-day Burma and reached the islands some sixty thousand years ago by way of a long-defunct land bridge. Marco Polo, who probably did not visit them but heard about them second-hand, noted that they did not have a king. He described them as "a most brutish and savage race, having heads, eyes, and teeth like those of dogs. They are very cruel, and kill and eat every foreigner on whom they can lay their hands."[13]

Before the British took over the islands the Andamanese had almost no contact with the outside world.[14] The population may have stood at 5,000–6,000. Since then it has dwindled to a few hundred at most. They were divided into some ten tribes each of which spoke a different language, though most were mutually intelligible. Their material culture was rudimentary indeed. Perhaps alone among all the humans in the world, the islanders did not have the technology for kindling fire, though they did know how to preserve it and make use of it. Property consisted of relatively scanty clothing and ornaments, implements such as nets, buckets, bows, arrows, and similar items used for fishing, hunting, and preparing food. There were also simple shelters, made of widely available materials, to live in or under, but nothing that could not be erected by almost any individual within a few hours. As a result, division of labor and specialization were very largely limited to those that naturally follow from differences in age and sex.

The land and sea from which people drew their subsistence was regarded as belonging to all members of each tribe in common. Expanses of it would, however, be defended against encroachments by foreigners. A tribe might also expand at the expense of is neighbors. There were periods of famine, which could be caused either by an expanding population or by some natural disaster. Normally, though, the surroundings provided enough for everyone. Food and other items belonged to whoever had gathered, hunted, or made them. Partly because there was no need, partly because so many organic products are hard to preserve over time, there was no propensity towards monopolizing, hoarding, or trading in material objects. Exchange was limited to reciprocal gift-giving. It took place mainly at appropriate times such as feasts and was sufficiently universal and frequent to preserve a condition of rough economic equality. After all, what was there to own? There was no government in the sense of a clearly distinct person or persons endowed with power and/or privilege others did not enjoy.

Still it is necessary to take note of the following facts: First, common forms of address clearly distinguished between husbands and wives, parents and children, seniors and juniors. Since kinship was almost the only relationship that tied different people together, this led to numerous gradations as well as sharply differentiated rights and obligations.[15] Second, one basic principle on which the bands were built was that anyone who had food was obliged to share it with those who did not. However, in the words of the great anthropologist who studied the islands, "should a young unmarried man kill a pig he must be content to see it distributed by one of the older men, the best parts going to the seniors, while he and his companions must be satisfied with the inferior parts. The result of these customs is ... that the younger men do not do so well as their elders."[16] Old men, in other words, were in a position to control some food they did not produce. The same, incidentally, was true of other band societies around the world, such as the Agta of Luzon and the Yanomamo of Paraguay. Conversely, feminist scholars have complained that women used to get less than their fair share. If so, then this was probably because men, who did most of the hunting and offshore fishing, produced the food containing the most protein. They used this fact to enhance their status.[17]

Third and perhaps most important, some individuals were supposed to possess greater supernatural powers than others. As the same anthropologist says, "these specially favored persons corresponded, to some degree, with the medicine men, magicians, or shamans of other primitive societies."[18] Depending on which island they came from, they were known as *oko-jumu* or *oko-paiad*. They were supposed to control the weather; an idea, we may safely assume, has never occurred either to a bonobo or to a chimpanzee. The outcome was that everyone was anxious to be on their good side. Though they did not necessarily have authority, let alone power, over others, they certainly had more than their share of influence. Briefly, even in *the* simplest known human society of all, simpler even than the tribes of the highlands of Papua/New Guinea, some people were considered more equal than others. Indeed it might be said that, to the extent that any kind of organization existed both inside and outside the family, it both rested on inequality and perpetuated it. Furthermore, as the fact that the young were obliged to feed the old and the existence of shamans shows, relationships were not governed solely by personal prowess, as among animals. Other factors also made themselves felt.

Unlike the Andamanese, Australian Aborigines had the technical means to kindle fire.[19] Their habitat was as isolated but poor in resources and infinitely larger, making for a more nomadic lifestyle. Yet in some other ways they were similar. Some Andamanese are Negritos, meaning that they have short stature, dark skins, and so-called "peppercorn" hair. This has caused some anthropologists to suggest that the two groups are somehow related. People lived in bands based on kinship ties, though in both cultures a closer examination would show that many of those ties were not natural but fictive and formed by adoption. While there were no rulers, within each band parents had some authority over the young and seniors over juniors. In particular elders, thanks to their supposed proximity to the spirit-world and their ability to influence it, enjoyed respect. Often they could obtain resources from the young and make their views prevail.[20] One author has suggested that they manipulated the young men, making them fight each other. Based on these factors as well as sex, each individual knew his or her place and had his or her carefully defined rights and duties. To that extent there could be no question of equality. Too, within each tribe some bands were superior to others.

A third people that might be cited in this context are, or were, the Nuer of the Southern Sudan. Like the Andamanese and the Aborigines, the Nuer had no rulers, no institutions, and no government. It is said that their community was best described as an "ordered anarchy."[21] The technology at their disposal was more developed than that of the others. However, they too had few material possessions. Those they did have were simple enough to be manufactured out of locally available materials by almost anyone for his or her immediate needs. Land, forest and sources of water were "owned" by the whole tribe in common. What puts the Nuer on an altogether different level from the other two, though, is the fact that they were herders and possessed cattle. From it they drew an important part of their nutrition as well as many other necessities. So important was cattle to the people's life that wealth was measured almost exclusively in terms of the number of heads a person or family owns. Competition for it was very keen. Some had more heads, others fewer. However, here was also an elaborate system of obligatory exchange between families. It took place as a result of births, weddings, and deaths, but also in the form of blood-money. Usually it kept inequality within fairly clear bounds.

As among the Andamanese and the Aborigines, Nuer fathers had some authority over children, uncles over nephews, and older siblings over younger ones. As among the Aborigines, some persons were supposed to have better access to magic powers than others. This turned them into natural leaders. Particularly important were the so-called prophets. Supposedly possessed by some god or gods, they were able to predict the future and initiate military expeditions (although they did not command). A close analogy is the Prophetess Dvora in the Old Testament book of *Judges*. In her own words, she caused the people to wake up and rise against their oppressors.[22] Yet she neither accompanied the ensuing military expedition nor had the authority to order anybody about. Female prophetesses, incidentally, are not unknown in other cultures either.

To return to the Nuer, their prophets did not represent or symbolize anybody or anything. Though the spirit rested on them, they did not have authority, let alone formal authority and the power to make it felt. Yet they certainly did have influence. That the line separating the two things is often a fine one hardly requires saying.

The Nuer resembled the Australian Aborigines in that some clans considered themselves aristocratic (*diel*) and were considered to be so by others. Others were associated, or *rul*. In case of murder, people belonging to the former class were entitled to claim more blood money that those of the latter. Apparently the distinction was based on the fact that the individuals forming the clans in question consist of pure-bred Nuer. In this they differed from others who had an admixture of Dinka blood brought about in the past by means of war, capture, and adoption.[23] Here, in other words, we see ancestry playing a role in shaping the social pecking order. But ancestry was only one of the factors involved. Some lineages, though specifically known to be "new," enjoyed elevated status. It was derived from the fact that they were considered to have superior power in relation to cattle. That included the ability to heal sick beasts or make barren cows have calves. Indeed the standard work on the Nuer, one of the best anthropological studies ever written, is full of expressions such as "senior" and "dominant."

The mere fact that some clans were larger than others would tend to make them more influential. The Andamanese, the Aborigines, the Nuer, and many others prove that even the politically least developed, materially most egalitarian, societies on earth recognized that different individuals are related in different ways. They also recognize, of course, that individuals have different abilities. It is these differences that caused differing individuals to have different rights and duties. Those guilty of violating those duties and those rights might find themselves severely punished as the rest, incited and organized, but hardly commanded, by some of the more equal, turned on them. It is unlikely that any of these societies were based on the assumption that everybody does, or should, enjoy exactly the same status, rights, and duties as everyone else.

So far we have been dealing with inequality among individuals and clans inside given societies. Going one step further, few if any even of the simplest societies regard their neighbors as equal to themselves. The eponymous—meaning that it covers both a tribe and the language its members speak—term Dinka simply means "people." The Dinkas' Nuer neighbors, of course, see things the other way around. The best translation of the word Bantu, widely used across Africa and variously pronounced Watu or Batu or Bato or Abantu or Vanhu or Vandu, is said to be "human." The implication, namely that everyone else is sub-human or nonhuman, hardly needs to be spelt out. Lokono, the name of a tribe and a language in the Caribbean, also means "people." The Blackfoot Indians of Montana and Alberta called themselves *Niitsítapi*, the "Original People". Yup'ik, the name of some Inuit groups that inhabit both sides of the Bering Strait, is a composite word. It is derived from *yuk* meaning "person," and the post-base *-pik* meaning "real" or "genuine." Thus its literal meaning is "real people."[24]

While people designated themselves as superior, the names they gave others indicated inferiority. The Sotho-Tswana of South Africa regularly add the prefix *Ama*, meaning "unfamiliar," to the names of other peoples besides themselves. The Greeks called foreigners *barbaroi*, barbarians. The implication was that they could not speak properly and were less than fully human. As Aristotle later put it, they were, "by nature, slaves," unable to govern themselves but in need of a master (*despotes*; in Greek, the word can refer both to a slave-owner and to a political ruler) who, of course, towered above his subjects and was anything but equal with them.[25] Other examples abound. There probably has hardly been a clan, tribe people, or nation whose members did *not* place themselves at the apex of creation. Doing so, they regarded most, perhaps even all, foreigners as inferior to themselves. In some laboratory experiments people were arbitrarily divided into groups and made to compete against other groups of the same kind. Though the people inside each group hardly knew each other, let alone the members of the opposing group, they quickly started to feel their own superiority. Proving, perhaps, that we are programmed to do just that.[26]

Whether or not band societies are "good" or "bad" depends on the perspective one adopts. Enlightenment explorers and the *philosophes* who followed their accounts and interpreted reality for them lived in a society that was highly unequal. Starting with the king, the upper classes, actively assisted by the Church, weighed down heavily on the lower ones inside what has been aptly called "the fiscal-military state."[27] Many of them greatly admired the equality, and consequently the freedom from oppression, that "savages" in distant lands supposedly enjoyed. Volume after volume celebrated their simplicity, their honesty, their courage, their generosity (also in the sense that they shared their women and gave them to anybody who wanted them), in short their nobility. A perfect example of the genre is Diderot's *Supplément au Voyage de Bougainville*. Written in 1772, it was banned during his lifetime and only published after the Revolution when it quickly became a classic. Even better known was Jean-Jacques Rousseau (1712–1778). He neatly summed up the matter when he wrote that "man was born free, and he is everywhere in chains."[28]

Nineteenth-century travelers, imperialists and ethnographers tended to take the opposite view. The customs, particularly in respect to sex, which their predecessors had interpreted as noble and exalted, they saw as bestial. As with Rousseau, every "savage" was supposedly equal to every other and did not have any authority over him. Thus the communities in which they lived were understood as mere "hordes." They lacked the organization needed for taking large-scale collective action, let alone building and maintaining a sophisticated civilization. It was recognized that individual "horde men" might be well-built, strong, and very brave. That, for example was how many Europeans saw the Maoris whom they met in New Zealand.[29] Henry Rider Haggard (1856–1924), a famous English traveler and novelist, described the Maasai of Kenya as "ferocious or awe-inspiring," "enormously tall ... and beautifully though somewhat slightly, shaped; but with the face of a devil."[30] Winston Churchill, writing of the Dervishes whom he fought at Omdurman in 1896, could not praise their courage highly enough.[31] However, socio-economic equality, translating as it did into weak political authority, made them easy to conquer and even easier to look down upon.

A third group, the socialists, took a kind of middle way. Most of them bitterly opposed European colonialism in other continents. Instead they chose to follow Rousseau, celebrating the absence of private property and the egalitarian nature of the simplest societies known to them. Marx himself, in some of his early writings, explicitly turned his face against the "alienation" that the division of labor entailed.[32] On the other hand the more realistic among them, including Marx himself during his mature years, were well aware of the fact that such egalitarianism is incompatible with the needs of a sophisticated industrial civilization. Had it been imposed, it would have without question caused nine-tenths of the people living in that civilization to starve to death within a few years. When Marx spoke about the future he did not aim simply at reproducing some kind of idealized tribal past. Private ownership over the means of production would indeed be abolished. However, the ensuing society would somehow operate at a much higher level than its antediluvian predecessors.[33]

Looking back, it appears that all the participants in the debate were wrong. A closer examination of the facts would have shown that hordes of perfectly free men and women enjoying equal authority, status and access to resources of every kind, including each other's sexuality, have never existed and probably could not have existed. To paraphrase Hobbes, perfect equality, like its concomitant perfect liberty, can only exist when each individual lives alone in a desert, where it is meaningless. Even the simplest known societies were, to a considerable extent, based on inequality. While there were neither permanent social classes nor institutions, different people were caught up in what were often extremely complex networks of deference, rights and duties. Deference was due, and rights and duties were differentiated, according to age and sex. The existence of some individuals who, often on the basis of their age and/or supposed access to the divine, were more equal than others was recognized. The capacity for exercising leadership, essential for raiding and war, was also important.

Even where differences among the members of any group were small, the members of each society invariably felt themselves superior to those of others within their groups. This perceived inequality was even stronger among different groups. These attitudes of superiority were almost certain to be reciprocated. Both people and groups spoke of each other, and treated each other, accordingly.

*

A fortiori, the same applies to chiefdoms. The transition from band societies to fully developed, hierarchically organized, chiefdoms must have been an extremely complex process. Occasionally it may also have worked in reverse as chiefdoms disintegrated and fell apart because they were decapitated by war and conquest. The difficulty is not only that there are countless intermediate rungs, but that each anthropologist seems bent on producing his or her own hierarchy which is incompatible with that outlined by the rest. Some speak of elders, some of big men, some of priests, some of war leaders, some of chieftains. Others see segmented or acephalous (headless) societies, or sodalities, or stratified societies. Others still see extended families and moieties and clans and tribes and nations; not to mention centralization and its opposite, decentralization.

Inequality may be either permanent or periodical (the technical terms for this seem to be simultaneous hierarchy and sequential hierarchy respectively). The abovementioned book of *Judges* provides a good example of the latter. During a period when "there was no king in Israel [and] each man did what is right in his own sight," each time the people were oppressed by some foreign people, a judge would make his appearance.[34] Claiming to be the Lord's emissary and accepted by others as such, he—on one occasion she—energized them and led them out of their troubles. Having done so he went on to judge them until his death, after which things returned to normal. Some judges tried to pass their authority to their sons, but generally without lasting success.

The most important factors responsible for the move towards chiefdoms were probably as follows: A growing population, which led to increased contact among people and made some form of government necessary; the development of material culture, including in many cases the discovery of metal-working, which led to specialization, exchange, and hoarding;[35] and war. The last factor named, war, might itself be considered part consequence, part cause, of the

other two. The three factors were combined in an endless number
of ways. For example, overpopulation could lead to war, conquest,
and the establishment of a new social hierarchy in which the vic-
tors ruled and exploited the losers. This must have happened many
times all over the world. However, when James Cook first landed
on Hawaii he thought he could observe the opposite. The islands
seemed to contain fewer people than the available resources would
allow; a fact he attributed to constant internecine warfare.[36]

At the apex of every chiefdom stood a paramount chief—almost
always male, rarely female. His needs, demands, and commands
took precedence over those of everyone else. He was surrounded
by lesser chiefs, many of whom were his relatives, such as uncles,
brothers, sons, and nephews. Others became associated with him
by marrying his female relatives, thus cementing their political alliances with him. Together they formed a highly privileged upper
class based, in essence, on kin. As in the simpler societies, some
of the kin relationships were fictive and had been artificially constructed by adoption. The chief had a disproportionate number of
wives (often, wives of very unequal status). That, in turn, led to
a disproportionate number of offspring. Even in the rare societies
that were officially monogamous, such as Homeric Greece, chiefs
regularly built up large harems consisting of female slaves.[37] Polyg-
yny meant inequality in the sense that, whereas some had as many
women as they wanted and to spare, others had to go without. Many
chiefs also had retainers, i.e. a number of men who were dependent
on them and worked directly for or under them, and whom they
could use, among other things, to enforce their will on recalcitrant
subordinates and subjects.

The chief also commanded a greater share of whatever commodities were considered most valuable, such as cattle, or animal

skins, or feathers, or cowry shells, or precious metals, or structures in which those commodities, as well as food, were hoarded. Even more important, his access to those commodities did not depend on the consent of others. As far as his domains stretched, essentially it was limited only by the need to prevent excessive dissatisfaction and revolt. The chief adorned his body with every kind of precious object not available to commoners. Many chiefdoms also had sumptuary laws which reserved such objects for the sole use of the chief and his immediate subordinates.

The paramount chief's living quarters were much better than those of anybody else. Some lived in huge fortresses or palaces that provided room for thousands of retainers of both sexes. He had authority over everyone else, often including the authority to put those who displeased him or whom he found guilty to death. However, his own person was considered sacrosanct. That sanctity might easily extend to detachable body parts such as hair, nails, and even foreskins. The chief's wives and relatives of both sexes, and even many of the objects, animate or inanimate, he owned were also on the list. Particularly important in this respect were regalia, such as diadems, scepters, plumes, armbands, and certain kinds of dress and furniture. They were carefully guarded and normally worn or put on display on certain festive occasions.

Chiefs owed their position either to their own politico-military prowess, real or reputed, or to inheritance. Whatever the answer, invariably their privileges were buttressed by religion. Often their ancestry was supposed to go back to the tribal god or gods. Alternatively their predecessors, or they themselves, had been appointed as the earthly representative of the divine being(s). In the Old Testament, the term for this is "the chosen of the Lord." To emphasize the role of inheritance, the chief ancestors' masks, or mummies, or any symbolic objects associated with them, might be carefully preserved. Some of the objects associated with chieftainship, such as the famous Ashanti golden stool, had supposedly come down straight from heaven. To further reinforce the link with the divine, the chiefs' principal life events, such as birth and death, were both widely celebrated and attended by taboos. For example, during his investiture people of all ranks might be prohibited from having sex. At the time of his death they might not be permitted to touch metal utensils, or sound certain drums, and so on.

To house the ceremonies surrounding chieftainship, while at the same time preventing disturbances, palace and temple were usually built in such a way as to form a single complex encircled by a palisade or wall. Inside the complex, palace and temple were linked by a "sacred way" used for holding formal processions. All this put the chief in a position where he was simultaneously his own high priest. In this capacity it was his right as well as duty to conduct certain rites and ceremonies on which the welfare of the community supposedly depended. Conversely, where for one reason or another there was no chief and the ceremonies could not be performed, natural disasters, such as locust, or forest-fire, or drought, or the latter's opposite, flooding, might well follow. The *Heimskringla*, or *Chronicle of the Kings of Norway*, regularly notes that, in the days of this or that early medieval chieftain, the ceremonies were performed and the land was fruitful (or not). The need to maintain continuity was a strong incentive to ensure an interregnum did not happen. To make doubly sure, the dates on which the various ceremonies were held tended to coincide with events in the agricultural year.[38]

Under the aristocracy—from the Greek word *aristoi*, "excellent ones"—came commoners. Often they were known by all kinds of derogatory names. In early Greece they were called *thetes* (laborers) and *kakoi* (bad ones). In Thessaly they were known as *penes iui*, meaning either toilers or poor men. The Natchez Indians of Oklahoma spoke of "stinkers." Many chiefdoms also had distinct populations of serfs and/or slaves who occupied the bottom of the hierarchy. The total number of classes might therefore be as many as four, as in Anglo-Saxon England and pre-Christian Scandinavia, or even five, as in Tahiti and Hawaii. To make things more complicated still, in some chiefdoms, presumably those whose origins owed much to war and conquest, members of the upper class or classes were ethnically distinct from those of the lower ones. In that case they would probably take care to maintain the separation by means of prohibitions on intermarriage as well as various tattoos, clothing, personal ornaments, etc. Thus "real" inequality was artificially emphasized and accentuated.

The Old Testament book of *Joshua* provides a good example of such an ethnically-based society. Having conquered Palestine during the fifteenth century BC, first the Israelites turned the Gibeonites into "hewers of wood and drawers of water."[39] Later, during the government-less period of the Judges, they themselves were repeatedly subjected by foreign invaders who enserfed them. In 1990–1994 the contrast between the Tutsi and Hutu of Rwanda and Burundi led to a vicious civil war and genocide; even though the two peoples speak the same language, and even though they are all but indistinguishable.

The important point is that, in all this, there was not even a pretense at equality. From the chief down, superiors, while engaged in an unending game of musical chairs among themselves in which the prize was power, ruled and exploited. Commoners either accepted their fate or were destroyed. Often they only had access to economic resources provided they paid some kind of tribute to their superiors; whether in the form of sharecropping, or forced labor, or the duty to hand over choice goods. That might even include their daughters. That was how the famous "Amazons" of Dahomey (Benin) originated. Far from being independent warrior women, they were officially the king's concubines, recruited by means of an annual levy.[40] If he did not necessarily sleep with all of them—they were too numerous for that—he certainly had the right to do so. Commoners also depended on their betters in order to communicate with the divinities that be. as for political rights, they had none.

In the *Iliad* Odysseus is shown beating Thersites, a man with no lineage and no military prowess to boast of, simply for daring to speak up in the assembly. The assembly itself roared its approval; never mind that there was much truth in what Thersites, an eloquent if exceptionally ugly man, had to say.[41] In the absence of any formal institutions that could have served society as a corset, inequality in front of the law, or perhaps one should say custom, was just what held the community together. An orderly life was only made possible by the fact that some had precedence over, and greater rights than, others. All over the socio-politico ladder each individual had a place of his or her own as well as clearly distinct rights and duties. As long as those duties and those rights were upheld, peace, if not necessarily liberty and justice, prevailed.

Needless to say, things worked better in theory than in practice. Both in the Greek epics and in the world at large, violent conflicts, up to and including civil war, were frequent and brutal. They could involve people inside each class as well as those belonging to different classes. If only because the polygamy practiced by the paramount chief and his relatives meant that he had many of the latter, coups and fights over the throne were not so much the exception as the rule. A chief's death was particularly likely to result in conflict. As a result, dynasties seldom lasted more than two or three generations. At times, so downtrodden did members of the lower classes feel that they rose in more or less spontaneous action, more or less successfully. Neighboring chiefdoms also clashed; over water, over agricultural land, over pasture, over all kinds of property, and over women. Provided one side did not exterminate the other, the normal outcome of a victorious war would be even greater inequality than before.

✳

Clearly, the rule governing animal nature is not equality but inequality. Among mammals which live in groups, primates specifically included, no two individuals have ever had exactly the same status. In the event they did, they certainly did not hold it over time. Life itself, zoologists claim, is one long struggle to reach the highest position as soon as possible, stay there for as long as possible, and take advantage of the nutritional and sexual privileges that accompany it.[42] The struggle is waged with every means, often including violence. The enjoyable aspects of those privileges apart, winners are rewarded by reproductive success. Some individuals obtain far more chances to spread their genes than others.[43] Turning now to humanity, it turns out that both eighteenth-century philosophers, inspired by warm admiration for "savages," and nineteenth-century ethnographers, inspired by profound contempt for them, were wrong. Everything is relative, yet even in the simplest known societies, equality is far from perfect. No people, not even the Andamanese, seem to have lived in a society where access to resources was equal, everything and everyone belonged to everyone else, and no individual had the authority to command or the duty to obey. Whatever social organizations existed were not only based on inequality, but consisted of it.

In summary, all human societies recognize differences of age and sex which translate into differences in the ability to produce food as well as different rights and duties. Those factors apart, it seems reasonable to surmise that some of the oldest justifications for inequality originated in magic, spirit-worship, religion, or whatever a sense of the supernatural is called. That was the thesis of late nineteenth-century anthropologists such as James Fraser in *The Golden Bough* (1890). They theorized that at first, prophets, shamans, and assorted miracle-workers were able to translate their knowledge into influence. As influence gradually grew into authority, authority into power, and power into property and privilege, chiefdoms emerged. However, history suggests that things did not proceed in such a simple linear order. Excavations in Russia show that, even 30,000 years ago and long before the so-called agricultural revolution made permanent settlements possible, some people were buried along with comparatively vast wealth. Others were interred with hardly anything at all. The former were probably chiefs, the latter commoners.[44] How it came about we simply do not know. Furthermore, among humans as well as many animals, inequality, accompanied by deference—meaning inequality that is *recognized*—was exactly what held the community or group together. Had it been otherwise, individuals competing for material and sexual resources, would presumably have torn one another to pieces. Not just occasionally, as is actually the case, but all of the time.

Chapter 2

The Greek Miracle

The first people to discover ways of constructing a community based, in some ways, on equality were the ancient Greeks. Unfortunately information about that period tends to be very scarce. It is essentially limited to archaeological remains and the poems of Homer and Hesiod. There are also many mythological tales, such as those involving gods, monsters, and supernatural deeds. However, their mythological character, plus the fact that they were written down centuries after the events they claim to describe, renders their value problematic. There are also some odd bits and pieces in the writings of Greek historians who lived during the classical period. The fact that, during the so-called dark ages, writing was not practiced does not make things any easier.

Judging by those few sources, between about 1100 BC and 700 BC Greece was inhabited by groups occupying a middle position between band societies and chiefdoms. In the *Iliad*, the paramount chief is Agamemnon. To quote Thersites again, "[Agamemnon's] tents are full of copper and many choice captive women." Whenever a city was captured he took the best spoils for himself as, indeed, he was entitled to do. He was surrounded by lesser chiefs of whom Odysseus, judging by the number of warriors he was able to muster, was one of the less important. They are described as "generous;" from them he received "gifts," and over them he exercised a certain authority. That authority was sufficiently strong to make the other chiefs leave their homes, join him at a designated meeting place, and campaign for ten years even though none of them had personally been wronged by the Trojans' hands; no mean achievement, that.

Yet Agamemnon was no despot. Particularly interesting is his relationship with Achilles. As an individual warrior Achilles was more than a match for Agamemnon and both of them knew it. Yet the latter could tell the former that, if necessary, he would invade his, Achilles', camp and take away his prize, the girl Briseis. Doing so, he would teach Achilles "how much greater I am than you, and another man will shrink before declaring himself my equal."[1] This was because he had more warriors at his command, and presumably more treasure to pay them with, than anyone else; yet when Achilles withdrew from the war, Agamemnon could not coerce him. To bring him back he had to cajole, make promises, and hand over valuable property. Thus their relationship was based neither on authority nor on equality but on a certain balance. Furthermore, once the war had ended each sub-chief went home to his *asty*, best translated as "citadel." There is no indication that any of them continued to be under Agamemnon's authority, let alone paid tribute to him. Given that those homes were spread from Pylos in the western Peloponnesus all the way to Crete in the east, and that some of them were separated from each other not just by land but by sea, this is most unlikely to have been the case.

Chiefs are known now as *anax*, now as *basileus*. Throughout the poems the two terms are used interchangeably, often for the same person. Yet it is mainly the more powerful chiefs, including both Zeus and Agamemnon, who are called by the former title. They owed their positions to three factors, i.e. their politico-military prowess, their wealth, and their ancestry. The need to record ancestry explains why book II of the *Iliad* contains such a detailed catalogue of them, the peoples whom they ruled, and the number of ships each of them mustered when he went out to war. Furthermore, each time a Greek chief meets a Trojan one on the battlefield the first thing they both do is boast about their forefathers. Some claimed divine descent, but this fact in itself does not seem to give them much preeminence over the rest. The fact that Sarpedon is Zeus' own son does not prevent him from being killed by Patroclus. Others, though not descended from gods, are called "god-like."[2]

Of equality, social, economic, political or legal, there could be no question whatsoever. One proof of this is the fact that, conversations with divine beings aside, practically all the encounters, both peaceful and hostile, recorded in both the *Iliad* and the *Odyssey* took place between aristocrats. The commoners whom they led in such large numbers seldom enter the picture. It is true the *Odyssey* gives a somewhat more complete account of them than the *Iliad* does. That is because the hero, who spends years traveling far from home and from other chiefs, is more dependent on them than he would normally be. We meet peasants, herders, artisans, doctors, and soothsayers, although the poem seldom mentions them by name. That only happens if, as in the case of the unfortunate Thersites, they opposed some chief, or else when they assisted him, as some members of Odysseus' household did after he had returned home from his travels.

Understood as historical sources, the trouble with the Homeric poems is that, like the tales of mythology, they received their final form centuries after the events they claim to describe. During those centuries an entire civilization, the Mycenaean, vanished from the earth. The country was repeatedly invaded, and systems of socio-political organization underwent radical changes. From Hesiod, who probably lived slightly later than Homer, we learn that some people were wealthy and powerful, others poor and humble. The former often oppressed the latter, and indeed the poem known as *Works and Days* can be read as a protest against that oppression. Still the poet does not demand to have equality imposed and the chiefs deposed, only that they should be just.[3] That apart, few details concerning the way society functioned are provided.

The best proof that chiefdoms had once existed is the fact that, even during the classical age, many Balkan tribes had not yet engaged in *synoikysmos*, the "fusion of households" into a single polis. Peoples such as the Illyrians, the Thracians, and the Aetolians continued to live in what were called "*ethne*," variously translated as nations, groups, or swarms. Each "nation" was headed by an *ethnarch*, meaning, rather precisely, chief. City-dwelling Greeks looked down on them and regarded them as backward. Of the Aetolians, Thucydides says that they were a warlike people. Yet they lacked fortified cities, lived in open villages, and only wore light armor.[4] Of the Thracians, the New Cambridge Ancient Cambridge History says that they formed a chiefdom that had "a quasi-feudal character" complete with "vassal rulers."[5] They left hardly any written records, however, which is why little is known about them.

Additional evidence is provided by the names of the subordinate divisions which, in one form or another, continued to be present in many classical city-states, Sparta and Athens included, for centuries after they had been formed. The divisions were known as tribes,

2. THE GREEK MIRACLE

fraternities, descent-groups, and clans. Just how egalitarian, or un-egalitarian, these communities and their members had been before they were joined together and fused into a single *polis* is impossible to say. The role they played in the latter's life often shifted and is hard to understand. However they may have been organized, originally they seem to have consisted of leaders and followers. One modern scholar, seeking to prove that they were not based solely on kin, has translated tribe (*phulon*) as "leader group." By this he meant a temporary organization thrown together by a chief in order to carry out a specific task.[6]

Given this unpromising background, how did the Greek chief-doms avoid developing into even more unequal bureaucratic or feudal polities—a process which, as we shall see, was the common fate of countless similar societies around the world? Certainly the idea of equality, with all its complex socio-economic-political implications, cannot have reached Greece from the Orient. True, socially, economically and politically the Middle East during this period was much more advanced than Greece, a small and relatively poor country. We also know that, since at least 1200 BC, commodities and ideas were traded in both directions. One thing the Greeks imported was the alphabet, which reached them at some time during the eighth century BC. However, there were limits to what could be learnt from this source. Starting as early as the third millennium, both Egypt and Mesopotamia were occupied by some of the most unequal and most hierarchical despotisms the world has ever seen. To convince oneself of this fact one only has to look at the pyramids. If there were any limits to the power of the Pharaohs, as well as the Assyrian, Babylonian and Persian kings, they were of a technical nature, not a legal one. The Greeks themselves always referred to the ruler of Persia as "the Great King." At least until the time of Alexander and his successors, they themselves had nothing of the sort.

Geography, the fact that the land consists of numerous valleys separated from one another by mountains, may have played a role in preventing Greece, too, from being unified under such an empire. However, other parts of the world are equally mountainous if not more so. Some, like pre-Columbian Peru, were nevertheless united by as hierarchic and as absolute an imperial power as any in the Old World. Others, such as Tahiti, remained split among numerous chiefdoms. Furthermore, the fact that certain peoples lived on extensive plains, as both the Australian aborigines and the Indians of North America did, in itself did not necessarily result in the rise of empires. As the Mongolians' ability to resist Chinese rule for millennia on end shows, large open spaces could be used just as well for escaping a central authority as for building it. Briefly, geography and the biosphere that goes with it can explain much. But on its own it cannot tell us why some societies developed in certain ways and others did not.

Cities, meaning permanent settlements containing a considerable number of people who did not make their living in agriculture but engaged in industry and trade instead, did indeed make their appearance in many places around the world. However, except for the Phoenician ones, about which we know very little, and those of Italy, on which more later, they were ruled by petty kings. Socially and politically their structure was at least as unequal as that of chiefdoms. Far from ruling themselves, many of them stood at the center of some highly-developed chiefdom. The Greek world itself contained at least one very important city of this kind. This was Pella, capital of the Macedonian kings who ended up by overrunning Greece.[7] To say, as one historian does, that "the [Greek] city-

state was the fruit of tensions within an agricultural world" and that
its rise "may have been much facilitated by the continuing simplicity
of economic patterns and by still almost primitive social structure
of the age" is not very helpful.[8]

Attempts have been made to link the rise of the classical polis from during the seventh century BC with the emergence of hoplite warfare.[9] Such warfare, waged by tightly-packed formations,
demanded very close cooperation among similarly armed, similarly
trained, heavy infantrymen maneuvering in step. Even commanders no longer waged separate duels against one another, as in the
Iliad. Instead they often fought in the ranks like everyone else.[10]
Thus the power of the community increased, whereas that of the
chiefs declined. The trouble with this interpretation is that phalanx-
like fighting formations, organized, paid for, and presumably commanded by monarchs or their appointees, were well-known both
in Egypt and Mesopotamia at least since the third millennium BC
on. After all, it does not take much intellectual effort to see that,
given suitable terrain, cohesive, disciplined, bodies of troops can do
certain things that mere skirmishers cannot do. Such bodies acted
as instruments of royal power, even its symbols. Yet there was no
question of them leading to equality or to democracy.

Some have tried to link the emergence of Greek democracy with
monogamy.[11] The fact that Greek men were only allowed to have
one wife, they argue, meant that more of them were able to marry.
This in turn led to a less varied rate of reproduction and greater
equality among the citizens. As already noted, however, this explanation ignores the fact that in practice, chiefs such as Agamemnon
and Odysseus could, and did, have as many women as they wanted.
The Romans were no less monogamous than the Greeks, and no
more so during the Republic than during the Empire. Yet this did

not prevent what started as a city-state on the shores of the Tiber from growing into one of the most hierarchical empires in the whole of history. Furthermore, the collapse of Rome laid the basis for European, i.e. Christian, feudalism. Christianity always expected each man and woman to have only one legitimate spouse at any one moment. Yet Christian feudalism resembled the empire in that it was perfectly compatible with, indeed based on, the crassest forms of inequality.

A third explanation, rarely mentioned in the literature, is a change in the way religion was organized. As we saw religion, meaning some kind of claim of closeness to the gods, has as good a claim as any to be the earliest basis of inequality first, and then of government. However, that does not apply to the world as it emerges from the Homeric poems. Instead the *Iliad* presents us with two priests, Charises (the father of Briseis) and Kalchas. Both serve the gods, pray to them, and sometimes have their prayers answered. Yet neither is said to be their scion. Nor does either of them rule over anybody or anything. Begging Agamemnon for the return of his daughter, Charises in particular cuts a somewhat pathetic figure. Conversely the Homeric chiefs, even those who are said to be descended from gods or to be god-like, do not explicitly base their right to rule on that fact. Nor do they act as their own head priests. Their authority is secular, not religious.

When, why and how the Homeric chiefs surrendered their special ties with the gods and ceased to rely on divine backing to buttress their secular rule we have no idea. But clearly it was one step, and a very important step, towards the classical city-state and the kind of equality that sometimes prevailed in them. The magistrates who governed city-states did not, in the main, owe their positions to the gods. Conversely, Greek priests were for the most part magistrates like all others.[12] Other explanations as to the origins of the city-state abound, but none so solid that no holes can be punched into it. Better, then, to take the *polis*, a self-governing city state, for granted, and trace the nature and development of our subject, equality, within it.

✳

In practice, to do so means focusing on two city-states out of several hundred: Sparta and Athens. In the case of the former this is because, in some ways, it carried equality further than any other. This feat, along with its celebrated military prowess, made it famous throughout Greece. The latter qualifies because the available evidence about it is relatively abundant and because it saw itself, and was often seen by others, as the "School of Hellas." Besides, already in antiquity the two were widely understood as presenting radically different, even opposed, political systems as well as ways of life. Thus examining them both represents the best way to understand them both.

In both cities, essentially the move towards the polis meant the dismantlement, sudden or gradual, of earlier, kin-based, organizations. Their place was taken by a single arrangement based on geographical location and citizenship. In Sparta, the reforms were said to be the work of Lycurgus. Whether he really existed and, if so, when, we have no idea. Though descended from an aristocratic lineage, he was no ruler; Plutarch, writing perhaps eight centuries after the supposed event, says that "he had a nature fitted to lead, and a power to make men follow him."[13] Nor do we know much about life in Sparta before Lycurgus's time. Herodotus and Thucydides both vaguely refer to a period of unrest and civil strife around the middle of the seventh century BC. Indeed, Herodotus claims that prior to the reform, Sparta was "the worst-governed city in Greece."[14]

Concerning the motive, we have the testimony of Thucydides, a well-informed realist if ever one there was. He says that "most Spartan institutions have always been designed with a view to security against the helots." The latter were a semi-servile population that probably came into being in the wake of the wars against another Peloponnesian city, Messenia, during the first half of the seventh century BC. Aristotle in the fourth century BC wrote that the helots, enslaved and mal-treated, were "an enemy constantly sitting in wait of the disaster of the Spartans."[15] It was to prevent them from trying to free themselves that the Spartans turned their city into an armed camp. They must have felt, quite rightly, that they were sitting on a volcano.

Still following Plutarch, whose account is the most detailed by far, the most critical step in producing the *homoioi* ("equal ones"), or Spartiates as they were known, was to take away all privately-owned land and put it into the hands of the state. Previously "there was a dreadful inequality in this regard, the city was heavily burdened with indigent and helpless people, and wealth was wholly concentrated in the hands of a few. Determined, therefore, to banish insolence and crime and luxury, and those yet more deep-seated and afflictive diseases of the state, poverty and wealth, [Lycurgus] persuaded his fellow-citizens to make one parcel of all their territory and divide it up anew, and to live with one another on the basis of entire uniformity and equality in the means of subsistence, seeking pre-eminence through virtue alone, assured that there was no other difference or inequality between man and man than that which was established by blame for base actions and praise for good ones."[16] Each lot was sufficiently large to maintain a man and his wife in good health, but nothing more.

Along with each lot came a number of helots who worked the land for its Spartiate master. This put the Spartiates in a position where they could devote their lives entirely to military training. Learning how to advance, how to retreat, and how to best use their weapons, they turned themselves into "professors of war."[17] Not a man to be content with half-measures, Lycurgus also had movable property gathered and redistributed. To prevent the return of inequality by way of trade and hoarding, gold and silver were banished. Henceforward the Spartans had to make do with an iron currency that was clumsy to use and only suitable for making the smallest purchases. Outside Sparta it was worthless and soon became the object of derision. With the disappearance of money, Plutarch says, every kind of vice also vanished. Not only luxury, but vagabondage, harlotry, the kind of deception practiced by soothsayers, and other societal ills simply disappeared.

Lycurgus' quest for equality also led directly to another and "most exquisite" reform. This was the establishment of common messes or, to borrow a term from modern anthropology, men's houses. Here Spartiates took their meals and spent their nights. They were even obliged to continue to do so for some time after they had married, visiting their wives in secret. Admission to the messes and to citizenship in general depended on completing a prolonged training course known as the *agoge*. It started at the age of seven and lasted until the age of about twenty. So rough and arduous was it that Aristotle considered it more suitable for beasts than for men. To support the mess to which he belonged, each member had to provide his share in food. Men who, for one reason or another, had lost their lots and could no longer contribute dropped out of the system. That, in turn, led to the loss of their status as Spartiates.

Such was the importance Lycurgus attributed to equality that it
applied even to death. Not only did he prohibit any kind of objects
to be buried with their owners, but tombs were not supposed to
carry the names of their occupants. The only exceptions to this rule
were men who had been killed in battle and women who had died
in childbirth. He accompanied his socio-economic reforms with
political ones. Sparta, Plutarch says, had long been ruled by two
basileis. "[The Spartans] felt that their kings were such in name and
station only, but in everything else were nothing better than their
subjects" and prone to the same human weaknesses.[18] As a result
the city tended, now towards the excesses of tyranny, now towards
the instability of democracy. To correct this problem Lycurgus appointed a Senate made up of twenty-eight men over sixty years old
serving for life. As each one passed away, the popular assembly,
comprising all adult male Spartiates, chose another by acclamation.
Their function was to act as a "sort of balance for the ship of state,
putting her on a steady keel."

Finally, either Lycurgus or one of his successors—our sources
differ on this point—instituted the ephors, or "overseers." Five in
number, they were elected annually and charged with supervising
the kings. The Senate and the kings had the sole right to convene
the assembly and submit business to it. However, in case the latter
tried to handle matters of which the ephors did not approve they
were entitled to adjourn it. In all this, the major deviations from
equality were the fact that private individuals could not speak in
the assembly; that only old men could be elected to the Senate; and
that the kingship was hereditary and limited to members of just
two families, the Agiads and the Eurypontids. When somebody
asked Lycurgus about this his response, presented as a typical example of "Laconian" brevity and pungency, was to tell the man to "go

and first establish democracy in your own household." Here it is
worth noting that, in Plato's view, the real rulers were the ephors.
Though democratically elected on an annual basis, they ran the city
as "despots." The kings, he says, were mere generals.[19]

Many modern historians believe the reforms were not carried
out by a single person but gradually over a much longer period, and
only later attributed to Lycurgus. Even if the latter existed, clearly
he had to overcome considerable opposition and did not accomplish everything at once. Much more important for our purposes,
equality among the Spartiates was achieved at the cost of the helots.
Not only were they enslaved, but each year the magistrates would
formally declare war on them. Thereupon Spartan youths, armed
with daggers, would ambush them and kill those of them they saw
fit. Other ways of humiliating them also abounded, all under the
cover of laws so firmly implanted that they were considered almost
sacred. So bad was the treatment the helots suffered that Plutarch
for one doubted whether the laws in question could have been instituted by Lycurgus himself. They must, he thought have been added
later on.

Another class of less-than-equals was the *perioikoi*, literally
"those around the house." They were free but not equal; while they
did serve in the army and, later, the navy, they were not allowed
to marry Spartan citizens and did not have any political rights.[20]
That, however, was by no means the end of the matter. A series of
wars during the sixth century BC gradually put Sparta in control of
the entire Peloponnesus. Probably relying on a system of unequal
treaties much like those later used by Rome to govern first Latium
and then the rest of Italy, it became the center of the Peloponnesian
League. In our sources, most of which originate in Sparta's enemy
Athens, the Spartans are regularly called Lacedaemonians. Appar-

ently the term referred to citizens, *perioikoi*, and subject-allies with-out distinction. On occasion it may even have included some of the helots who served in the army as porters and other noncombatants.

Thus regarded, Peloponnesian society was organized as a pyra-mid with very steep walls and a flat top. Of all the members of the hierarchy it was only the Spartiates, occupying that top, who were in any sense "equal." Even in their case, as Lycurgus him-self made clear, equality did not quite imply democracy, i.e. the right to equal participation in government. Returning to Plutarch, originally there were nine thousand Spartiates and thirty thousand *perioikoi*. Add the subject-allies and the helots—to say nothing of women and children—and it is clear that the "equals" formed a very small part of the total, perhaps as few as 3 to 4 percent. Even that was just the beginning of the story, not its end. Herodotus says that, by the time of the Persian Wars in 490–480 BC, the number of Spartiates had fallen to eight thousand.[21] According to Plutarch, Lycurgus provided for each newly-born male child to be examined by "the elders of the tribe" to which the father belonged. Those found healthy were allowed to live and were assigned one of the nine thousand lots.[22] To ensure the number of Spartiates remained steady, it would have been necessary for each father to leave behind one, and only one, son on average. Whether that was in fact Ly-curgus' intention, and if so, how it was done in practice, we do not have the foggiest idea.

Around the middle of the fifth century BC the process whereby the number of Spartiates declined accelerated. To quote the invalu-able Plutarch again, "in the reign of Agis [king Agis II, who died in 401 AD], gold and silver money first flowed into Sparta. With money came greed and a desire for wealth prevailed through the agency of Lysander [the Spartan general who defeated Athens and brought the Peloponnesian War to an end], who, though incorruptible himself, filled his country with the love of riches and with luxury, by bringing home gold and silver from the war."[23] Loot apart, additional money came from Persia. At this time the Persian empire was subsidizing Sparta, thereby permitting funds to be diverted from the state into the pockets of private individuals. Having grown rich, the latter were able to buy their fellows' *kleroi*, plots of land, turning the former owners into a landless proletariat and disenfranchising them. The constant wars and the numerous casualties must have pushed things along. Aristotle says that, in Sparta, landed property tended to be concentrated into the hands of rich widows.

By the time of Aristotle (384–322 BC) there were fewer than 1,000 Spartiates left. Plutarch says that, at the Battle of Leuctra in 371, BC the number of Lacedaemonians present stood at 11,000. If so, then the Spartiates formed a small minority even in the army. At the accession of King Agis IV in 244 BC the figure had gone down to just 700. During the third century BC several attempts were made to arrest the decline. This was done by emancipating *perioikoi* and helots, requisitioning the land, and redistributing it among the citizens. As one may imagine, the reforms did not exactly meet with everyone's approval; one of Agis' successors, Nabis (who reigned from 207 to 192 BC), even executed the last remaining members of the two traditional royal families. He also forced the women of Sparta to marry the newly emancipated men.[24] It was a case of too little, too late.

Taking 650 BC as the proximate date at which the most important reforms were put in place, equality in Sparta, as far as it went, lasted until late in the Peloponnesian War, that is about two and a half centuries. From that point on it started declining. On one hand, inequality raised its head. On the other, maintaining equality

by failing to augment the number of *homoioi* had a disastrous effect
on the power of the state. Ultimately nothing was left of the famous
Spartan prowess except a handful of youths. In a special ceremony
attended by tourists, they allowed themselves to be flogged to death.

Let us move on from Sparta to Athens. Here we find that equality, known as *isonomia* (literally, "equality in front of the law"), only
started taking hold towards the middle of the sixth century BC.
It was associated mainly with the names of two famous reformers,
Solon, who lived from about 638 BC to 558 BC, and Cleisthenes
who must have been active during the years just before 500 BC. Like
those of Lycurgus, Solon's reforms covered both the economic and
the political fields. In the present context, both are of considerable
interest.

The reform that, at the time and later, acquired the greatest
fame was the *seisachtheia*, literally "the shaking off of burdens."[25]
The meaning of the phrase is not quite clear. However, it seems
to have been related to ownership over land. Previously Athenian
law made land inalienable, meaning it had to remain in the hands
of the males of each tribe. A somewhat similar arrangement is described in the Old Testament book of *Numbers*.[26] The outcome was
that debtors, unable to sell or mortgage their farms, were forced to
enter into some kind of proto-feudal relationships with creditors or
even sell themselves and their families as slaves. *Seisachtheia* probably meant that doing so was prohibited. Outstanding debts were
cancelled, people who had already entered into one of the two relationships just mentioned retroactively released from them. The
move did not mean that slavery was abolished. Both Athenian individuals and the state could, and would, continue to own slaves.
What changed was the fact that the slaves in question could not be

Athenian citizens. From this point on, in other words, all Athenian citizens were, by definition, free.

To prevent extreme economic inequality from re-emerging, Solon put in place a series of sumptuary laws designed to prevent the rich from flaunting their wealth. An even more important policy was the way he limited the amount of land any single individual was permitted to own. Even so, the danger existed that those who, though freed, had lost their land would now turn into an urban *Lumpenproletariat.* Evidently it was with this problem in mind that Solon sought to put the economy on a new basis by stimulating industry, trade, shipping, and the circulation of money. Some ancient historians claim that he was also the first to introduce coinage. This is probably false; but there can be no doubt that, to speak with Aristotle, without rough economic equality and a strong middle class, neither Greek democracy nor the polis itself would have been possible.[27]

The precise details are disputed and do not matter much. Before Solon the principal institution was the Areopagus, an aristocratic body that, like the Roman Senate, comprised all former magistrates. Day-to-day administration was in the hands of nine archons, or governors. They served for one year and were selected on the basis of noble birth and/or wealth. Just who did the selection, as well as carried out the inquiry archons had to undergo as their terms of office ended, is not clear. Apparently it was done in such a way as to leave real power in the hands of the Areopagus and the "well-sired" aristocrats who sat on it. Solon took control over the archons away from the Areopagus and handed it to the popular assembly. He may even have given the lowest classes the right to vote, though this is uncertain. He also set up a new body known as the council. It numbered four hundred men and was charged with preparing business for the popular assembly to debate and vote on. In this case, too, it is uncertain whether the members of the lowest classes were allowed to participate.

The net effect was to broaden the basis of government—a clear step towards equality, even though some have argued that Solon's real purpose was to preserve inequality by granting the lower classes some of their demands.[28] This he did by dividing the citizens into four classes according to the amount of property they owned. The richer any man, the higher the office or offices for which he was eligible; however, the lower classes were still excluded. Having done his work—probably not all at once—Solon, like Lycurgus before him, left the country. Shortly thereafter civil unrest started, ultimately leading to the ascent of a relative of Solon's, the tyrant Peisistratus. In 527 BC Peisistratus died after a reign of nineteen years, passing power to his son Hippias. In 514 BC, two youths named Harmodius and Aristogeiton killed Hippias. A contemporary inscription praises them for making their country "*isonomic*," or legally equal.[29] An Athenian drinking song, preserved by a much later historian, says that the pair, having made Athens a place of *isonomia*, would remain famous forever.[30]

Some modern historians have argued that, at this time, *isonomia* meant no more than equality among aristocrats.[31] Even if that was the case, before long the concept started marching in lockstep with democracy. The next important move in this direction was made by Cleisthenes. With him we enter the great period of Athenian history and its incomparably brilliant achievements in every field of life. Just as the reforms attributed to Solon were probably linked to the emergence of hoplite warfare, so those of Cleisthenes owed much to the development of the Athenian navy and its warships, the famous triremes. Triremes required thousands of oarsmen to work them. They could only be recruited among those who had nothing to offer the state except their muscles. In return, they had to be given the vote and admitted into the assembly—if that had not already been accomplished by Solon. The laws prohibiting members of the lower classes from taking up office also went by the board.[32]

By redistributing the population according to their place of residence rather than according to the tribes to which they belonged, Cleisthenes also pushed forward the process whereby all citizens were fused into a single body. The Areopagus continued to lose power in favor of the council, the number of whose members Cleisthenes increased to five hundred men. In 462 BC, forty years after Cleisthenes's innovations, the Areopagus was finally deprived of most of its remaining functions at the hands of a radically democratic politician by the name of Ephialtes. Here it is necessary to point out that all this was done neither at once nor easily. Instead the reforms took place amidst ferocious political struggles between "conservative" aristocrats and "progressive" democrats. One of the victims of those struggles was Ephialtes, who was assassinated in 461 BC.

Ephialtes's successor was the great Pericles. Under his leadership, which lasted for some thirty years, Athenian democracy assumed its classic form. One indication of this was the appearance, besides *isonomia*—formed out of *iso*, equal, with *nomos*, meaning usage, custom, or law—of a whole series of closely related concepts. Among them were *isogeria*, meaning an equal right of all citizens to address the various political assemblies; *isophsephos*, i.e. one man, one vote; as well as *isokratia*, or equality of power. Of *isonomia* itself Herodotus has a Persian nobleman say that it was the "fairest word of all."[33] Nothing like this democracy had been attempted before. And nothing like it was to be attempted again for many, many centuries to come.

Under this system the sovereign body was the popular assembly. It alone had the power to pass laws, make treaties, declare war or peace, and appoint the most important magistrates (the rest were selected by lot, thus giving every male citizen a chance to participate in government). All magistrates served for one year and had to submit their accounts to the assembly after leaving office. To make sure that participation in the government would indeed be open to all, magistrates and jurors were paid from the public treasury. Not content with this, the Athenians also insisted on *isonomia* in the sense of equality in front of the law. Both before and since in most polities, different laws were applied to different classes of people. Very often the most powerful people, be they kings or emperors or tyrants, were not subject to any law at all. Not so in classical Athens. In it, absolute obedience to the law was required from all without distinction.

To buttress *isonomia* still further, people were prohibited from hiring lawyers. While this could not prevent them from having others write their speeches for them, in court they were obliged to represent themselves. The courts' own impartiality and immunity to bribes was guaranteed by the large number of jurors who looked after each case—as many as 500 or, in the case of the most important lawsuits, 1,000. They too were selected by lot with the aid of an ingenious mechanism specially developed for the purpose. All this worked, as it was intended to, in favor of equality and against patronage on one hand and corruption on the other. In the words of Thucydides, it provided everyone with a share of "the good things in life."[34]

Thus both Sparta and Athens, each in its own way, were based on equality. Nevertheless, and as the different terminology used in each city suffices to show, they were anything but similar. On the one hand, the *homoioi*, and on the other, those who lived in *isonomia*, developed two radically different political, economic, social, and cultural systems. The contrast permeates the work of Thucydides and, especially, the speeches he puts into the mouths of various leaders on both sides. Of those, by far the most important one is Pericles's funeral oration, delivered early in the Peloponnesian War into which he led Athens to its eventual destruction.[35] Together, the speeches paint a clear, if perhaps overdrawn, picture of both polities. Spartans were specialists in violence, the Athenians were well-rounded (although no slouches in violence themselves). Spartans were secretive and lived in comparative isolation at the center of their peninsula, while Athens was open to foreigners from all over the world. Spartans were conservative, Athenians were always looking for new things. Spartans were restrained and disciplined, Athenians enterprising. Spartans were stolid and lacking in initiative, Athenians were famous for their quickness of mind. Although Athenians were brave and entirely capable of waging war, their city was anything but an armed camp. Above all, says Pericles, the Athenian democracy, unlike some other polities, was made up of free men living under their own rule. While guaranteeing equal justice to all citizens, it also enabled those who wanted to do so to serve the state to the limits of their ability.

Taking Cleisthenes' reforms just before 500 BC as the real starting point, and apart from a brief period around 400 BC, Athenian democracy, and the *isonomia* on which it was based, lasted until 338 BC. In that year the city was brought under Macedonian control and lost its independence, though for centuries afterwards it did remain a center of learning and culture. Both the Spartan and

Athenian versions of equality have been extensively studied by contemporaries and successors alike. And it is to what they had to say of it that we must now turn our attention.

During the last twenty-five centuries or so Sparta in general, and the form of equality in which its citizens lived in particular, has had a very mixed press. To Xenophon, an Athenian who spent some time living in Sparta during the first half of the fourth century BC, Lycurgus's laws represented "the utmost limit of wisdom."[36] He was particularly enamored of the military system. Plato around 400 BC also admired the city, though less for its military prowess than for the kind of socio-economic equality among the *homoioi* that it provided and which he saw as a prerequisite for both stability and justice. He even used it as a model for the polity he outlined in his greatest masterpiece, *The Republic*. Plutarch, too, seems to regret its passing away. That is evident not only from his biography of Lycurgus but also from the many exemplary sayings of "true" Spartan men and women he collected in his *Moralia*.

Others were more critical. To recount the opinions of a few of the more famous historians, Herodotus was concerned about the power of the two kings who, unusually for Greek city-states, inherited their positions. In a passage that foreshadows criticisms of equality from his time to the present, he also mentions the "despotism" of the law required to enforce equality and maintain it.[37] Similarly Polybius, the second-century BC Greek historian, has a lot to say about the crimes Nabis committed in his attempt to restore equality to Sparta, when he murdered people right and left.[38] Seventeen hundred years or so later Machiavelli thought that the chief weakness of Sparta, as compared to Rome, was its reluctance, extreme even by Greek standards, to admit foreigners into the citizenry. Yet Machiavelli well understood that keeping foreigners out was an absolute prerequisite for maintaining the kind of equality that existed among the *homoioi*. Sparta, in other words, was built on a contradiction. It was a contradiction that could only end, and eventually did end, in its downfall.[39]

Passing to the Enlightenment, most French and British thinkers rejected Sparta's militarism. Like Herodotus (and Thucydides) before them, they noted the suppression of the individual by the state, his complete subordination to the demands of the latter, the consequent loss of liberty, and the tendency to neglect of letters and the arts. All of those, of course, were themselves both cause and consequence of the famous Spartan combination of frugality and equality, specifically including equality of wealth.[40] Perhaps surprisingly, in view of his subsequent reputation as the grandfather of both Communism and Fascism, one of those who attacked the Spartan version of equality was the great philosopher Georg Friedrich Hegel (1770–1831). To him it was destructive of the "free individualism" that was, or ought to be, the supreme goal of any polity.[41]

Not everybody saw things in this way. To the Abbé Gabriel Bonnot de Mably (1709–1785), another well-known author of the time, the economic equality imposed by Lycurgus was meant to create free men. Not in the sense that they were free from the demands of the state, to be sure; but such as would be free from the desire for wealth, thus opening the gates to virtue.[42] Most famous of all was Mably's close contemporary Rousseau. He used Sparta as a weapon in his lifelong struggle against the inequality he understood as characteristic of the modern world. The Spartans' forceful words and deeds, he wrote, were preferable to Athenians babblings.[43]

Addressing the National Assembly in May 1794, Robespierre

himself had high praise for Sparta. Amidst a historical background
consisting of inequality, selfishness, and greed, he said, "it shines like
a star."[44] This was two months before he was deposed and executed.
The list of nineteenth-century public figures who wrote admiringly
about Sparta could be continued forever. To many militarists on
both sides of the Rhine, the kind of equality the city represented
was a necessary, if under modern conditions impractical, prerequisite for recapturing its exceptional prowess at war. Especially in
France, however, many republican radicals also upheld it. Continuing where Rousseau had left off, they saw Sparta as the incarnation
of civic virtue. Too often, they did not allow the fact that the equality was forced and life itself regimented to the nth degree to disturb
them too much.

The Nazis, as usual, added a peculiar twist of their own. For
them the Athenian version of equality, going hand-in-hand with
democracy as it did, was effete and effeminate. Insisting that the
Spartans were northern "Dorians," Third-Reich historians claimed
that they maintained their equality, and with it their greatness (as
long as it lasted) by rigorously excluding the members of inferior
races and refusing to mix with them in any way.[45] The *homoioi*,
in other words, were a model. The helots *deserved* to be treated
like dogs, enslaved, exploited, and even killed. In all this the Nazis
took the opposite line from Machiavelli. Arguably they made their
country share Sparta's fate by leading it into a war against the entire
world; one which, however excellent their armed forces, owing to
their lack of numbers they could not win.

In the case of Sparta, critics' views concerning the *homoioi*, the
kind of life they led and the price they paid, tend to be overshad-
owed by their attitudes to the city-state's militarism and prowess in
war. Whether or not we agree that the city enjoyed *eunomia*, "good

laws," Spartan equality was of the kind that usually prevails inside an armed camp. Personal freedom did not exist. Everyone was elevated or, depending on one's point of view, reduced to a common denominator. It certainly did not open a path towards democracy; politically speaking, equal rights did not prevail. By contrast, opinions surrounding Athenian equality are always hard to separate from those concerning its democracy. Already with Herodotus, the two have often been identified, even confused, with one another. In Athens equality led to and implied democracy, while democracy in turn promoted equality.

Foreshadowing Anatole France's quip that "the law in its majestic equality prohibits both rich and poor from sleeping under the bridges and stealing bread," several ancient writers criticized the Athenian kind of equality for not going far enough. Especially prominent were Phaleas of Chalcedon and Hippodamus of Miletus. Both wrote during the last decades of the fifth century BC. Phaleas, who is only known to us from Aristotle, pointed out that, though a sort of civic and political equality had been achieved, socioeconomic gaps had not been closed. Inequality in these fields was the inevitable result of a society which, forsaking agriculture and the system whereby each man had his own lot of land and provided for his own family, engaged in industry and trade instead. Hence he proposed all artisans be reduced into public slaves, which would also result in their removal from the body of citizens. Two other reforms would complete the picture. The first was the gradual redistribution of landed property by regulating dowries in such a way that the poor would only be allowed to receive them, and the rich, to give them. The second, which may have been borrowed from Sparta, was the same education for everyone;[46] but for this, all other kinds of equality would be meaningless.

Much better known than Phaleas was Hippodamus of Miletus, an architect who was said to have originated the gridiron plan for cities. Even today, his work may still be seen in the streets of the Athenian suburb of Piraeus. As is also the case in many American towns today, the plan reflected the wish to maintain a certain kind of equality among the inhabitants. Hippodamus too sought to correct the socio-political imbalance by imposing a form of communal ownership. The difference was that the citizen body, and thus the right to both to enjoy civil rights and to participate in politics, would remain intact. Land, still considered the most important resource of all, was to be owned by the community. Part of it would be dedicated to the gods, part would support the soldiers, and part feed the farmers.[47] To this Aristotle responded, with good reason, that Hippodamus had neglected to say who would work the soldiers' land. Moreover, a functional separation between soldiers and farmers would never work. There was, in the plan, nothing to prevent the former from dominating the latter.

Fourth-century BC members of the Cynic (from *kynos*, dog) school also hoped to establish equality by abolishing property. However, theirs was the equality of the mendicant and the beggar who owns nothing and has nothing to lose. As one of them, Diogenes, the philosopher who lived in a barrel and asked Alexander to move aside so as not to obstruct the sun, said, men should be distinguished from one another only by their virtue and by nothing else.[48] The outcome would have been the dismantlement of the polis, indeed of any kind of organized polity. That was something the Cynics realized and even looked forward to.[49] Other critics still, notably Thucydides, took the opposite tack. To them, the trouble with democracy and the *isonomia* with which it was largely synonymous was that they went much too far. To use Plutarch's excellent metaphor, what was wrong with Athens was that it lacked a steady-ing "keel." In its absence the assembly, largely made up of peo-ple who were without property and easily swayed by demagogues, veered now in one direction, now in another. It always risked going to extremes. As many incidents during the Peloponnesian War in particular illustrated, a sane, balanced, continuous policy was very hard, perhaps impossible, to devise and maintain.

The greatest critic of all was Plato. He differed from the rest in that he looked at the question from both sides at once. On one hand he shared the idea, very widespread at the time, that economic inequality would necessarily lead to conflict, perhaps civil war, and suggested that it be abolished. His class of guardians was to hold everything, including even their wives and children, in common so that the distinction between "mine" and "thine" would disappear. Only thus could a truly united city be built. Yet Plato's guardians were to be sharply distinguished both from the workers below them and the philosopher-ruler(s) by whom they were led. Whatever the precise arrangements, and they are anything but clear, obviously there was to be no equality in either rights, or duties, or function. Indeed the whole thing was to be based on a "noble lie:" namely, that the division into classes was not artificial but nature-made.[50] Plato, an aristocrat if ever one there was, also joined Thucydides in criticizing the other side of democracy. That included its "feverish" nature, its encouragement of unrestricted competition among indi-vidual (and equal) citizens, and its inability to keep a steady course. Indeed he compared the ruler in a democracy to a trainer in charge of some big and dangerous beast. To avoid being eaten, he is forever forced to follow the beast's every whim.[51]

Here we cannot trace all the things that have been said about the Greek version of equality from antiquity to the present. It is, however, worth pointing out that ancient critics were interested mainly in what equality did to those who had it. Either they argued that it did not go far enough, or else that it gave rise to certain problems, or both. By contrast, much of modern, particularly liberal and social-ist, criticism focused on how exclusive Greek equality was. In Sparta only a small and diminishing fraction of the population consisted of *homoioi*. In Athens equality probably covered more people— perhaps 50,000, or 10 percent, in a population estimated at half a million. Neither in Sparta nor in Athens (nor in any modern state), did resident aliens possess political rights. Slaves, both state- and privately-owned, had hardly any rights at all. Though Solon did much to make Athens more egalitarian, he also passed a law against slaves practicing gymnastics.[52] Everywhere women were perpetual wards; unattached widows and courtesans apart, they could only live under male protection.

Concerning the first and the second of these groups, no ancient writer seems to have suggested that the situation was unjust and that they be incorporated into the citizen-body. To the extent that this was in fact done, not only in Sparta but in other cities too, it was the result of dire necessity. At times it brought the polities in question to the verge of civil war. With women the situation was different. Here and there, the possibility of giving women equal rights became the subject of discussion. One of those involved was the great comic playwright Aristophanes. In his play *Ecclesiazusae*, "Women in the Assembly," he portrayed an imaginary polis run by women on behalf of women. Property would be held in common and economic work carried out by slaves, as in Sparta. Inside the citizen-body, sexual exclusiveness would be abolished so as to give even the ugliest peo-ple of both sexes an equal chance of sleeping with the best-looking specimens of the opposite one. Probably Aristophanes' purpose in

writing the play was to criticize the Idea of equality, women's equality included, by pushing it to absurd lengths. However, we do not
really know.

Plato, too, discussed the emancipation of women at some
length. To enable women to participate in the affairs of the polis
on an equal basis and play their part as guardians, he suggested that
they be given an education similar to that of men. Like so many
subsequent feminists, he also wanted to see them "liberated" from
the need to look after their children. Probably he saw such arrangements as just, useful, and even essential, though utopian. In the
end, however, no Greek polis ever turned women into citizens, let
alone extended equality to the point where they would be equal with
men.

In both Sparta and Athens equality, whatever its precise form,
was rather exclusive. Inside each city it only embraced a fairly small
part of the population. Externally, it was jealously guarded so that
for foreigners to gain access to it, and share in it, was extremely
difficult. In Athens doing so became more difficult with time, not
less. Attempts to change course were sometimes made, but regularly defeated.[53] During Hellenistic times some cities might form a
loose league and give each other's citizens some limited rights. As is
currently the situation in the European Union, however, they never
even approached a common citizenship. Citizens did not see themselves as an accidental gathering of people. Rather, they believed
they were sharing some kind of common ancestry.[54] It was the sacred task of each city to defend the heritage which represented its
essence, distinguished it from the rest, and justified its existence.
When Aristotle sent his students to collect the "constitutions," or

politeai, of no fewer than 158 cities, what he meant was not merely the political framework but the way their social, cultural and even religious lives was organized. Had the material survived, it would have provided a matchless picture of every aspect of Greek civilization in every significant polis—but unfortunately only the volume dealing with Athens remains.

Internal exclusivity meant that, inside each polis, only part of the population enjoyed equal rights. None was a democracy as the term is understood today. Both in antiquity and later some would go further, arguing that what equality existed came at the expense of liberty (in Sparta) and stability (in Athens). Others considered it as fake; merely a device whereby a relatively small group of people, namely adult male citizens, dominated the rest. External exclusivity meant that there were strict limits to how large any polis could reach without ceasing to be what made it unique. This exclusivity goes far to explain the limited success city-states enjoyed in foreign policy and war, and why they eventually gave way to different, larger and more powerful polities. In the end equality, appearing for the first time in history as a consciously held and, to some extent, realized ideal, flickered and went out. Yet it was never quite forgotten, and it continues to make its impact felt right down to the present day.

Chapter 3

The Proud Tower

Greece was not the only place where city-states, meaning in this context independent, urbanized settlements, rose and developed. Others appeared in the ancient Middle East, Asia—primarily along the Silk Road—and Meso-America. Most were ruled by hereditary chiefs or petty monarchs. The book of *Joshua* mentions dozens of them, each ruled by a *melech* (king, in Hebrew). In respect to equality they do not seem to have differed significantly from the chiefdoms we have discussed. A few developed more egalitarian systems. The Old Testament mentions Philistine office-holders called *sranim*.[1] It has been suggested that the Greeks of 800 BC may have been familiar with the organization of the seafaring Phoenician city-states on the coast of what is Lebanon today and derived some of their political ideas from them.[2] However, so little is known about the city-states in question that the matter must remain uncertain.

Much later Carthage, itself a Phoenician city, had a sort of Senate as well as magistrates called *suffettes*. However, the right to elect and be elected seems to have been limited to the members of a wealthy aristocracy.[3] Carthage may have had the potential to turn itself into a different and much larger kind of polity. However, since it was defeated and destroyed by Rome, which also wiped out any literary sources its enemy may have produced, we shall never know. All other city-states, by refusing to extend citizenship and accept outsiders on an equal basis, remained rather small. Many probably did not have more than a few hundred citizens. Sooner or later they fell victim to polities that, organized on different principles, were much larger than themselves. The one exception to the rule was Rome. The small city on the banks of the Tiber pulled itself up by its bootstraps over a period of centuries and grew into one of the largest and most powerful empires ever. Hence the way equality developed, or did not develop, in Rome is worth examining in some detail. The more so because, as much of our political terminology shows, its shadow has continued to linger right down to the present day.

Like Dark Ages Greece, Italy during the first half of the first millennium BC was inhabited by tribes each of which had its own chief or chiefs. Some of those tribes continued to exist more or less unchanged into historical times. Others apparently developed urban centers where political, religious, and economic life was concentrated. Looking back, the most important urban center was Rome itself. Originally it was ruled by kings who passed their positions to their sons. However, after the last one, Tarquinius Superbus, was deposed in 509 BC the city turned itself into a republic. Yet Rome did not follow either the Spartan or the Athenian trajectory towards greater equality among its citizens. Instead, for some four and a half centuries after the abolition of the monarchy it remained what one can only call an aristocratic republic.

The republic in question knew neither the Spartan principle of socio-economic equality nor the Athenian one, of which Pericles had boasted, of *isonomia*. Instead, the population was divided into three classes, i.e. the Senators, the Knights, and the common people. Membership in the upper classes was based on descent and property. Moral conduct also counted for something, since the censors who reviewed the lists every five years had the right to remove those of whom they disapproved on such grounds from the rolls. Of equality before the law there could be no question whatsoever. So large were the gaps between the classes that for a member of the lower ones to sue his superior was almost unheard of. And when it came to punishment, Senators, in particular were exempt from its most degrading forms.

The political differences between the classes were, if anything, even more important. Like the Greek city-states, the Roman republic was governed by elected magistrates who served for one year. As in the Greek city-states, it was the assembled people who elected them. It was the assembled people, too, who made the most important decisions, including the passing of legislation and declaring war and peace. In fact Rome had not one but two, later three, different popular assemblies. In the two oldest of those, the *comitia tributa* and the *comitia centuriata*, citizens did not vote as individuals but by the tribe or century to which they belonged. In both, things were organized in such a way as to heavily favor first the members of certain tribes, and then those of the upper classes. Thus some people carried far more voting weight than their numbers would warrant.

As its name indicates, the third assembly, known as *Comitia Plebis Tributa* and created specifically for the common people, was not organized on the principle of one man, one vote either. However, we do not know exactly how these things worked or the extent to which they later changed, if indeed they did. Originally only senators, known as *patres conscripti* (registered fathers) could claim leading positions. Later, as members of prominent non-senatorial families joined the senators, this changed. The two elements gradually merged, but that was as far as the process went. As long as the Republic lasted political power remained firmly in the hands of the aristocracy, specifically the Senate whose members, like those of the Athenian Areopagus and (perhaps) some similar body in Carthage, were made up of former magistrates.

At present, expressions such as "aristocratic republic" smack of exclusiveness and that worst of all bad things, unequal rights. Many ancient historians, particularly Polybius and Livy who in this respect were following Aristotle, saw things in a different light. They thought that Rome's "mixed constitution," consisting of monarchic, aristocratic and democratic elements, served to restrain all three and prevent them from being carried to excesses. Far from being a handicap, the constitution represented the real secret of the city's exceptional success. So firmly rooted and so self-evident was inequality that even popular reformers such as the Gracchus brothers and Julius Caesar were descended from highly aristocratic families, the Cornelii and Julii respectively. The former had included more magistrates among its members than any other. The latter traced their origins back to the Trojan leader Anchises and the goddess Venus.[4] Among the few important exceptions was Gaius Marius, the great late second and early first-century BC politician, reformer, and military commander. According to Plutarch, his father was a laborer. However, since Marius ran for office in his native city of Arpinum, the modern Arpino in central Italy, and married into that city's elite, the claim was probably made for political reasons and false.[5]

The rather sharp class distinctions characteristic of Rome also explain the role played by another form of social organization, i.e. clientage, that classical Greece only knew in a much weaker form, if at all. Clients were neither relatives nor slaves. They did not form part of their patrons' households and were free citizens. The only exception to this rule were manumitted slaves whose importance grew as time went on. Clients entered into a semi-formal relationship of faith (*fides*) with some person who was richer and more powerful than themselves. Both parties were supposed to assist each other with money, with political influence (working from the top to the bottom), during elections (reaching from the bottom to the top), and in the courts. Several first-century BC warlords even had enough clients to recruit armies, or at any rate the nuclei of armies, from among them.[6] So useful was clientage to both sides that it was carried over from the Republican age into the Imperial era; from Augustus on, many emperors tried to present themselves as *patrones* of the Empire as a whole.

As in all other ancient polities, city-states included, Roman equality, to the extent that it existed at all, was limited to adult male citizens. It did not embrace the very considerable fraction of the population made up of women, children, slaves, and of course foreigners. As Machiavelli wrote, though, where Rome differed from the rest was in its ability to expand. The process started early in the fifth century BC. Much of it was accomplished by war, a field in which Rome was as proficient as any polity before or since. As a rule, the Romans neither destroyed Italian cities they had defeated nor enslaved their inhabitants. Nor, on the other hand, did they incorporate their former enemies into their own polity by bestowing citizenship on them. Instead they demonstrated their own political genius by signing treaties with them, giving them limited rights such as *connubium* (the right to intermarry with Roman citizens) and *commercium* (trade). Technically the polities that were treated in this way were known as *foederati* or allies. This meant they no longer had the right to conduct an independent foreign policy, which was handled almost entirely by the Senate at Rome.

Another measure the Romans often took was to set up colonies on conquered land. The system enabled Rome to maintain a number of citizens, hence of soldiers, far larger than that which any other contemporary Mediterranean polity could muster. It is estimated that, in 225 BC, the Republic had under its authority about 770,000 men of military age. Of those 273,000 were citizens, 85,000 Latin colonists, and 412,000 allies.[7] The system was both complex and explicitly based on inequality. Few details are available; quite probably the Romans were following their famous principle of divide and rule. Still it was sufficiently robust to withstand and overcome even the mortal danger presented by Hannibal's invasion during the last years of the third century BC. Only in 90 BC, centuries after the whole of the peninsula had come under Roman rule, did the various Italian allies finally wake up and demand full citizen rights for themselves. The resulting "Social War" was as ferocious as any. In the end the allies got what they had asked for.

The merger between citizens and allies and the establishment of civic and political equality among them did not end the story. Throughout the second century BC socio-economic inequality had increased. The countless wars Rome fought, the enormous demands those wars made on the available manpower, and the uneven distribution of the vast amounts of booty that flowed into the city were the primary causes. As a few became fabulously wealthy, many grew much poorer than they had been. They were forced to sell their land to the owners of the great estates and move into the city where they became a shiftless proletariat. During the 130s these problems for the first time gave rise to serious political trouble which grew into a whole series of civil wars. The wars lasted for about a century before Augustus, by establishing the Principate, finally put an end to them. The outcome was for one man to be elevated to dizzying heights above all the rest. Even the title Augustus took for himself, *Princeps*, perhaps best translated as "first in rank" or "paramount," leaves very little doubt on that account.

Under Augustus and his successors Rome gradually developed into a monarchy. Whatever equality had existed was obviated and numerous measures taken to accentuate the gap that now separated the emperors even from their greatest subjects; for example, after a short time it was only they and their relatives who were still allowed to celebrate triumphs. Some emperors did so even though they had never taken the field. Some were worshipped as gods and/or declared divine after their deaths. During the third century AD, more and more they demanded to be recognized as living gods. The more elevated and the more absolute the emperors became, the more their subjects lost any rights they may have had. Until the end of the second century AD, and at any rate under "good emperors" such as Augustus, Vespasian and the Antonines, at least the pretense that the Senate and the senatorial families whose members filled its ranks shared the government with the emperor was maintained. From that point on, though, even the pretense no longer prevailed as military commanders, who were often from the lower classes and from outlying parts of the empire, regularly fought each other for the throne.

Also starting with Augustus, emperors very often appointed themselves *pontifex maximus*, supreme priest. In this capacity they mediated between their subjects and the world of the gods. The inequality that was the result of the elevation of one man over all the rest was accentuated by developments at the bottom of the pyramid. As everyone and everything became firmly subject to the emperor, distinctions between citizen and noncitizen became less important. The so-called Constitutio Antoniana of 212 AD, which gave citizenship to all the empire's inhabitants, carried this process to its logical conclusion. Differences between freemen and slaves, once very great, also tended to lose their significance. There was even some improvement in the status of women, who in practically all societies before and after Rome were considered inferior to men and subordinate to them.[8] The shape of the social pyramid had changed. In theory, it reached the point where, instead of tapering towards the top, it consisted of a mighty pillar on which, like Nelson on his column in the Center of London, stood a single man. All around him stretched a social terrain that was increasingly flat.

In practice, things were not pushed quite so far. No man, however mighty and however competent, could rule all the rest on his own without the help of associates, big and small. To enlist and maintain their collaboration he had to give them some kind of *quid pro quo*. Men continued to vary enormously in power, rank, and property. A few governed provinces, commanded armies, gathered vast wealth, and either wrote or had written for them books that celebrated their glorious deeds. Countless others owned nothing, worked the fields like so many beasts of burden, and died almost as if they had never existed. In Rome and other empires, some emperors did their best to impose justice. A stele erected by one of the earliest emperors, the "god-chosen" Hammurabi around 1772 BC, says that the objective of issuing a code of law was to ensure that the strong would not oppress the weak.[9] Still the code, and many similar ones, drew very sharp distinctions between noblemen and commoners, commoners and slaves, and also between men and women. In the case of murder, the amount of blood money required to be paid therefore varied accordingly.

Only in two respects did equality prevail in Rome. First, adherents of the Stoic school of philosophy asserted the natural equality of all human beings. All, slaves included, had sprung from the same stock. They lived under the same skies, had the same biological makeup and needs, and were equal under natural law.[10] There was nobody so low born, so degraded, that he (or she) was incapable *ab initio* of being virtuous.[11] People should remember this and try to assist each other and treat each other as kindly as circumstances permitted. However, Stoics never made any kind of organized attempt to tear down existing political, social and economic inequalities. How could they, given that they tended to be upper class men with an emperor, Marcus Aurelius, at their head? Second, to quote Caligula (reigned 33–37 AD), who prided himself on his lack of shame in his behavior and readiness to tell the truth, the emperor could do anything to anyone at any time he wanted, including cutting his or her throat.[12] He did not even have to give his reasons. The situation in other empires was usually similar.

*

Apart from the Hellenistic monarchies, centering as they did on cities, and from China, on which more later, most of the world's remaining empires seem to have been rather less urbanized than Rome. Unlike Rome, these empires grew directly out of chiefdoms. They skipped the city-state, never acquiring any of the latter's characteristics even as a more or less distant memory that could be contrasted with the present, as in the slightly nostalgic writings of the Roman historian Tacitus. As was also the case in parts of nineteenth-century Africa, some chiefdoms were sufficiently powerful and well-organized to be called kingdoms.[13] Indeed as far back as we can look, one African potentate, the ruler of Ethiopia, always called himself "emperor." Not accidentally, he was a Christian. Like some of his less celebrated counterparts in West Africa, who converted to Islam, his power was closely linked to the use of writing for religious purposes. Whether the difference between all three types of monarchies, chiefdoms, kingdoms and empires, is one of principle or merely of degree has often been debated at length. In respect to equality, though, the latter answer seems closer to the truth.

Here we do not need to follow the development of these polities, some of which were among the most powerful of all time, in any detail. Suffice it to say that, wherever we look, we find paramount chiefs using every sort of political and military method to subordinate other peoples, or tribes and turning themselves into emperors. Sometimes the populations over whom they ultimately came to rule in this way were quite homogenous, as in Egypt before its conquest by Persia in the sixth century BC and also in China. Apart from the ill-understood period when the former came under the rule of the Hyksos, as well as those when the latter was ruled by the Mongols and the Manchu, there were no major cultural differences between the emperor and his elite on one hand and the mass of his subjects on the other. All this was even more true of Japan, an exceptionally homogeneous empire that also formed a separate culture.[14]

In most other empires the situation was different. In ancient Mesopotamia there were the Akkadians, Assyrians, Babylonians, among others. Empires repeatedly appeared, expanded, ruled, and eventually collapsed. Similarly in Iran, Elamites, Persians, Parthians, and other peoples fought each other, defeated each other, and ruled over each other for centuries on end.[15] Before the Aztecs there were the Toltecs and before them, the Olmecs. The Aztecs themselves ruled over an entire host of subject peoples. Many of them were unwilling and looked forward to nothing so much as the opportunity to rebel and throw off the bloody yoke,[16] which was one reason why Cortés and his handful of men were able to defeat them so easily. The Inca, too, were a conquering tribe that gave their name to an empire made up of a complex patchwork of languages, cultures, and peoples.[17] The same applies to the Mughal Empire the foundations of which were being laid just at the time when, on the other side of the world, the Aztec Empire was being conquered.[18] Another empire of the same kind was the Ottoman. Reaching its greatest extent between about 1500 and 1700, it only collapsed at the end of World War I. By then, thanks partly to the fact that equality was unknown, Europeans referred to the Porte as "the Unspeakable Turk."

In their quest for support, most emperors turned to religion and claimed some kind of divine descent. Even if they did not, they saw themselves as appointed by god and headed the religious establishment of their empires. Pharaoh was supposedly the son of Amun Ra. One pharaoh, Akhenaten, who reigned from approximately 1353 to 1336 BC, tried to replace him with the sun god Aton. The experiment did not work and after his death it was quickly abandoned. In any case it did not constitute an attempt to increase equality by renouncing the ruler's divine status—such a thought could never have entered Akhenaten's head. It was merely a question of replacing one deity by another deemed more suitable for the task.[19] Many reliefs show Mesopotamian emperors of various periods and nationalities conversing with their gods on an almost equal basis. To make sure the viewer does not confuse the one with the other, some deities are seated. Others are provided with a pair of wings. Outside the Middle East thing were similar. Sapa Inca, the title of the Inca emperor, is variously translated "child of the sun" or "paramount chief." Japan's Imperial dynasty is supposed to be descended from the sun-goddess Amaterasu. Until recently the emperor *was* a deity (*kami*). Even now he is known as *Tenno Heika*, "His Majesty the Heavenly Sovereign."

One of the most important and long-lived official ideologies that underpinned government and justified the unequal power that some people exercised over others was Chinese Confucianism. Unlike most other civilizations, China did not have a supreme god. In some sense, indeed, it did not have any gods at all. As a result, instead of claiming to be descended from the supreme god, Chinese emperors carried the title Son of Heaven (*Tien*) and claimed to rule over All under Heaven. The way Confucius described the universe, all the inhabitants of All under Heaven were part of a single, though vast, family. Inside that family, everyone and everything had its place which was also mandated by Heaven. Moderns were duty-bound to respect ancients, inferiors, superiors, youngsters their elders and women, men.[20] All these obligations were supposed to be reciprocal. In return for being revered, served and fed, superiors owed inferiors guidance, protection, and benevolence. Confucius himself emphasized that reciprocity—"do unto others as you would have others do unto you"—stands at the very heart of his teaching.[21]

In this system the central value was harmony, not equality. Social life was to be based on the recognition that all people (and, according to some of the master's followers, all things, but that is less important for our purpose) have their proper station in life. They should be treated, and should treat others, accordingly. In this sense, indeed, harmony was consciously meant as a substitute for the inequality nature had created and which was an essential prerequisite for any civilization. Laws, or rather codes of conduct, were not formalized but had to be planted in the people's hearts and minds instead. The means for doing so were goodwill, example

and education, not prohibitions and punishments. This in turn reflected the belief that everybody, however low his or her position in
life, had the *potential* to become virtuous. In this sense at any rate,
everyone had indeed been born equal to everybody else.

Assuming he was a genuine historical figure, Confucius lived
and worked shortly before 500 BC, during the Period of the Warring States. Centuries later his doctrine was made into the official
Imperial ideology, a purpose for which, owing to the heavy emphasis on harmony, duty, and hierarchy, it was well suited. Confucius
himself was careful to treat officials of different rank differently.[22]
In 140 BC examinations in his ideology were instituted which every
aspirant to the Imperial Civil Service had to pass. So successful was
the system that it lasted for two millennia. During the Cultural Revolution Mao Tze Dong ordered all Chinese to "criticize Confucius"
for the subservience he demanded. The criticism was justifiable, for
the sage quite explicitly aimed his teachings at the elite, not "the
common people."[23] Concerning the latter, all Confucius had to say
is that they needed to be kept firmly in their place. But as powerful
as Mao was, his wishes availed him nothing. In present-day China,
Confucius' doctrine remains as influential as it has ever been.

Not everyone was happy with this way of looking at things. On
one side of Confucianism was Daoism. Like Confucianism, it can
be seen as a religion, a philosophy, or both.[24] Also like Confucianism, it opposed written laws—"too many laws make the empire decline." It differs in that it puts the individual, not the community, at
the center of things. It recognizes that different people have different ways of attaining *Dao*, meaning "the proper path," "excellence,"
or "a state in which the gap between the existing and the desirable
is closed." To be sure, the rights, tasks and duties of the king were
very different from those of the commoner. Still, and it is here that

Daoism and Confucianism differ, everyone is theoretically able to achieve his *Dao without reference to anyone else*. In this sense all are equal. The *Daoist* hero, if that is not an oxymoron, is the perfectly self-contained individual. At the same time, so attuned is he to the world that he achieves everything without doing anything.

Such a doctrine is not easy to reconcile with the existence of a system of government based on inequality. Both within and without China it could be used, and occasionally has been used, to deny the need for any government at all.[25] Hence it is not surprising that we find, on Confucius' other side, the so-called "legalist" tradition. Once again, the background is formed by the Period of the Warring States. Here the emphasis is on avoiding chaos and maintaining order. This is to be achieved by means of powerful laws known as *fa*. The Emperor must have them written down and applied to all his subjects equally.[26] Transgressions are punished with the utmost severity. Except that there is no personal god, we are back with Hammurabi and countless similar despots. Their common goal was to raise themselves so high above all the rest that they could treat them, or tread on them, as equals—an idea, of course, that was rarely if ever realized in practice.

Rulers in monotheistic societies differed from the rest in that they could be neither divine nor semi-divine. In Judaism this even applied to King David, the most favorite king of all. The most they could aspire was to be God's chosen, or anointed. Jewish groups which believed in the divinity of certain human beings, as the Christians and, much later, the followers of Sabbatai Zevi did, usually ended up by leaving Judaism altogether.[27] To further emphasize the vast gulf that separates men from God, the Jewish prayer book gives the latter the exalted title, "the King of the Kings of Kings," no less. As long as Jews lived in the *galuth*, or diaspora, they also failed to develop a rabbinical hierarchy. Certainly some rabbis were much more influential than others and were revered by their followers. However, there was no formal hierarchy so that none had authority over their colleagues. What Rabbi X permitted Rabbi Z often prohibited, and the other way around. Hence the well-known Jewish saying, "make [choose] yourself a rabbi."

During the second half of the eighteenth century things started changing. The principle that no man could be divine or semi-divine remained in place. However, Hassidic Jews gradually started investing their rabbis with almost magical qualities of devoutness and wisdom. In this they became more like Sephardic Jews in Africa and Asia who had long had a special class of saintly rabbis. In some ways they resemble Christian Saints. They even carry out similar functions such as intercession by prayer, fortune-telling, blessing, and healing. Their homes are the objects of pilgrimage, their tombs places where prayers are launched and feasts celebrated. Of late such rabbis have been multiplying like the proverbial rabbits. Both Hassidic and Sephardic rabbis often pass their status to their offspring. More recently, the establishment of the State of Israel led to the creation of an official Rabbinate that is part of the civil service. As a result, those rabbis who are part of it—not all are—have been formed into a regular hierarchy. With every passing year the two processes, the one coming from below and the other from above, are causing the kind of equality rabbis used to possess to be thrown overboard. Traditional Judaism also had certain laws that distinguish between priests (*cohanim*), Levites, and ordinary people. But their importance is relatively minor.

No more than their Jewish colleagues could Christian rulers be gods, living or dead. By way of doing the next best thing Constantine (reigned, 306–337 AD) became a saint. Even the fact that he executed his son Crispus and had his wife Fausta scalded to death did not prevent him from being put on a par with the Apostles, no less. Constantine's mother Helena was also beatified. Charlemagne was made a Saint (by Antipope Paschal III, 1164–1168), but subsequently the Church withdrew its recognition. Other Christian rulers also held their positions *dei gratia*. By contrast, early Christian congregations formed small, powerless minorities in a pagan sea. They drew their members mainly from the lower classes and were as egalitarian as any communities have ever been. Some even adopted a communist lifestyle including common property, common living quarters, common meals, and in the catacombs, common burials and common graves.[28] The Apostle Paul regularly addressed his letters to entire communities, not to specific people within them. Furthermore, during the first three centuries Christians were often severely persecuted. Always fearing to be betrayed as Jesus himself was, leaders could exercise influence but had to tread very carefully when wielding authority.

Later things changed. In heaven, the saints were carefully graded according to their importance. Here on earth, once the Church had emerged from the underground and was officially recognized as the carrier of the state religion it lost no time in building an enormously elaborate hierarchy that consisted of patriarchs, hegemons, cardinals, archbishops, bishops, deacons, and a whole host of less important dignitaries. Each of them occupied a different rank, possessed different powers, and enjoyed different privileges. As any number of Episcopal residences shows, the gap that separated the purple-clad princes of the Church from the simple parish priest was quite as large as those that prevailed in the secular world. In the West during the early middle ages the Christian hierarchy, staffed by trained priests who could read and write, was often centuries in advance of the other types of government that existed.

Furthermore, the ecclesiastical hierarchies were integrated into the secular ones. First in the West, later in the East too, senior priests lived much as noblemen did. Many noblemen, especially cadets who did not inherit the family estates, joined the Church. To be sure, they could not leave their offices to their offspring. But they could, and often did, pass them to their nephews. Nor, until the Counter-Reformation, were they prevented from having stables full of concubines. In the West some of the more powerful ecclesiastics, the Pope included, ruled their own principalities and defended them by the sword. In both West and East religion was systematically used to buttress inequality, justify it, and enforce it if necessary. The main difference was that the Byzantine emperor was simultaneously head of the Greek Orthodox Church. Not so the Western emperor who had to suffer a rival, the Bishop of Rome. The Pope was seldom under his control and almost never completely so. Wherever one looked, equality existed only in the eyes of God, if indeed it existed at all.

Moslem rulers resembled Jewish and Christian rulers in that they could not be gods. However, just as their Greek Orthodox counterparts were heads of the eastern Church, they could very well be Caliphs (heads of the faithful). Islam was at first a tribal religion. While Mohammed led his "Companions" (*Ansar*) it is important to recall that he was a refugee who had been forced to flee his native city of Mecca. As a result, all he could rely upon were example and persuasion, not formal authority. Yet even the *Quran* itself contains several verses that prohibit believers from questioning social inequalities, claiming that they were instituted by Allah in person.[29] Whether these are later interpolations, as some scholars believe they are, will not be discussed here. What is indisputable is that, once Islamic expansion had begun in earnest, things changed. Moslem rulers, running a huge empire, took over or developed much more hierarchical structures than those their people had previously possessed.[30]

Nevertheless there have always been some Islamic voices suggesting equality. Much the most important form remained equality before God, which few doubted. Inside the mosque every man had to prostrate himself just like everyone else. Arguably this form of equality was of great assistance in enabling Islam to penetrate the extremely un-egalitarian societies of India and West Africa, regions where it established a permanent, and in the eyes of many very troublesome, presence. Islamic scholars also considered equality before the law and socio-economic equality. On occasion, even the possibility of granting equality to Jews and Christians (*dhimmi*) and women was debated. Some medieval scholars may have been influenced by Plato whose works reached them in more or less faithful, more or less abbreviated, translations.[31] Few if any of these ideas were ever realized in practice. Rather, as was also the case among Christians, equality before God served as an excuse not to institute it on earth. In this sense Marx's quip that religion is the opium of the masses rings all too true.

It is, however, necessary to add that the Moslem clergy, or *ulama*, remained surprisingly egalitarian. Caliphs might be the successors of Mohammed and the heads of the faithful. However, they were not religious scholars. Society did recognize that some scholars were better than others. Their reward was to receive more elevated titles, to become better known, and to attract more students. Some Islamic scholars served as judges, but it was the secular authorities who appointed them and controlled them. Even Shiites, who are more inclined to grade such scholars than Sunnis are, did not develop the formal organization, i.e. a church, needed for one Ayatollah to force his views on all the rest. That only happened in Iran after the fall of the Shahanasha ("King of Kings") in 1978 when the country became an Islamic Republic. In that form of republic, the religious establishment is superior to the secular one rather than *vice versa*. Whether, following the so-called "Arab Spring," something similar will take shape elsewhere remains to be seen. It was precisely because no monotheistic ruler could be a god that all three religions could introduce the strange—strange in the sense that, historically speaking, it is rather exceptional—belief that all believers are equal in the eyes of God. In theory they were ready to take in anybody regardless of race, color, nationality, sex, and previous creed. Their God was far mightier and far more remote from mankind than in most other religions. He was, said the great scholar Maimonides (1138–1204), "the mover who was not moved."

Regardless of just how they themselves were, or were not, related to God, and also of how egalitarian the various religions and doctrines were, rulers in all the empires listed above resembled Caligula in that their power was absolute. Conversely, subjects had no rights whatsoever. In a very real sense they were the rulers' slaves. To the sixteenth-century French political scientist Jean Bodin, that fact was precisely why the Ottoman Empire had grown as powerful as it was. In most places, so far did an emperor stand above other mortals that they were expected to approach him while crawling on their bellies as if they were worms or ants. In ancient Persia, anybody who so much as accidentally touched him was, unless clemency was exercised, executed on the spot. By agreeing to her kinsmen's request that she speak to Asahuerus (Xerxes) without asking for permission first, Esther, who was his favorite concubine, put her life in jeopardy.[32] In the *Arthashastra*, one of the most sophisticated political treatises ever which was allegedly written by Kautilya (ca. 350–283 BC) as a guide to the rulers of the Mauryan Empire, equality is not even mentioned.

Everywhere emperors surrounded themselves by elaborate hierarchies without which their rule would have been impossible. Inside each hierarchy some owed their positions to the fact that they were related to the emperor by blood, marriage, or adoption. Others were elevated because of their aristocratic status, i.e. descent, whereas others still were appointed on the basis of loyalty and competence. Some entered the hierarchy from the aristocracy, others made their way up from the bottom. Inside each hierarchy there was a constant jockeying for power. In the end, everything depended on getting the emperor's ear. In many places independently rich and influential people who were not a part of the imperial hierarchy did indeed exist. However, being outsiders, their position was often as precarious as that of the hierarchy's members, if not more so.

In one way or another, all these problems were duplicated by the empires' smaller relatives, i.e. kingdoms and chiefdoms. What really set empires apart was the fact that their heads' pretensions to supremacy (in other words, their unequal status), went far beyond their own territories. The aforementioned Hammurabi claimed to rule the entire earth. His Assyrian and Persian successors made the same claim. Somewhere along the way they also invented the title King of Kings. Roman and Byzantine emperors claimed to rule the *oikoumene*, or inhabited world, even though they knew quite well that, in reality, that was not the case. Otherwise, why make the occasional forays into Scotland and Mesopotamia? Medieval Holy Roman Emperors claimed to be the heads of the *Respublica Christiana*, if not the entire world.

These claims often resulted in strange incidents. Visiting Paris in 1377, Emperor Charles IV mounted the white horse reserved for King Charles V of France without asking for permission first, even though France was not part of the his empire. No wonder that in a contemporary illustration, the king looks annoyed.[33] A Japanese delegation visiting Beijing did not pay the emperor the respect the latter claimed was his due. Loath to break relations, he generously "forgave them" for their ignorance. Sultan Suleiman the Magnificent issued a proclamation saying that King Francis I of France had prostrated himself in front of his throne (in reality, he had suggested an alliance). Ivan the Terrible of Russia called Queen Elizabeth I of England "a mere maiden."[34] Yet the claim of absolute superiority was far from being a harmless quirk. It meant that anyone who elected to wage war, even a defensive war, against an emperor was, by definition, a rebel and treated accordingly. How many millions paid with their lives for this idea is impossible to say.

Before leaving empires behind, it is necessary to return to the most important quality that distinguished them from the city-states discussed in the previous chapter. As we saw, the very fact that city-states rested on citizen-bodies whose members were, in some important ways, each other's equals formed a formidable obstacle to their unification and expansion. No group has ever been eager to share its privileges with others; as a result, in most cases those obstacles remained insurmountable. Empires, being based on in-equality, even if it was only a "soft" inequality dressed in Confucian etiquette, did not suffer from this disadvantage to nearly the same extent. From antiquity down to quite recent times, in principle and very often in practice they were able to swallow up many smaller polities, city-states included, and incorporate many peoples with-out having to worry about this aspect of the problem. An empire might be defined as a polity that, precisely because it was *not* rooted in equality, was able to do all those things. But for inequality, most empires could hardly have become what they were.

To be sure, there was a price to be paid. Everywhere superiors, regardless of whether it was by status, religion or nationality that they differed from subordinates, had to devote a considerable part of their resources to holding them in their proper place. When that effort failed, as it notoriously did in the case of the Aztec, Inca, and Mughal empires, the entire elaborate structure came crashing down like a house of cards. Not so long ago the same happened first to the various European colonial empires and then to the Soviet Union. Yet considering how mighty some empires became, and how long they lasted, it seems to have been a price they were well able to bear.

*

Not every empire or kingdom succeeded in preserving its centralized structure over extended periods. Partly this was because distances were often very great and communications very poor. To relay information from the capital to the frontier and back might take weeks or more.[35] To assemble an army and march it to a trouble spot took considerably longer still. As a result, provincial governors and officials could not be strictly controlled. The point might come where they were able to leave their positions to their offspring. Understood as a political concept, feudalism was invented during the Enlightenment. As we saw and as we shall see again, the thinkers of that period were obsessed with "equality." "Feudalism" stood for the opposite of equality as well as anything else associated with the "dark" or "Gothic" ages, as the middle ages were known.[36]

Since then feudalism has been defined in as many ways as there are historians. The term itself probably comes from *feudum*, a fief.

A close relative is *beneficium*. It stood for a system of government, indeed a kind of social order, under which, in return for fealty and military service, lords agreed to take subordinates under their protection. Whether this arrangement always meant that the subordinate, or vassal, was given an estate, complete with serfs, to live on has been hotly debated. Clearly, though, this was often the case. Others define feudalism as a regime where the aristocracy rules by right; others still as one that, in contrast to both the ancient polis and the modern state, drew no sharp distinction between the public and the private.[37] Indeed it could almost be said that the public realm did not exist; government was based not on abstract principles but on personal loyalties. Such a system seems well attuned to human nature. That, in turn may explain why many feudal regimes around the world have often been very long-lived indeed. From our point of view it does not matter. What does matter is the fact that, if there is one thing all forms of feudalism have in common, it is the inequality that those who first described it saw as its essence.

European feudalism, with which we are mainly concerned here, seems to have grown out of two separate developments. One was the progressive weakening of the Roman Empire during the fourth and fifth centuries AD. It created a situation where the center could no longer control the provinces. As a result, leading men in the latter started making themselves practically independent. Significantly, by this time the term *clientes* had come to mean a band of armed retainers. Thus assisted, these leading men tried to defend their estates, plus those members of the population who put themselves under their protection, against the various tribes that were repeatedly invading the empire. The other new development was the consequences of the invasions themselves. The first process worked from the center to the provinces, the second from the provinces to the center. As they unfolded, many previously free people were gradually turned into serfs.[38]

Once they had settled down as a new ruling class, the conquering tribes also changed. Their social system became less egalitarian and more hierarchical than it had been at the time they were first described by the early second-century AD Roman historian Tacitus.[39] Although the *Chronicles of the Kings of Norway* originate in Scandinavia where there were few indigenous people to conquer and feudalism proper never established itself, it can help us by providing a graphic description of the step-by-step way inequality developed. At first, we are told, chiefs dined in the midst of their men with everyone sitting side by side on long benches. Next, they moved themselves to the head of the table. Next, another table was joined to the first so as to form a T; next, the crossbar of the T was raised and put on a dais. Slowly but surely, chiefs were elevated and metamorphosed into kings. The final step was to interpose a curtain between the king and his queen and everybody else. Only on special festive occasions was the curtain removed so that everyone might see the royal couple eat. From there it was but a short step to instituting ceremonies during which they alone ate while everyone else was obliged to watch.

Further south, several centuries passed during which any number of relatively small, relatively weak, kingdoms coalesced, all the time fighting each other tooth and nail. Beginning in 768 AD Charlemagne, surely one of the most remarkable characters who ever lived, made a determined attempt to put at least some of the pieces together again. It is said that, as part of the process, he even tried to learn how to read and write, though without much success.[40] In 800 he had Pope Leo III, who was his protégé, crown him emperor in Rome. Yet in the end his efforts were to no avail.

After his death, which took place in 814, his empire was divided among his sons and fell apart. This marked the opening of what most historians see as the "classical" period of feudalism.

Although family ties were necessarily important, feudal society was not based on kin to quite the same extent as chiefdoms were. What really counted was fealty on one hand and serfdom on the other. Both, but fealty in particular, created a reciprocal set of rights and obligations. Fealty was formalized by means of ceremonies, gifts, oaths, and, later, written documents. The duties of both lords and vassals were laid down by custom. As a result, considerable variation existed both from one place to another and over time. In theory a simple chain led from the highest prince, i.e. the emperor or king, down to the lowliest squire. From him it went on to the serfs who lived on his land and worked it for him. The difference was that, whereas fealty was supposed to be individual, voluntary, and subject to periodical renewal, serfdom was collective, compulsory and hereditary.

As things were, there was often nothing to prevent the same vassal from swearing fealty to, and holding lands from, several lords simultaneously. This made the situation much more complicated. Several lords might share the same village or group of villages among themselves, and the same lord could owe fealty to several superiors. In theory even emperors could be somebody else's vassals and owe homage for some of the lands they held. This sometimes happened in practice as well. As late as the second half of the sixteenth century the French political scientist Jean Bodin considered that, in the whole of Europe, there was only one ruler who was truly sovereign in the sense that he did *not* have a superior for any of the countries, provinces, districts, and estates he governed. He was, of course, referring to the King of France.[41]

To add to the confusion, rank did not necessarily reflect power and wealth, nor power and wealth, rank. The outcome was a vast body of aristocrats no two of whom were exactly each other's equals. Titles, some of them derived from Latin and others from the various Germanic languages, varied from one place to another. As time passed, they tended to become more numerous and more elaborate. Under the emperor there were kings, arch- or grand dukes, dukes, princes, earls, counts, and viscounts, to mention but a few of the better-known ones. Many men carried not one title but several; the longer the list, the better. Some terms, such as prince and baron, carried a double meaning. They might refer to men of a specific rank; but they might also describe whole groups of aristocrats whose ranks were not necessarily equal. Queen Elizabeth I of England systematically used the title "prince" to gloss over the fact that, as a woman, she was different from other rulers.[42] The title "knight" could cover any aristocrat who had been dubbed as such regardless of his rank. Conversely, commoners could not be knights even if they were armed like knights and fought like them. In time this prohibition, rather than being relaxed, grew stricter still.

So self-evident was inequality that the myths which, in the absence of history proper, traced the origins of each people and group, did not mention it.[43] Feudal society has often been characterized as being made up of three classes: warrior-aristocrats who fought, priests who prayed and, in doing so, formed a separate hierarchy parallel to the secular one, and peasants who worked. There is some truth in this, but it is also an oversimplification. In some regions, chiefly mountainous ones, relatively egalitarian tribal societies survived. In others a steep hierarchy became entrenched early on. Not all property was feudalized, i.e. held from some lord in return for fealty. In various places so-called freeholds survived. As economies became more monetized from about 1300 onward, land gradually ceased to be the only form of wealth so that the hierarchy that was based on it was disrupted. There were probably always some soldiers and office holders who, instead of receiving a *feudum*, were fed and/or paid directly by their lords. After 1300 the number of paid personnel probably increased. Finally there were the towns, enclaves in a feudal "sea." Over time many were able to emancipate themselves from the control of those on whose land they were built. Doing so they acquired "privileges," literally "private laws".

The term "privilege" takes us into the very heart of feudal society. We today live in a world where, in theory at least, the same law, duly enacted by the authorized organs of the sovereign state, applies to everyone. Nothing could be more foreign to the Middle Ages when each group, and sometimes each individual, was subject to a different set of laws. Often they were subject to several different ones, some of them conflicting. Secular men and women came under one kind of law, ecclesiastics under another that was made by different authorities on the basis of different procedures. Not unreasonably, Henry VIII of England complained that clerics were "only half my subjects."[44] Nobles, commoners, serfs, slaves (some countries still had them, particularly during the early part of the age) and townsmen all had, or had imposed on them, separate systems of law. Crossing from one province to another within the same kingdom, different laws often applied. Each time a province was added, the first thing a ruler had to do was to swear that he would maintain the existing laws, different from the rest though they might be. All this is nicely summed up by the motto of the British royal family, which dates to the middle years of the fourteenth century: *Dieu et mon droit*.[45]

Separate systems of law meant different courts and different procedures. They also entailed different rights and restrictions—for the members of the upper classes, needless to say, there were more rights than restrictions. That fact, perhaps more than simple vanity, explains why competition for noble titles, and the coats of arms which displayed them for all to see, was as keen as it was.[46] In Western Europe feudalism-fealty and serfdom included-slowly started giving way to different types of socio-political systems from about 1400 on. However, the shift towards capitalism and absolutism did not mean that inequality grew less pronounced. On the contrary, the growing power of the modern state, which in many ways was based on a firm partnership between the kings and their nobilities, caused it to be accentuated even more. The system of state monarchy reached its height under the reign of the "Sun King," Louis XIV.

Depending on the time and the place, the privileges nobles enjoyed included access to court: "The Fountain of Honor," to use a British expression. On that, everything else depended.[47] Next there was exemption from taxes. Far from paying them, many nobles had the right to levy them in the form of tolls. These levies came on top of forced labor or *corvés*, which Adam Smith regarded as the most iniquitous of all.[48] Nobles exercised a monopoly on some official posts and had preferred access to others. That was true both in the secular and ecclesiastic bureaucracies, both in civilian life and in the armed forces. In France during the last years before 1789, to adduce but one example, the officer corps actually became less democratic than it had previously been.

Nobles also had the right to be tried by their peers. They were exempt from judicial torture as well as certain kinds of punishments considered degrading; viewed forest and countryside as their exclusive preserve where they alone had the right to hunt; were allowed to wear certain clothes as well as a sword; and had an exclusive right to defend their honor by means of a duel. Especially for officers, in many places the latter was also a duty. There were also some prohibitions, including one on marrying commoners. This did not prevent aristocats from accessing lower-class women who were seen as easy prey. But it did mean that those who tried to formalize their unions might face difficulty in getting the marriage recognized and in passing their titles, privileges and property to their wives and off-spring. Often nobles were also forbidden to engage in commerce, an occupation understood as incompatible with gentility and honor.

Under king, priests and aristocrats came the so-called "Third Estate," made up of respectable bourgeois in the towns. Begin-ning already in the Middle Ages, the towns were havens of equality compared to the countryside. At any rate, there were no serfs in them—"urban air makes free," as the saying went. Yet they were criss-crossed by neighborhood associations, fraternities and guilds, all of them made up of different people with very different civic functions, rights and duties.[49] Such political rights as existed were normally available only to a small group of rich patricians. They alone elected the magistrates, held municipal office and represented the towns *vis a vis* the higher ups.

Many people also recognized a Fourth Estate consisting of urban and rural laborers as well as itinerant riff-raff of every kind. Unlike their betters, these people did not have representatives who attended the meetings of provincial and national parliaments. A clear geo-graphical boundary also existed. Traveling from west to east, once past the Elbe towns became fewer in number and serfdom more widespread.[50] In some ways serfdom became even stronger than it had been before. Until well into the nineteenth century even *corvés* persisted. As readers of Gogol know, in Russia serfdom was little different from slavery.

In the West, however, the system was not always as watertight as seems to be the case at first glance.[51] Study, self-acquired wealth, service and sheer competence might enable a person to rise both within the class to which one belonged and from one class into another. Both military service and the Church provided such venues. While women rarely joined the quest on their own, under certain circumstances they could advance themselves by successfully identifying an up-and coming man and marrying him. Men who climbed the ladder in this way could even see their newly-acquired privileges formally confirmed by the authorities and leave them to their offspring. Upward social mobility, as well as its opposite, might well stretch over several generations. Some countries took a different path, and advanced faster towards modernity than others did.

Compared to the city-state in which Rome originated, and the chiefdoms in which all the rest did, empires were extremely unegalitarian. Indeed one could argue that inequality, often buttressed by alleged divine descent or mission and enforced by mighty armed forces as well as sophisticated bureaucratic structures, was precisely the factor that tied them together. Some empires were remarkably long-lived—one need only think of ancient Egypt, China and Japan. Others, such as those of Mesopotamia, and the Middle East as well as Mexico, succeeded each other. Generally the more homogeneous an empire, ethnically speaking, the longer it lasted, though nothing endures forever. The life of even the most homogeneous empires was punctuated by so-called intermediate periods during which emperors lost control both over provinces and the men who governed them. Such periods might last for decades, sometimes centuries. Supposing civil war did not lead to a total collapse, the outcome was decentralization and feudalism. Thus the line separating empire from feudalism was often a flexible one. That explains why historians have so often wondered whether the term may or may not be applied to the Arab Middle East, Persia, India, and Japan in addition to Europe.

Another way to see feudalism is as a regime under which different groups and individuals, instead of being uniformly at the mercy of an emperor, each have their own *independent* rights in the form of privileges. Thus defined European feudalism, on which we have focused here, lasted from the fall of Rome and the establishment of barbarian kingdoms at the end of the fifth century AD to the last years of the eighteenth. During that period one may discern a move from relatively "flat" chiefdoms to full-blown feudalism and from there to absolutism. It is true that the early modern state was based less on fealty and the distribution of land and more on money and service. Yet privilege, much of it hereditary, played no less a role in 1776 AD than it had in 476 BC. Some emperors were "absolute" and so powerful that they could cut off the head of each of their subjects equally. Others, standing at the apex of "feudal" structures, were not. In both cases, the organizing principle was not equality but its exact opposite. All the polities in question were "Proud Towers," deliberately designed to enforce and preserve inequality as perhaps *the* most important means of maintaining social order and stamp out any attempt to resist it.

Chapter 4

Islands in the Sea

It is unlikely that all the peoples that ever existed were capable of understanding the idea of equality. However, its opposite, oppression—meaning the unjust exercise of power by superiors over inferiors—has always been understood perfectly well. History bristles with attempts, many of them very violent, to end it and put something better in its place. Such struggles often merged with ideological and religious conflicts, revolts aimed at throwing out foreigners and achieving national independence, coups mounted by one person to take over power from another, and many similar conflicts. Quite possibly that is one reason why they so rarely succeeded in achieving their aim. Even if they did, usually it did not take long for a different but no less unequal order to establish itself. Here only a few of the struggles in question can be considered. They will have to stand for the rest.

Given how great the ancient city-states' contribution to the development of equality was, they form a good starting point for discussion.[1] The background was formed by a growing polarization, after about 400 BC, between rich and poor. Changing inheritance

laws, the growth of trade of industry, the influx from the time of
Alexander on of huge sums of money from the newly-conquered
Middle East, and later the impact of Roman warfare on Greek soil,
all contributed to this. The repeated attempts by some Spartan kings
to put back the clock, augment the number of citizens, and restore
equality have already been noted. These attempts were launched
from above, but in most other places the pressure came from below. The total number of known cases, spread all over the Mediterranean, is about sixty. Among those affected were several very small
city states located on Aegean islands. However, Syracuse, much the
largest city of all, also felt the impact. Now the *demos* acted on its
own, now it was led, or as was more often the case, misled, by a
would-be tyrant.

The most important reform demanded, and sometimes carried
out, was the redistribution of land and the establishment of *iso-
moira*, "equal lots." With it came the cancellation of debts. Often
the confiscation of property and the manumission of slaves were
added. However, the latter measure in particular had more to do
with the desire to increase the number of citizen-soldiers than with
any deeply-rooted ideal of putting an end to injustice and establishing equality. Some of the struggles were mainly political by nature.
Others resembled the one waged by Nabis and were extremely violent. In Argos in the Peloponnesus in 370 BC, the entire ruling
class was simply wiped out.[2] A few of the movements involved did
succeed seizing power, carrying out their programs, and maintaining themselves for a number of years. So, for example, the regimes
established by the tyrants Clearchus and Apollodorus in their re-
spective cities, Heracleia and Kassandreia, in 364 and 280 BC. The
former held out for twelve years, the latter for four. However, whatever equality was established never lasted for long. In many cases it

was probably not established at all. This is evident from the fact that many cities, Syracuse included, experienced not just a single revolution but several successive ones. Clearchus, before he was murdered, pronounced himself to be an incarnation of Zeus. He even named his son Kaunos, "The Thunderer," after one of that god's epithets.

Polybius says that Rome, whose legions put an end to Greek independence in 146 BC, "abolished democracies and established governments based on property qualifications."[3] After that we only hear of isolated attempts to change the social-economic order, such as the one that took place at Dyme, in Achaia, in 116–114 BC.[4] However, that does not mean Rome itself was free from attempts to establish greater social, economic, and political equality. One of the most prolonged struggles opened almost immediately after the abolition of the monarchy. It was waged by peaceful means, ending only in 287 BC when many of the political demands of the lower classes, or *plebs*, were finally granted.[5] The change made it easier for commoners to become magistrates and, later, senators. However, it did little to change the aristocratic character of the Republic. It did even less to establish legal and socio-economic equality among citizens. Throughout the second century BC gaps between rich and poor continued to grow, finally leading to civil war and the establishment of the empire with all its hierarchy.

In addition Rome, and to a lesser extent Greece, also experienced huge slave revolts, especially between 140 and 71 BC. Certainly the slaves resented the way they were treated and wished for freedom. That apart, though, very little is known about their programs, if any. Especially in Greece, some revolts were successful in that the slaves succeeded in throwing off the yoke and setting up independent communities that lasted for a few years. Some modern authors have argued that, far from wishing to abolish slavery on the way to equality, what the rebels really wanted was to become slave-owners themselves. A society without slaves seems to have been beyond their imaginations.[6]

Other parts of the world also had their revolts.[7] As in Greece and Rome, often the rebels' motives were hopelessly mixed. Socio-economic conflicts, religious struggles, national uprisings, and palace coups abounded. As the rebels sought and received aid from their rulers' neighbors, many revolts developed into "international" wars. Still, equality before God apart, the people of no other continent seem to have developed it even as an ideal. Neither the Egyptian revolt against Persia in 460 BC, nor that of the Abbasids against the Umayyads in 747 AD, nor that of the Bulgars against Byzantium in 1185 AD, to mention but three, were inspired by it. To the contrary, often it was a question of local elites rising against centralizing policies originating in the imperial capital and aimed at reducing their privileges. Russia during the seventeenth and eighteenth centuries experienced several large revolts in which serfs and Cossacks joined forces against their betters. However, none of them was directed against serfdom as such. In most cases the goal was less to bring about a new type of equality-seeking regime than to reduce oppression by substituting good rulers for bad ones. The same was true in Japan before the Meiji "Restoration" of 1867–1869. All the various rebels had in mind was to correct abuses, not to abolish the Samurai class itself.

Only around 1790 did the quest for equality start playing any role at all, and then only because the idea was imported by, and from, the conquering West. Influenced by the French Revolution, some of the slave revolts that broke out in the Caribbean during his period proclaimed the equality of men of all races.[8] Later on, the Chinese Taiping Rebellion (1850–1864) introduced its own version

of equality. The movement's goals included the seizure and social-
ization of land and the suppression of private trade. Confucianism,
Buddhism and Chinese folk religion were to be abolished. Their
place would be taken by a bizarre form of Christianity according to
which the leader, Hong Xiuquan, was Jesus' younger brother.[9] The
fact that, earlier in Chinese history, equality was seldom mentioned
explains why in modern discussions of the topic, the focus is almost
always either on equality between Chinese and Westerners or on that
which is supposed to exists between men and women.[10] Others refer to equality in the context of Chinese Communism. The latter
itself was a Western import and one that only lasted for forty years,
until, after the bloody paroxysm known as the Cultural Revolution,
it was gradually dismantled step by step.[11]

In medieval and early modern Europe, governed first by empire, then by feudalism, and then by "absolute" monarchies, rebellions explicitly aimed at achieving a greater measure of equality were
somewhat more frequent. Why this should have been the case is
hard to say. At the popular level it owed much to the early days
of Christianity. Confucius was a high government official, Mohammed a well-to do merchant. But Jesus and his early followers
were poor. In the words of the New Testament, "it is easier for
a camel to go through the eye of a needle than for a rich man to
enter the kingdom of God."[12] Some of the leaders may also have
been influenced by the lingering memory of the Greek city-state as
transmitted by Plato above all.

Much the best known socio-economic revolt of the middle ages
remains the French Jacquerie of 1358. It is supposed to have been
named after the padded jackets worn by the French peasants. The
"deep background" was formed by the intense hatred of the serfs,
tied to the soil and subject to all kinds of exactions as well as, too of-

ten, contempt and ridicule, for their self-appointed betters.[13] Having risen in arms, the Jacques killed, burnt, and raped, but whether their leader, Guillaume Cale, ever developed any sort of ideology, let alone an egalitarian one, is not clear. Perhaps this is because, among the accounts we have, not one is sympathetic to him and his men. In any case it only lasted for about three weeks before being followed by repression no less brutal than the rebellion itself.

Across the Channel the English peasantry was bearing as many burdens as the French, including rent, tithes, forced labor, restrictions on movement and marriage, and more.[14] Resistance, known to us mainly from court cases, was endemic. In 1381 it exploded into open, organized, riots. The peasants' leaders explicitly sought to end serfdom and establish equality. In the famous words of one of them, a priest named John Ball: "When Adam delved and Eve span, who was then the gentleman?"[15] "From the beginning," he went on, "all men were created equal by nature." Servitude was the product of oppression, introduced by evil and unjust men who went against the will of God. Had the latter really wanted to create serfs, surely He would have done so from the time of genesis on.

Members of the establishment also understood what it was all about. In the words of the poet John Gower (1330–1408), the rebels foolishly demanded that there should be no lords, but only kings and peasants. This idea, namely that nobles of all sorts should be done away with and the bad king replaced by a good one, was typical of the middle ages and we shall meet it again. Unlike the Jacquerie, the revolt was suppressed with minimal bloodshed. Its leaders, including John Ball, were tried and executed. Some historians believe that the movement signified the beginning of the end of serfdom in England. Even if that is true, it does not mean that society became more egalitarian; only that the existing feudal forms of inequality were gradually replaced by early capitalist ones.

The largest revolt of all was the German Peasant War of 1524–1525.[16] The 1525 document known as the Twelve Articles of the Black Forest, which lists the things the peasants wanted abolished, reads almost like a register of aristocratic privileges.[17] They included the exclusive rights of nobles to use open spaces, forests and waterways for hunting, hewing wood, and fishing; their right to demand forced labor; all kinds of fees, tolls, and taxes they imposed; as well as the entire relationship between superiors and inferiors known as serfdom. In the background was the Reformation which was in full swing. Hadn't Christ shed his blood for everyone, from the highest to the lowest? And hadn't Luther himself gone on record as saying that, since Jesus was the sole superior, "All have the same right, power, possession and honor"?[18] So popular were the Articles that they were printed 25,000 times, a vast number for those days. Luther, however, needed the nobility to wage his fight the Catholic Church. Using his normal vitriolic language, he called for the "bands of robbers" to be "crushed, strangled, stabbed, both undercover and in the open, by whoever can do so, like mad dogs."[19] In the end they were suppressed—at the cost, it is said, of a hundred thousand dead.

There were many other peasant revolts.[20] Other revolts still took place in the towns. Often the rebels were guildsmen who took on the ruling patriarchate in quest of greater, not to say equal, social and political rights. In Flanders alone between 1306 and 1313, Saint Omer, Bruges, Aardenburg, and Ypres all witnessed uprisings of this kind. The next two centuries saw many more. Quite a few led to bloodshed on both sides. However, few if any succeeded in the sense of producing greater social equality for any period of time.

Perhaps the most interesting town-centered revolt of all was that of the Anabaptists. Once again, the background was shaped by the Reformation. The Anabaptists challenged both the religious order and the social one. Not surprisingly, both Catholics and Protestants persecuted them might and main. In the spring of 1525 the principal Anabaptist leader, Thomas Muenzer, conducted a short-lived experiment in egalitarian communism in the town of Muehlhausen in Thuringia. He then put himself at the head of some 8,000 armed peasants, but was defeated at the Battle of Frankenhausen. Captured and tortured, he confessed his belief in eradicating socio-economic differences by distributing "everything among everybody." His enemies claimed that this also applied to women.[21] He was executed and his body parts were put on display on the city walls.

In 1534–1535, the Anabaptists made another try at the north German city of Muenster. Having seized it, they canceled all debts, allowed their own people to occupy empty houses, and organized a communal feeding system. Whether these measures were temporary, meant to enable the town to withstand a siege, or were supposed to become permanent is not clear. As in the case of Muehlhausen and Muenzer, the Anabaptists' enemies accused them of instituting a community of women. As at Muehlhausen, too, the uprising ended with the rebels' defeat. It did not have any successors.[22]

Whereas in other continents, the call for equality hardly played any role in uprisings, in Europe at least traces of desire for it can be occasionally found. That is not to say that demands for it were not mixed with a host of other motives, religious, national, political, and personal. Often the attempts to establish it occasioned rivers of blood, as numbers of the more equal classes were mercilessly massacred. However, most attempts to impose equality by force were put down fairly quickly. Kings, nobility, rich townsmen, or some combination of the three more privileged classes put an end to them, often engaging in bloodshed even greater than that previously committed by their opponents. The few rebel communities that held out for more than a few months often turned into tyrannies. Once that happened their leaders tended to undermine the equality they claimed to pursue by seizing every sort of privilege for themselves.

For example, Jan van Leiden, the leader of the Muenster Anabaptists, surrounded himself with so much pomp and circumstance that he was called "the king." Taiping ideology, one of the few outside Europe to concern itself with equality at all, stressed the redistribution of property as well as strict separation between the sexes even within the family. Yet far from imitating his alleged elder brother and leading a life of poverty, Hong Xiuquan took any number of concubines and lived like a king. His principal lieutenants did the same. The quest for equality, in other words, failed even when it succeeded.

＊

In the words of Paul the Apostle, "For all you who have been baptized into Christ, have put on Christ, there is neither Jew nor Greek; there is neither slave not freeman; there is neither male nor female."[23] As far as faith goes, this kind of equality his been maintained to the present day. That did not apply to the things of the world. Whereas early Christian communities were indeed egalitarian, once Constantine put an end to persecution in 313 AD most of them were integrated into society at large. Not only did the Church itself become much more hierarchical than it had been, but many lay aristocrats converted to the new religion. They saw equality, if they thought about it at all, as the last of their concerns.[24] Four

and a half centuries earlier, both in Greece and all over the rest of
the Mediterranean, city-states had lost their independence and with
it their democracy and equality. Simple band societies and tribes
without rulers apart, practically the entire world was governed by
chiefdoms, empires, or feudal systems.

One place where equality might still be found was in the monasteries (from the Greek *monos*, meaning either single or alone). Both
Islam and Zoroastriansm reject monasticism, though the former has
always had its share of dervishes, or hermits, who led a solitary life in
the desert. It was, however, known and practiced in many parts of
the Old World. Buddhist monasticism, like Buddhism itself, developed in northern India in the midst of an extremely unequal society
made up of castes. Originally there were just four. But later on their
number increased until there were hundreds, if not thousands. of
different ones. The members of each had different rights and different duties. So sharply delineated were the differences between them
that their members would not even intermarry as, in many cases,
they still don't. Some modern scholars believe that the system, hierarchic as it is, facilitated the maintenance of social order.[25]

Under the Tibetan variety of Buddhism the Dalai Lama is, in
theory at any rate, an absolute ruler. He is supported by an entire
hierarchy of lesser lamas. Elsewhere, however, Buddhism does not
recognize any kind of officials who exercise authority over others.
There is, in other words, no Church of which monasteries form a
part and by which it is held accountable. Like its Christian coun-
terpart, Buddhist monasticism assumed many different forms, some
of them much stricter than others. Everywhere, though, the principal method for distinguishing monks from their lay surroundings
and establishing equality among them consisted of a prohibition on
personal property. Monks were not allowed to touch, let alone pos-

sess, money and other valuables. All they could call their own were two sets of special clothing, a bowl, and a drinking cup. Medical aids such as trusses and eyeglasses were also permitted. Dress and haircuts were the same for everyone. Dainty foods, many forms of comfort, and, not least, marriage and sex were prohibited. To cut their links with the outside world, monks had to assume new names. In all these ways equality was imposed, lived, experienced, assimilated, or otherwise made real.

Inside the monasteries, the difference between public and private life is abolished. The latter only exists when the monk is in his cell, asleep; not even the dreamer, let alone others, can control dreams. Socially the only distinctions are those between veteran monk and novice, guru and student. Yet nobody is forced to join a monastery or remain in it against his or her will. Nor must novices take formal oaths in order to become monks. Gurus become gurus when they themselves feel they have something to teach and can attract students. Students choose their own gurus and change them whenever they see fit. Punishments are inflicted, if that is the word, by the assembled community as a whole. They cannot include deprivation of food, let alone a physical beating. Mostly it is a question of confessing, repenting, conciliating and, where appropriate, atoning and compensating. However, repeated transgressions of a sufficiently severe kind can lead to expulsion.[26] Expulsion, of course, also means cutting the monk from his source economic support, forcing him either to beg or work for a living.

This kind of egalitarianism leaves open the question how some of the larger monasteries, in which many dozens of monks may live together and which in time may accumulate considerable assets, are administered. In the absence of a formal hierarchy, typically a monastery will be run by a senior monk who is neither too young nor too old for the task. He is elected by the remaining monks, all of whom have an equal vote in the matter, on the basis of a recommendation by his predecessor; Thailand differs from the rest in that it is the lay contributors who vote. The usual term of office is three years, sometimes more. The head may have assistants but not subordinates. Monasteries survive with the aid of benefactors who donate money or food. By so doing they hope to earn merit and save themselves from spending their next lives as, say, caterpillars. Monks also ask for contributions from visitors who spend some time in them.

On the inside, these monasteries maintain equality by virtue of the fact that there is hardly any property, little formal authority, and no specialization or formal division of labor. The fact that all relationships can be entered into and terminated at will helps prevent strong hierarchies from being created. The links between the monasteries and outside society are also voluntary. It is "religious" belief, not authority and power, that counts. Enormously sophisticated as Buddhist doctrines are, in all these ways monasteries are about as egalitarian as, though very dissimilar to, the simplest known societies. More important still, the monastic movement cuts right across the caste-system by which it was, and for the most part is, surrounded. Instead of birth being destiny, as in the world at large, it promises anybody who joins and stays in it the chance of being reborn, so to speak, and have an equal shot at reaching nirvana, the perfect peace of mind.[27] That is just what, in the eyes of many, makes it as attractive as it is.

Still, equality could only be carried so far. True, nobody was forced to become a monk. But neither were monasteries obliged to accept anybody who applied. They could, and did, turn away the misshapen, the debtor, and those who had committed a crime and were seeking to evade punishment.[28] Furthermore, a great many monks only spent a number of years at the monastery. This prevented the emergence of strong hierarchies, but it also meant inequality between permanent and transient residents. Among the former some had less *dharma*, spiritual enlightenment, others more. In China, at any rate, lists of the latter were carefully maintained. Not every monk with *dharma* became an abbot, and not every abbot had *dharma*. Still there was a link between it and the ability to have oneself elected. Most of the larger monasteries also had officials in charge of various departments such as the treasury, the sacristy, and guests. There might even be a provost responsible for discipline. The officials' other function was to supervise the abbot. He was not a dictator; if he broke the rules, or disposed of the monastery's property without consulting the remaining officials, he could be impeached and expelled. Such events were rare, but they did occur.[29]

On a day-to-day basis questions of priority had to be settled; not everyone could be given everything at the same time. Talk about "everybody" electing the senior monk in charge and "everybody" deciding what to do with those who had violated the rules is good and well. However, such an approach could, and on occasion did, lead to factionalism and strife. The weaker the country's lay government, the more abbots depended on their own resources in maintaining and enforcing order. To do so a wide variety of methods were used. Even murder was not unknown. In any case, not every trifle can justify a call for everyone to meet and decide. Other arrangements, some of them quite complex, had to be made, and in doing so it was inevitable that some people would carry greater weight than others.[30] Finally, in Sri Lanka and some other places monasteries can and do own land, either such as was donated to them or they acquired by purchase. They live on the labor of those who work it, an arrangement quite compatible both with traditional feudalism and with modern capitalism. Some have grown fabulously rich, particularly in works of art. What equality exists, in other words, is limited exclusively to the space within their walls.[31]

Early Judaism had some people known, in English, as nazirites (from the Hebrew *nazir*, monk). They took vows, usually temporary, to abstain from alcohol, refrain from cutting their hair, and avoid coming into contact with unclean matters such as dead bodies.[32] However, they did not have to give up marriage and sex. Two outstanding Old Testament representatives of the genre are the Judge Samson and the Prophet Samuel. Both were married, and the latter had children. Samson was a somewhat uncouth slayer of Philistines, Samuel a lifelong servant of the Lord with a strong interest in politics. However, the nazirites never formed an organized movement or tried to set up monasteries. Their contribution to equality was zero.

The situation with Christianity was entirely different. Starting in the second century AD, perhaps even earlier, some converts to it started withdrawing into the desert. In doing so they may or may not have been linked to Judaic sects such as the Essenes who, between about 200 BC and 100 AD, led a communal lifestyle in various parts of the Holy Land.[33] The earliest Christian hermits wanted to be far from temptation and devote themselves solely to worshipping their God. As also happened in the Far East, at some point they became more sociable and started joining together. The outcome was so-called "cenobitic," meaning "cell-based," monasteries. In them each monk or nun was assigned his or her cell. However, meals, prayer, and study took place in common. By the year 346 AD there were said to be 3,000 such communities in Egypt alone, and their number kept growing. Similar ones appeared in other parts of the Roman Empire such as North Africa, Judea, Syria, and Asia Minor. Ethiopia, though it was never part of the Empire, also had them.

Very little is known about the way early monasteries were organized—but starting with the first one, said to have been founded by the Egyptian St. Pachomius in 326 AD, all had abbots (from *av*, Hebrew for "Father"). What really distinguished Christian monasteries from Buddhist ones was the rise, first in the Middle East and then in Europe, of a strongly-organized Church. As early as the second century AD it started developing an elaborate hierarchy with patriarchs, hegemons and presbyters and, in the West, their Latin equivalents. It would be going too far to say that the Church absorbed every hermit who chose to live alone in some remote place, worship God, and atone for his sins—some, no doubt, did so precisely to escape its clutches.[34] However, headed as it was by an Emperor in Constantinople and by God's own deputy in Rome, it did seek to control every institution and integrate it into its own hierarchy. In 451 AD the Council of Chalcedon explicitly ordered that no monastery should be established without permission from the local bishop and that all monks should be subject to him.[35] In the West this also entailed a change in the way abbots were chosen. Instead of simply being elected by all the monks or designated by their own successors, they had to be consecrated by the local bishop who thus acquired the right of veto.

Some fifty years before the Council took place Saint Augustine (354–430 AD) had composed several sermons and letters concerning the way monks and nuns ought to live.[36] The first, and most important, point is that everybody should work for a living. That having been settled, the principal virtues he recommends were poverty, fraternity, charity, and of course chastity. While the Saint explains each of them at length, he also pays some attention to administrative matters. Each nunnery, he says, should be headed by a mother superior. She should rule by conciliation, as far as possible, but should also have the power to expel a wayward nun if that became necessary. She should have four assistants, one whom was to take care of the sick, one of the cellar, one of the wardrobe, and one of the library. The significant point is that, already at this early time, it was neither the abbess nor the nuns but the bishop who laid down many of the details. However, it is possible that Augustine was writing principally for his own household.

Probably the best-known Rule of all is that of St. Benedict.[37] It served as the inspiration for countless others, to the point that Charlemagne had it copied and distributed throughout his empire. Benedict was a hermit who had left Rome to lead a solitary life in the wild, rugged country further south. Having attracted a considerable following, in 529 he founded the Monastery of Monte Casino which still exists. The Rule itself shows strong signs of being based on several earlier ones, including those of St. Pachomius and St. Augustine. It goes to some lengths to establish equality, prohibiting private ownership of anything and prescribing a just distribution of such things—mainly clothing and small personal items—as monks are allowed to have. It also ordains that undesirable work, such as kitchen duty, be shared equally by all the monks in turn. Next, Abbots are strongly urged to treat their monks equally. Any social distinctions they may have brought with them from the outside world must be ignored. Instead they should be treated solely on the basis of their merit in the service of God.

The single most important injunction is contained in the prologue. It orders monks to "take up the strong and most excellent arms of obedience, to do battle for Christ the Lord, the true King."

Those are much stronger terms than any Buddhist would have used. In fact they would have been seen as contradicting everything that the monastic life and Buddhism itself stand for. The impression of a powerful, hierarchically-based, organization is reinforced by the articles that follow. To list the most important ones only, Article 5 repeats the injunction for obedience which must be prompt, ungrudging, absolute, and unhesitating. The objective is not just to make an orderly life possible but also, and even more importantly, to teach humility. Article 21 provides for every group of ten monks to be ruled by a dean. Articles 23 to 29 focus on discipline, including a long list of punishments to be inflicted on monks who have violated the rules. Starting with a private admonition, it proceeds through public reproof and solitary confinement all the way to excommunication and corporal punishment. Article 54 prohibits the monks from receiving letters or gifts without the abbot's permission. Article 58 lays down procedures for accepting new monks into the organization; once the monastic vow has been taken, it is binding for life. Finally, Article 71 repeats the injunction for the monks to obey the abbot and his appointed officials.

The so-called *Rule of the Master*, a similar document written by an unknown monk at roughly the same time in roughly the same region, also stresses the monks' duty to obey their superiors. Monks, it says, do not live "according to their own discretion or obeying their own desires and pleasures." Instead, walking "by the judgment and command of another, they not only exercise self-control in [their] desires and pleasures and do not want to do their own will even if they could, but they also submit themselves to the authority of another. Living in monasteries, they wish to have an abbot over them and not bear this title themselves."[38] Again we find a lengthy list of punishments that abbots and their subordinates, the deans, may use to discipline recalcitrant monks. Those who, having been excommunicated, still persist in their evil ways may even be "confined and whipped with rods to the point of death."[39] Unless they obtain the abbot's permission first, monks are not even allowed to fast more, or pray more, than the Rule prescribes. To enforce equality, hierarchy and strict obedience were required.

Both the Benedictine Rule and the *Rule of the Master* put great emphasis on the need to prevent monks from spending their time in idleness, which Heaven forbids, but work instead. The former in particular has become famous for its slogan, *ora et labora* (pray and work). Much of the work was done inside the monasteries, in the form of study on one hand and maintenance work on the other. Some monastic orders also had their members perform more productive labor. For example, the *Rule of the Master* recommends that articles manufactured inside the monastery be sold at somewhat less than market price. Cistercians, whose order dates to 1098, specialized in agriculture and played an important role in land-reclamation. The Humiliati, who go back to the same period, specialized in textiles. Some monasteries generated part of their income by providing lodging to guests. They also promoted holiness in the form of prayers, amulets, and so on.

In return they asked for, and received, contributions from the laity. Some of the most important contributions consisted not of money or goods but of arable land. Here the *Rule of the Master*, written though it was at an early point in the development of Christianity, is instructive indeed. "All the lands of the monastery should be rented out so that a secular lessee is burdened with all the field-work, the care of the estate, the clamors of the tenants, the quarrels with neighbors—a man who does not know how to be concerned exclusively about his soul and whose interests in the present life are limited to the world ... On the contrary, those who have become spiritual men do not entangle themselves in worldly affairs."[40] The need to look after one's economic needs was detrimental to the soul. Thus equality inside the monastery, as far as it went, could only be established at the price of preserving inequality outside it.

Nor was it always a matter of entering voluntary agreements with lessors and tenants. As the middle ages took hold, many monasteries received or purchased not only land but entire villages and the people who lived in them. Thus monasticism was perfectly compatible with serfdom, even slavery, in the outside world. In fact, the Council of Chalcedon had prohibited monasteries from taking in runaway slaves. Since medieval monks tended to be far more literate than the laity they were well-known as hard masters. Here and there attempts were made to set back the clock and return to the original poverty and egalitarianism that had characterized Jesus and his disciples. Among the best-known are those of the Franciscans and their offspring, the Capuchins. The Franciscan Rule commands that "those brothers whom the Lord favors with the gift of working should do so faithfully and devotedly, so that idleness, the enemy of the soul, is excluded yet the spirit of holy prayer and devotion, which all other temporal things should serve, is not extinguished. As payment for their labor, let them receive that which is necessary for themselves and their brothers, but not money. Let them receive it humbly as befits those who serve God and seek after the holiest poverty."[41] It is worth noting, though, that much of the "labor" consisted of begging. In return for alms, monks gave their blessing.

All these strict injunctions may have done something to increase equality among the monks themselves. However, on the whole they did not work well. No sooner was the Order established (in 1233) than it began to grow as rich as any other. Throughout the thirteenth century, this gave rise to endless disputes as to how "poverty" should be interpreted and the surplus wealth distributed. Did poverty mean that the monks themselves had to do without? And how about the Order? Should it be allowed to keep the property it had begun to amass, usually from donations and wills, or should everything be transferred to the Church and the Pope in Rome? For being on the wrong side of such disputes, some monks were delivered to the Inquisition and paid with their lives. A mere look at the some of the many splendid Franciscan monasteries scattered in various countries will show that the Order did little if anything to change the way the world works. Not only did both ecclesiastical and secular hierarchies continue to exist and prosper, but the abbots of most monastic orders fitted into them rather comfortably. Far from promoting equality, so wealthy were many monasteries that numerous secular rulers laid greedy eyes on them. During the Reformation they took the opportunity to seize their property and disband them, sending the monks into the streets.

In Catholic countries things went on more or less as usual. In 1563 the Council of Trent, in its efforts to erase some of the evils that had led to the Reformation, reconfirmed poverty as one of the bases of religious life.[42] However, neither before nor after this was there much of an attempt to prevent inequality. Some monks had always come from well-to-do backgrounds. Joining the monastery, they brought along luxury items for their personal use. Others continued to receive support from their families. Some, instead of living in simple "cells," had at their disposal complete furnished flats, including kitchens and toilets. They employed lower-ranking monks as servants and might even have their own coats of arms. The promise

of such benefits must have been one reason why many nuns in particular took the veil in the first place.

The outcome was to turn the apartments in question, rather
than the common premises, into the centers of their occupants' lives.
All this flew directly in the face of the ideal of monastic equality.[43]
The Church's repeated attempts to stamp out the practice failed.
Many donors saw to it that some of the property they gave should
benefit the entire institution, effectively bribing it. Abbesses and
abbots could console themselves with the thought that those who
brought property along with them were only allowed its use. At
their death, it would revert to the organization in which they had
spent their lives.

Eighteenth-century Lisbon, the quintessential "priest-ridden"
city, alone had thirty-two monasteries and eighteen nunneries in a
population of a little over a quarter million and other Catholic cities
were not far behind. Starting in the second half of the century and
continuing during the French Revolution, many Catholic countries
set out to clip the wings of organized religion. Doing so, they put
monasticism on an entirely new basis. In the Habsburg Empire under Joseph II (reigned 1765–1790) alone, one-third of all religious
houses were closed and had their property confiscated. The number of monks and nuns was reduced by two-thirds.[44] During the
nineteenth century, the same thing happened in many other countries ranging from Greece to Mexico. The remaining monasteries
and their inhabitants were made subject to the civil law like everyone else. Abbots, monks, and their ecclesiastical superiors lost many
of their privileges and a considerable amount of their power. One
of the most important lost privileges in this respect was the power
to prevent monks from leaving their monasteries by inflicting various punishments upon them. Many forms of income considered

incompatible with the ethos of capitalism were also lost. Later the same happened in the declaredly secular countries of the Far East such as India and China.

In the end, monasticism did survive the onslaught of secularism, liberalism, and even the militant communism of Stalin and Mao. However, everywhere it was put on an almost purely voluntary basis. These developments did not change the fact that Christian monasteries remained part of the ecclesiastical hierarchy and the hierarchy retained its authority. Whether the changes have made the lives of monks and nuns more or less egalitarian than they used to be in earlier periods is very hard to judge. All one can say is that here and there, the islands after which this chapter is named still exist and try to make their influence felt.

The kinds of equality in the imaginary worlds created by various writers ran parallel to those which existed, or did not exist, in the real one. To start with Plato as the author of the most celebrated utopia of all, he was a fervent admirer of Sparta. That is not because he was a militarist. As he wrote, war is neither educational nor a game. Yet he knew full well that, in the long run, no community can survive without armed force.

To Plato, the origins of external war were luxury, the effeminacy to which it led, and the enemies it attracted. Hence he rather liked Spartan frugality. Certainly he did not mean his guardians to lead a luxurious life.[45] Even more important was the fact that, to him, civil war was "the worst thing in the world."[46] All these reasons led him to suggest a form of equality at least as extreme as any that has been imagined before or since, though whether it was to be maintained not only among the guardians but among the workers as well is not clear. In the Republic, so perfectly harmonized is every individual both in relation to all the rest and to the community that both liberty and justice, here understood not as equity but as a formal process, are rendered superfluous and disappear.

Even so, inequality remains. Rulers, guardians and workers form a clear, and very rigid, hierarchy. The guardians themselves are rewarded on the basis of merit and performance, chiefly in war; the rulers, meeting in secret, decide who mates with whom and how often. These rather unattractive features of the Republic may explain why several other authors put forward their own, much more libertarian, schemes. Writing shortly after 300 BC, Euhemerus ("Good Day") suggested a society made up of artisans, soldiers, shepherds, and land-workers. Houses and gardens apart, private property is unknown. All work is organized by the state. Every man does what he can, brings the fruit of his labor to the common storehouses, and receives equal supplies to meet his needs. Only the priests, who rule the entire structure, receive a double share. The outcome is a life of bliss. Writing perhaps three quarters of a century later still, Iambulus imagined the Island of the Sun. There, not only private property but family life and even the division of labor have been abolished. Such are the lengths to which equality is carried that everyone is expected to carry out all tasks, from running the state to the most menial ones in turn.[47] Both writers dress their utopias as accounts of journeys made. Both are perhaps best understood as later-day mythographers who take equality as critically important towards the creation of an ideal world.

Confucius, a rough contemporary of Plato, thought that people should deal with things as they are, not with those that should be or which they would like to be.[48] Lao Tzu's Daoist followers were, if anything, even more insistent on this point. This may be why, like

the Europeans of the middle ages, Chinese sages rarely tried to paint
an imaginary picture of a living, functioning community to replace
the real one. However, they sometimes did produce short poems,
or else a few lines of prose, that wistfully describe the ideal life. For
example, the fourth-century BC philosopher Mencius paints a brief
picture of an ideal society sharply different from the poverty and
war so ubiquitous during the Period of the Warring States in which
he lived. Government is humane. People dress in silk, everyone has
meat to eat, the young are deferential, and the elderly enjoy leisure.
A drinking song attributed to Cao Cao (155–220 AD) also describes
a society in which no official comes to knock on the door. Barns are
full, the prisons empty, and people treat each other so kindly that
no formal system of justice is needed. Plants, animals, and insects
are covered by "the dew of grace."

Subsequent texts generally take a similar line. By far the most
famous was *Peach-Blossom Spring*.[49] Dating to about 400 AD, the
English version is just under six hundred words long. It led to countless interpretations, expansions, and imitations. Plying his trade, a
fisherman glides over a quiet stream. Suddenly the bamboo groves
open. In front of his eyes lies an enchanted place far from, and
unknown to, civilization. People live not in towns but in picture-
window villages. Though they do work in agriculture, abundance,
simplicity and affability reign. Nobody has heard of taxes, forced
labor, or emperors who send officials and soldiers to make people
pay, work, and join the armed forces. In some versions all hierarchical relationships are abolished. Only inside the family do "soft"
authority, and its opposite, deference, prevail. In other tales the
inhabitants are immortal, indicating that the authors have crossed
the line into fairytale land. As in Chinese philosophy in general,
though, equality as such is not mentioned.

To return to Europe, medieval utopias are less structured than Hellenistic ones.[50] One and all, clearly they were written by authors who knew what hunger is like. Their main purpose is to describe a place—one can hardly speak of an organized society—where everybody has plenty to eat and drink without working. Some of those places are located in the mythological past, others in distant, almost unknown, lands. Several seem to go back to the ancient idea of a Golden Age, particularly as drawn by the early first-century AD Roman poet Ovid.[51] "Somewhere, over the rainbow," as it were, everyone behaves in a prelapsian manner. Impiety, oppression, and lechery are unknown. There is neither strife, nor war. By implication, any formal system for exercising justice is superfluous. People never live in towns, rarely in villages. There are no families and no sex. Women, freed from the curse that was laid on Eve in *Genesis*, deliver in song and dance. Children are born about six years old and already able to walk and participate in the simple life everyone leads. People spend their time almost like so many cattle, amicably sharing an endless, but very fertile, meadow. Never mind that, as the authors must have known from their own observations, in reality free-ranging cattle are as concerned with dominance as most other animals.[52]

The illustrations that sometimes accompany the texts show the blessed dancing, bathing in the fountain of life, etc. To explain how they manage to live without working some of the legends have them drinking pure spring water, feeding on acorns and game, and wearing skins. Others speak of mountains of cheese and rivers of wine. Perhaps because there is plenty of everything to go around, equality is not so much discussed as taken for granted. There is, after all, nothing to compete for. Some authors seem to accept the "feudal" system, hierarchical as it is, as a given and are content to iron out its sharper edges.[53] Others attribute the pleasant world they are conjuring up to some benevolent king. Judging by these works, indeed, the good life simply *had* to unfold under a king or lord; even though, since everything and everyone was perfect, just what he did is not clear. With the death of that lord, the Garden of Eden ended.

Rabelais' Abbey of Thélème, which was presented to the world in 1532, still continues the tradition of the middle ages. Whether it does so seriously or by way of a spoofing is hard to say. In an unknown place far away, in the midst of splendid gardens surrounded by a fertile countryside, the giant Pantagruel has built a magnificent country house. In it, supported by a benefactor with unlimited resources at his disposal, lives a company of aristocratic men and women. They enjoy all the leisure in the world; one and all, they are "lively, jovial, handsome, brisk, gay, witty, frolick, cheerful, merry, frisk ... precious, alluring, courtly comely, fine, compleat, wise, personable, ravishing and sweet."[54] There are twice as many positive qualities on the list than letters in the alphabet. The Abbey has only two laws, namely "do as you will" and "be happy." Since there is no government, equality, though not explicitly mentioned, does prevail. And why not, given that there is no work to be done, no competition for resources, nor any need for defense, and everyone is polite and good?

Most sixteenth-century authors took a very different line. Much the best-known among them was Thomas More (1477–1535), Chancellor of England who was executed by Henry VIII for refusing to recognize him as head of the Anglican Church. His ideal society, as presented to us in *Utopia* (1516), follows Plato and is highly structured. It is also egalitarian in the sense that everyone is obliged—the emphasis is on obliged—to do productive work six hours a day. The only exceptions are a small number of gifted people who, freed from toil, are allowed to use their talents in fields such as study, administration, diplomacy, etc. As long as they deliver, they are always the same people. Since everybody (even women, More says) does productive work there is plenty of everything. Since everything is equally divided among all, poverty and hoarding are unknown. "Nobody owns anything, but everybody is rich."[55] But wealth does not luxury produce. As used to be the case in Mao's China, everyone wears virtually the same clothes and fashion, which More saw as a foolish luxury, hardly changes. All towns, of which there are many, are identical as far as local conditions allow. Inside each family, women are subject to their husbands, children to their parents, and youngsters to their elders. Elders sit at the head of the communal tables and receive the best helpings. Women and children are obliged to kneel and confess their sins to family heads.

Utopian households, consisting of several dozen people, are run by "reliable" old couples who keep an eye open. Officials, priests included, are elected annually, as are the members of the Council. More does not tell us whether women were allowed to vote, but we may take it for granted that they were not. Neither does he say anything about the way the chief executive, if one there is, was chosen and controlled. So well did the various magistrates exercise their function that they were regularly re-elected. Utopia did, however, have a large class of slaves. This shows how much strong the impact of antiquity on the author was. In fact there had been few slaves in Europe for several centuries past. Nevertheless, More could not imagine an "ideal" society without them.

Some slaves were "non-combatant prisoners of war [one shudders to think what happened to combatant ones], slaves by birth, or purchases from foreign slave-markets." Others were "either Utopian convicts or, much more often, condemned criminals from other countries, who were acquired in larger numbers, sometimes for a small payment, but usually for nothing." Others still were penniless foreigners who became slaves out of their own free will. It was slaves who did all the rough and dirty work. Those who worked in the open did so in chain-gangs.[56] Presumably most were male, for females so employed would not survive for long. In all this there was more uniformity than true equality. Neither inside the family, nor in all that concerns people with special talents, nor in respect to slavery did the latter prevail. Furthermore, the kind of order needed to maintain even such equality as did exist could only be maintained by Draconian methods. More has never heard of transparency; simply to discuss public affairs outside the Council was a capital offense. Leaving one's town without a passport was strictly prohibited. Get caught twice, and slavery is the penalty.

The utopian societies envisaged by More's immediate successors are equally structured. One of the most interesting is *The City of the Sun* (1602).[57] The author, Tommaso Campanella, was a Dominican monk. He was sufficiently heterodox and involved in various conspiracies in his Calabrian homeland to spend no fewer than twenty-seven years of his life in a variety of jails. Like More's Utopia, Campanella's city is located on a remote island. The inhabitants "came there from India, flying from the sword of the Magi, a race of plunderers and tyrants who lay waste their country, and they determined to lead a philosophic life in fellowship with one another." Both private property and the family have been abolished. "All those of the same age call one another brothers. They call all over twenty-two years of age fathers; those that are less than twenty-two are named sons." Every kind of labor, manual labor included, is considered honorable. Everyone loves the state and works diligently for it, though just what motivates them in doing so the narrator, a much-traveled sea captain, cannot say. He does, however, comment that they "burn with love" for their country. They are what Christian monks should be if only they could give up ambition and greed. The state, in turn, meets everybody's needs on an equal basis.

The ruler carries the title of Sole ("Sun"). He is high priest, chief executive, and supreme judge. Nobody can be Sole whose wisdom is not perfect; but how he is "chosen," or by whom, is not clear. He appoints three principal assistants called, in translation, Power, Wisdom, and Love. They in turn appoint their own assistants, creating an entire hierarchy. Power is in charge of war. Wisdom runs the highly-developed arts and sciences. Love's task is to look after the improvement of the race by making sure that the approved people sleep with each other in the approved manner at the approved, astrologically-determined, times. In this respect Campanella claims to have done better than Plato. The latter wanted to deceive his guardians, pretending that the relevant decisions are made by lot but secretly basing them on eugenic considerations. In *The City of the Sun* no such tricks are needed since everyone knows full well what is going on. Love based on sex, in other words, is abolished.

The objective of the entire system seems to be the promotion of human happiness by combining wise rule with a perfect knowledge of the arts and sciences. Thanks to this knowledge life is rich and colorful, not frugal and uniform as with More and, perhaps, Plato. Campanella's citizens live in communes. Everybody works and there is no slavery; to that extent *The City of the Sun* is perhaps more egalitarian than many other Western imaginary communities from antiquity to 1600 or so. Popular assemblies are attended by men and, remarkably, women. They hold regular meetings to criticize officials and replace them if necessary. However, this democratic system does not apply to Sun, Power, Wisdom, and Love. The four of them form a cabal; the one thing that can prevent them from abusing their positions is their own infinite wisdom.

Being of Indian descent, the citizens of *The City of the Sun* are not Christians but live happily enough with a religion that is a mixture of many different ones. In *Christianopolis*, Valentin Andreae (1586–1654) sets out to correct Campanella in this respect.[58] Whereas, in *The City of the Sun*, the basis of all good are knowledge and understanding, in *Christianopolis* that role is played is played by, what else, Christianity. The place is ruled by an aristocracy, or, to be precise, a triumvirate; "for though a monarchy has many advantages, yet they prefer to preserve this dignity for Christ." Possessed of every virtue and sworn to defend all of them, the three chief magistrates work in concert and balance each other so that tyranny is avoided. Yet how they themselves are chosen, whether they can be replaced, and if so by what means is nowhere spelt out. Under them is a whole hierarchy of officials, each with his own field of responsibility. Equality is assured, if at all, only by the fact that they prefer to rule by example so that none orders others to do what he does not do himself.

All three authors are very conscious of the fact that a rich, well-ordered community will attract enemies as a honeypot attracts flies. That is why they locate their utopias on remote, strongly fortified islands that are organized for war. None of them answer Aristotle's question as to how the soldiers can be prevented from setting up a military dictatorship and taking everything for themselves. With each of them it is clear that the government is strong, even very strong. That in turn means that whatever equality exists can only go so far. Where Andreae differs from More and Plato (but resembles Campanella) is that he considers all work honorable. Thus there is no need either for slaves or for a separate class of workers, though the question as to what will make people work remains largely unanswered. As with Campanella, Andrea's system is communist in that all products of labor are delivered to a central storehouse and equally distributed.

Andreae, good Christian as he is, keeps the monogamous family intact. Family heads, all of them men, who have more than thirty living relatives are given a medal. Each family lives in its own house and its members take their meals in it. Common production and ownership, but separate consumption; had Plato read the text, as well as that of More, he would have pointed out the contradiction in no time. He would also have prophesied that it would not work for very long.

✳

To repeat, probably not every society was able to understand the nature of equality. All, however, must have understood that of unjust oppression of inferiors by their superiors. That explains why, outside ancient Greece and until at least the middle of the seventeenth century, in all the countless coups, uprisings, rebellions, and civil wars that have punctuated world history, equality is rarely mentioned. Too often people could not even imagine it. Here and there were exceptions. However, all attempts to establish equality in practice seem to have failed. Often the failures were caused by the efforts of their opponents. Just as often, though, they were brought about by the fact that, no sooner had the leaders of a revolt seized power, they started making themselves more equal than the rest.

This leaves monasteries and "utopian" societies. Monasteries can only exist as islands in a larger society that protects them and meets their economic needs. Often this meant, and means, a highly un-egalitarian economic basis. Among the monks a certain kind of equality may indeed exist, but only as long as their numbers are kept quite small. Once their numbers grow past a certain point, some machinery for maintaining discipline is required, causing inequality to rear its head again. Utopias fall into two kinds. From Plato to Andreae, some are highly structured. Normally socio-economic equality prevails, but only at the cost of a powerful government that is neither egalitarian nor transparent. Another reason for this, as well as for the absence of liberty, is the need for defense and the hope to improve the human race by selective breeding. By contrast, Chinese utopias are located in secret places. Their security is assured, which enables them to do without strong government, in other words superiors and inferiors. That is even more true of medieval utopias, including Rabelais's. Not only are they inaccessible, but production, distribution and ownership have been abolished. People, not least Rabelais's aristocrats, live like free-roaming cattle. Either children come into the world without sex and already grown, as in the legends, or else they do not exist, as with Thélème. Otherwise they might spoil the fun and force the utopians, women in particular, to behave responsibly. Either inequality or dehumanization, it seems, is the choice utopia presents us.

Chapter 5

Liberal Equality

If the task of utopia is to sketch an ideal society, that of political theory is to understand the way real polities function and ought to function. The two are clearly related. Nevertheless, in spite of having a common origin in Plato, they are not the same. Like equality and democracy, political theory as a separate field distinct from both cosmology and theology originated in ancient Greece. Later, as democracy and equality disappeared, it was replaced by so-called mirrors for princes. As Machiavelli's *The Prince* shows, such works remained popular into the sixteenth century. The difference between mirrors and utopias was that they did not deal with imaginary societies but with real ones. The difference between them and political theory was that their purpose was to tell rulers how to rule, not to analyze government and politics as such.[1] Except in so far as they targeted the high and the mighty rather than ordinary men and women, in some ways they resemble modern self-improvement works such as *The 7 Habits of Highly Successful People*.

The leap from mirrors to modern political theory—and a huge one it was—was made by Jean Bodin. The years from 1562 to 1648 were punctuated by savage religious wars. First in France and the Low Countries and then all over Europe, Catholics and Protestants busily cut each other's throats. It was in the hope of putting an end to the wars and re-imposing order that Bodin, a lawyer who at one point worked for King Henry III, wrote his famous *Six Books of the Commonwealth* (1576). In this work he invented sovereignty and the sovereign.[2] Sovereignty meant two things. The first was the need to concentrate all power in the hands of a single person or body. That in turn implied the cancellation of all privileges and a return to the kind of rule under which everyone had equal rights, or, though Bodin did not dare say so openly, no rights. The second was that all sovereigns, since they could not and did not acknowledge any superior above themselves, were equal. The old idea which lay at the heart of feudal regimes in particular, about some rulers being superior and others inferior, was false.

Of the two ideas, equality among sovereigns proved more acceptable. By the late seventeenth century the Peace of Westphalia had turned it into an established fact. When Louis XIV, during the so-called "War of Devolution" of 1667–1668, tried to reverse it by demanding all kinds of lands to which he claimed the French throne held some ancient feudal right, all he succeeded in doing was to unite the rest of Europe against him.[3] However, abolishing "feudalism" and achieving equality inside each state took much longer. The definitive theoretical step towards the idea that all men—not women, that was only to come many years later—are equal was made by Thomas Hobbes (1588–1579). Hobbes was a lifelong bachelor who lived in the houses of the great and taught their sons. Embarking on the enterprise, one of the advantages he enjoyed was that early in his career he had translated Thucydides. A better way to master the topic can hardly be imagined.

On the face of it, to associate Hobbes with liberalism, from the Latin *libertas*, Is a strange thing to do. After all he envisaged the most absolute state in history in which liberty was merely the cracks left open between the sovereign's laws.[4] The "mystery," as it has been called, is readily solved.[5] Like Bodin, Hobbes wrote against the background of a bloody civil war during which he was in fear of his life and had to seek asylum in Holland. The war provided definite proof that the days when God and religion could act as the basis of government were gone for good. How, then, to realize his goal, which was to impose order at all costs?[6] There was only one thing to do: namely, to forget about God and go back to the beginning, back to "the state of nature."

In the primeval state of nature, Hobbes explained, everybody had a right to everything, which is the same as saying that nobody had any rights at all. In that sense everyone was exactly equal to everyone else. "Though there be found one man sometimes manifestly stronger in body, or of quicker mind then another; yet when all is reckoned together, the difference between man, and man, is not so considerable, as that one man can thereupon claim to himself any benefit, to which another may not pretend, as well as he. For as to the strength of body, the weakest has strength enough to kill the strongest, either by secret machination, or by confederacy with others, that are in the same danger with himselfe. And as to the faculties of the mind ... I find yet a greater equality amongst men, than that of strength ... For such is the nature of men, that ... they will hardly believe there be many so wise as themselves ... there is not ordinarily a greater sign of the equal distribution of any thing, than that every man is contented with his share."[7] Hobbes might well be speaking tongue in cheek, except that he is not.

Men are driven by an endless quest for power that only ceases with death. Hence, the outcome of natural equality is the perpetual warfare of all against all. However, humans are endowed with reason. To avoid a war which would be ruinous to all, they have agreed to sign a covenant, or social contract. Under that contract they give up all their rights and transfer them to the commonwealth, or state, or Leviathan, instead. At this point Hobbes pulls a second great innovation out of his magician's hat. The Greek polis and Republican Rome apart, in all previous civilizations rulers had ruled because, by virtue of the divine descent and/or support they enjoyed, or their ancestry, or their wealth, they possessed greater rights than others. With Hobbes, though, the right to govern was transferred, not to a person but to an abstract entity. All the ruler did was to "carry" that entity on his shoulders and embody it.[8] As the state, "a mortal god," took the place of a person, or persons, inequality became superfluous as a basis for government. Inside it everyone was equal. What power one exercised and what privileges one enjoyed originated in the office one occupied, not in one's divine descent or support, or ancestry, or property.

The principle of equality having been established, it proved to be dynamite. Over the next three-and-a-half centuries it spread like ripples in a pond. As we shall see, in a sense it was even subscribed to by Hitler and the National Socialists. It is true that not everybody agreed with Hobbes that all men were made equal by nature and that the only way to prevent them from tearing one another to pieces was to set up an absolute state. In fact some, such as the English philosopher John Locke (1632–1704), questioned both ideas. Reverting to some older ideas, Locke tried to derive equality from Christianity. At the same time he looked for ways to combine equality with liberty. The way to do so, he suggested, was to abandon the idea of a single absolute ruler. Inside the state, which by now was taken very much for granted, authority was to be divided among different powers. Each would have its own sphere, and they would balance each other. Most important of all, government was to be by consent of the governed. The people were to be given the opportunity to change their rulers when doing so suited them.[9]

In practice, liberal equality took a long time to establish itself even in England. For example, it was only in 1829 that the Catholic minority, which had been discriminated against since the days of Henry VIII in the first half of the sixteenth century, was fully emancipated. This measure paved the way to the abolition of many other hindrances and privileges left over from centuries of the *ancien régime*.[10] Outside England two countries in particular proved susceptible to the message: the American colonies on one hand, and France on the other. In America the Puritans, while in many ways conservatively-minded, at first sought to combine most of the different kinds of equality we have studied so far. That included equality before God, equality before the law, and socio-economic equality. In trying to achieve the last of those, they had the immense advantage of being able to divide a new country, or as much of it as they had acquired, among themselves. Yet they also wanted liberty. Since equality and liberty are, in principle, incompatible, such a system presupposed the kind of voluntary restraint only a community of saints can maintain.[11]

Not surprisingly, it did not work. Early on the Puritan settlements made their living mainly by scratching the earth. As they prospered and gradually derived a greater part of their income from industry and trade, liberty gained priority over equality as in many ways it still does in the United States. Socio-economic gaps among the settlements' members started opening up. With them came differences in political power. To the extent that decisions were not made in London, on the other side of the Atlantic, the colonies tended to be governed by oligarchies of rich men. Either they lived in the towns, as in the north, or else in the countryside, as in the south. Most did hold elections of some kind. But nowhere were they democratic in the sense that all adult men, let alone women, could participate in them. In most places the poor, the religiously dissident, or both were excluded—to say nothing of black slaves.

The other country where Locke's ideas found a favorable reception was France. The American colonies were small, poor, and far away. Not so France, which for a century and a half or so after the accession of Louis XIV was the most powerful country in Europe. The king's motto, *nec pluribus impar*, not unequal to many, proudly proclaimed that fact. The "feudal" aristocratic-clerical-military state weighed heavily on the lower classes. Yet France was also a developing industrial and commercial country. It had many towns and a numerous, prosperous, well-educated, bourgeoisie. All of this provided a fertile field for receiving the message of equality, meaning in the French case, above all equality in front of the law and the abolition of noble privilege.

The names of those who dabbled with equality read like a list of French Enlightenment "greats:" Voltaire, d'Alembert, Concordet, and Diderot, to mention but a few. Voltaire, while he did not often use the concept, spent a lifetime fighting against the privileges of the clergy and the nobility and trying to defend minorities, such as the Protestants, who were being discriminated against and persecuted. Jean le Rond d'Alembert (1717–1783) was interested in equality between the sexes, a field in which he was later followed by the Marquis de Sade. Marie-Jean de Concordet (1743–1794) also wanted more equality in France. However, thinking of Sparta, he worried about the impact too much of it might have on culture and the intellectual elite. Diderot had a lot to say about the unseemly inequality between "superiors" and "subalterns."[12] And with very good reason, for he himself spent time in prison as a result of a *lettre de cachet*, best translated as an arbitrary warrant for arrest, issued against him.

Many of these famous Enlightenment figures interacted with each other and influenced each other. Their concept of equality was so much in the air that a form of it even penetrated the walls of the monasteries. Some monks were affected—their superiors would no doubt say infected—by the prospect of breaking down the barriers between them and ordinary people in the service of the nation as a whole.[13] Still, the eighteenth-century author who took the idea of equality further than anybody else was Rousseau. Like Hobbes, Rousseau was a strong believer in a primeval state of nature that had existed before human society was created and history started moving. Unlike Hobbes, whom he never ceased to attack, he did not believe in the war of all against all. Perhaps most important of all, Rousseau was a truly superb writer. His romantic, not to say sentimental, style appealed to far more people than Hobbes' dry, wry analysis ever could.

In the *Discourse on the Origin of Inequality* (1750), Rousseau painted a portrait of the state of nature with which he has been associated ever since. That fact, of course, says as much about his readers as it did about the author himself. "Savages are not wicked precisely because they do not know what it is to be good, for it is neither the development of knowledge nor the restraint of law, but the calm of the passions and the ignorance of vice that keeps them from doing wrong." Echoes here of *Genesis* and the Garden of Eden, no doubt. They were, however, familiar with kindness for the unfortunate and for the weak. That was a quality Rousseau, anticipating de Waal, thought he could see even in animals.[14] "It is pity that, in the state of nature, takes the place of laws, moral habits, and virtues, with the added benefit that there no one is tempted to disobey its gentle voice…." It is pity that is the origin of tenderness, love, care, and even, since mothers risk their lives for their offspring, courage. It is pity, too, that inspires in all men the "maxim of natural goodness:" namely, "do what is good to yourself with as little as possible harm to others." Under such conditions, "inequality is scarcely noticeable … and its influence … is almost negligible."[15]

"The true founder of civil society [and of inequality] was the first man who, having enclosed a piece of land, thought of saying, 'This is mine,' and came across people simple enough to believe him." The failure to correct him was the origin of all crimes, wars, and murders. As populations grew the family, housing, tools, agriculture, and metallurgy made their appearance. So did specialization and the division of labor. More important still, people lost their innocence. They started seeing themselves through the eyes of others, leading to competition, vanity, influence, and authority. The "march of inequality" was jump-started. It has never ceased advancing since, giving birth to endless conflicts, revolutions, and wars. From these struggles "the monster," despotism, "gradually rearing its ugly head and swallowing up everything that it had seen to be good and sound" in society would rise.[16]

So what is the remedy? Rousseau's answer is found in *The Social Contract* (1762). The community he envisages differs from Plato's *Republic* in that there is no division into classes. That apart, it owes a lot to its predecessor. In both cases it is hard to say where political science ends and utopia begins. Meeting in assembly, all the men in a community sign a contract. In it, they surrender the kind of freedom that nature has endowed them with. So precisely determined are its articles that, no sooner are they changed or violated by anyone than they are rendered null and void, so that natural freedom is resumed. It reads: "Each one of us puts into the community his person and all his powers under the supreme discretion of the general will; and as a body, we incorporate every member as an indivisible part of the whole." "Immediately in place of the individual person of each contracting party, this act of association creates an artificial and collective body composed of as many members as there are voters in the assembly."[17] The gap between government and civil society is closed. Only the assembly in which the general will finds expression and by which it is expressed is left. Since nobody has any rights outside the general will or against it, everyone is by definition the equal of everyone else. In this "totalitarian democracy," as it has been called, the difference between freedom and unfreedom is abolished.[18]

Everything, then, depends on having at hand men (and, in their own way, women) who, out of their own free will, are willing to embark on such an experiment and able to live in the community of equals it would create. In his novel *Émile*, also published in 1762, Rousseau describes the way such people should be raised and educated. The details do not matter much. Guided mainly by his father, a master educator if ever one there was, the boy is introduced first to the physical world around him; then to the trade he will one day exercise; and finally to the world of sentiment. By sentiment Rousseau means the kind of understanding, feeling and attitudes needed to enable the individual to live in harmony with his fellow creatures without any kind of compulsion. All this is done gradually and by means of example, observation, and experimentation. Practice dominates, whereas books only play a relatively small role. Since discovering the world and becoming what one is constitute their own reward there is room for neither rewards nor punishments. Children are helped to glide into their own personalities, so to speak. So gentle is the process that they do not even notice it.

From beginning to end, the objective is to preserve and foster everything in them that is "natural." Doing so requires that people give up their birthright, i.e. the kind of freedom nature had given them. Rousseau's ideal community offers even less liberty and is less tolerant of individual differences than the sovereign who "carries" Hobbes' Leviathan on his strong shoulders. The latter, after all, is only interested in order. There is a paradox here. As with Plato, who put as strong an emphasis on education as Rousseau did, first people are given the most perfect education to help them become and remain what nature has made them. Next, on pain of being excommunicated, they must subordinate themselves to, and lose themselves in, the general will. In Rousseau's paradise things are taken to the point where everybody is obliged to wear the same clothes. Even if all of this were feasible, if that is the price of equality then who wants it?

Considering his own system Hobbes, like Bodin before him, sees it as equally compatible with monarchy, aristocracy, or democracy. He himself favored monarchy; in practice, however, once the principle of equality had been established that of democracy was not very far behind. Had not Herodotus, writing over two millennia before Hobbes, seen the two as marching together, indeed all but interchangeable? Locke himself never explained how government by consent should work, an omission that is almost certainly not accidental. Had he been pressed to the wall, probably he would have said that, to enable people to change their rulers if they wanted to, elections were indispensable. He would have added that, to prevent mob rule, the right to vote should be restricted to a minority, even a small one, of property owners, as was the case in the England of his day.[19]

But how could one reconcile such a system with the kind of equality Rousseau envisaged? Outside the family, either everybody was the equal of everybody else or he was not. Government by consent, both of the kind that existed in Athens and of that which Locke proposed, is nevertheless government. The temporary power of one man (a magistrate) over others (citizens) still means that power is, albeit temporarily, unequally distributed. To square the circle, Rousseau introduced two measures. First, magistrates were to be chosen not by elections but by casting lots. Second, sovereignty was transferred to the popular assembly. Its decisions would reflect "the general will" in which individuals were supposed to submerge themselves.

There were, however, problems. First, the idea of selecting any but the least important officials by lot is preposterous and unworthy of a serious thinker. Second, as he himself knew well enough,[20] a system of this kind was only practical, if indeed it was practical at all, in a small community where everybody lived with everybody else face-to-face. The model he had in mind was the Geneva of his youth which at the time, it was about the size of some of the larger Greek city-states. This was ironic, given that Rousseau's own father had been forced to flee Geneva after being caught poaching; in other words, encroaching on the privileges his betters, in this case the rich Swiss oligarchs, had reserved for themselves.

Perhaps even more than Plato's Republic, Rousseau's vision was destined to remain in Heaven—or, if one prefers, in Hell. Here on earth, others looked for other solutions. Ancient Greek democracy,

practically the only one before the modern age, was of the direct
kind. In classical Athens, all citizens were allowed to participate in
the assembly. At one point they even started to be paid for doing so.
Each citizen had one vote. All were entitled to address the assembly, and all could gain office either by lot or by getting themselves
elected. Briefly, whoever would take a part in public affairs could
do so. Pericles himself said that anybody who did not serve the city
in this way was an *idiotēs*, best translated as idle chatterbox.[21] This
was direct democracy in action. In point of creating civic and political equality among the citizens it has never been improved upon.
What is more, and precisely because it did *not* seek to enforce socio-
economic equality, Athenian democracy also offered more liberty
than most polities, real or imaginary, before or since.

However, in the absence of sophisticated means of transportation and telecommunication, direct democracy also meant that both
the geographical extent of the polity and the citizen body had to be
kept fairly small. Otherwise it would be impossible to gather everybody at the same place, present the various arguments, and take
the vote. We know that the Athenian assembly met about once every three weeks and that, on one particular occasion out of many
hundreds, 9,000 citizens were actually present. But that is all we
know. The way out of the dilemma was representation, the method
by which some people speak on behalf of others. Rousseau himself says that the idea "comes to us from feudal government, from
that iniquitous and absurd system under which the human race is
degraded and which dishonors the name of man."[22] Modern historians, perhaps because they do not have to live under it, no longer
see "feudal government" in quite so bad a light. However, they
do agree that it is there that the origins of representation must be
sought. Many European countries had parliaments in which the

three estates were represented. And what are parliaments if not in
stitutionalized meetings of representatives? Many towns with their
elected governing organs also made use of the system.[23]

In itself, representation did little to abolish inequality before the
law—perhaps, indeed, the opposite was the case. Politically, too,
inequality reigned. There never was any question of one man, one
vote, let alone an equal right to hold office. Forming part of the
lower classes, the great majority of people did not have any vote at
all. Locke himself rarely spoke of representation. Yet as early as the
opening years of the thirteenth century his own country had set up
"the Mother of Parliaments." Between 1683 and 1688 he could also
watch the system in action in the Netherlands where, like Hobbes,
he had sought refuge. Over there the Estates General, as well as the
Estates of each of the seven provinces, was in full bloom. Quite apart
from imposing some kind of control on absolute government, the
great advantage of representation was that it provided a potential
for combining equality—one man, one vote—with an unlimited
capacity for demographic and geographical expansion. Modern India, a country of no less than 3.2 million square miles and 1.2 billion
people, is able to hold regular elections. Though it is anything but
democratic, so does China whose territory is three times larger than
that of India.

Rousseau himself was well aware that his vision of a small community was incompatible with the powerful territorial states of his
day. It could be realized, if at all, only in the nooks and crannies that
might exist between them. Celebrated as he was, this fact caused his
ideas to be relegated somewhat to the sidelines from where they later
emerged in a truly terrible form. Meanwhile, starting where Locke
had left off, it fell to Montesquieu to work out the details. The key-
words to look for in *The Spirit of the Laws* are separation of powers,

democracy, and elections. Taking a leaf from the English system of
his day, Montesquieu also suggested a bicameral legislative in which
the two chambers would balance one another.[24] And how was a
system in which some governed others, albeit democratically, to be
reconciled with equality? Simple, Montesquieu answered: Equality
means "not that everybody should command, or that no one should
be commanded, but that we obey or command our equals."[25]

As he recognized full well, in reality things were not so simple.
But for socio-economic equality, political equality was largely meaningless. Lycurgus and Romulus, Montesquieu explains, were lucky.
The former found a polity thoroughly detested by all its members,
providing him with a unique opportunity to reform it as thoroughly
as he wished. The latter founded an entirely new one. Both, though
for different reasons, were able to make an equal division of property, meaning land (what happened to the previous owners Montesquieu does not say). Even so, their work was far from perfect.
Maintaining equality over time is at least as hard as establishing it.
Doing so requires a measure of frugality that was present in Sparta
but not, Montesquieu says, in Athens. Solon, while in charge of the
latter, had done his best to limit economic inequality by regulating
dowries as well as other measures;[26] but he only succeeded to a limited extent. As for Rome, it quickly outgrew any egalitarianism with
which it may have started out.

From these men, Locke and Montesquieu in particular, a
straight line leads to the War of the American Revolution. Thomas
Paine, the English-American journalist who, in 1768, anonymously
penned the enormously popular pamphlet *Common Sense*, took it
for granted that, "in the order of creation," men were originally
equal.[27] So how did they cease to be unequal, and how did oppression raise its head? "Government by kings was first introduced

into the world by the Heathens, from whom the children of Israel copied the custom. It was the most prosperous invention the Devil ever set on foot for the promotion of idolatry." In imitating them and setting up their own monarchy under King Saul, the children of Israel both went against their own ancient tradition and sinned against the Lord's will.[28] Next, they compounded the error by making kingship hereditary. "Where there are no distinctions there can be no superiority, perfect equality affords no temptation. The republics of Europe are all (and we may say always) in peace. Holland and Switzerland are without wars, foreign or domestic."

Contrast this with "monarchical governments." Driven by pride and insolence, and always threatened by would-be usurpers of every sort, they are "never long at rest." The one way to avoid oppression, then, was to institute republican government. To make doubly sure, both electors (voters) and representatives should be numerous and equal. We are getting very close—late eighteenth-century critics would have said perilously so—to Thomas Jefferson and the American Declaration of Independence.[29] "We hold these truths to be self-evident, that all men are created equal, that they are endowed by their Creator with certain unalienable rights, that among these are life, liberty and the pursuit of happiness. That to secure these rights, governments are instituted among men, deriving their just powers from the consent of the governed." While there had been attempts to institute equality before, nothing like this had ever been written to serve as the basis for a real-life government. In the words of the great Seal of the United State: a *novus ordo seclorum*, a "new order of the ages," had come into being.

Jefferson's words could never have been officially adopted by the Continental Congress if conditions had not been suitable. Especially compared with Europe, a certain kind of equality, and even

more so the idea of equality, did indeed prevail. The first reason for
this was that a "feudal" society had never existed. That meant that
descent, and the privileges it conferred in other countries, did not
count for much. Slavery apart, what lawful authority some people
exercised over others was solely by virtue of the public offices they
held or, in the case of indentured servants, a covenant both sides had
voluntarily entered. The fact that indenture was always temporary
diminished its impact. The second was the absence in many places
of a powerful government. Always in theory, and often in practice,
whoever wanted to could move west. Over there, a thin population
and primeval conditions prevented strong hierarchies from being
formed. The third was the lingering influence of Puritanism. It
continued to insist on equality in front of God; unlike most polities
at most time and places, most colonies had neither a state religion
nor a powerful ecclesiastical hierarchy to enforce it. As important,
in theory at any rate, it considered all work honorable.

Nevertheless, already in 1774 socio-economic gaps among the
inhabitants of the thirteen colonies were extremely wide. The top
quintile held 95 percent of wealth, whereas the next four only owned
5 percent.[30] Jefferson himself was well aware of these facts. His objective in waging a prolonged campaign against the Federalists was
precisely to prevent the gaps from growing larger still. By contrast,
what made Locke, and even more so Montesquieu, so popular in
America was precisely the fact that they had squared the circle. They
provided, or were believed to provide, a way of setting up and maintaining civic and political equality without any need to extend it into
the economic sphere as well. Paine himself had showed the way. He
mentioned Holland and Switzerland as models of democracy, which
by the standards of the day they certainly were. What he did not say
was that both societies were socio-economically unegalitarian. It is

true that there were no kings and that the aristocracy was relatively weak. However, political rights were concentrated in the hands of a wealthy oligarchy.

Once it had been established, American democracy did indeed guarantee a sort of political and civic equality. The circle of those who enjoyed that equality steadily grew. First the restrictions which, in many states, prevented the poor and the dissident from electing and being elected were removed. Much later blacks, women, and those aged between eighteen and twenty-one started marching, or were pointed, in the same direction. Today, the major exception is the system whereby each State, regardless of how large or small its population is, sends an equal number of representatives to the Senate. Civic equality has also been expanded. Minorities such as gays made advances and were, to some extent, put on an equal basis with the rest. Through all this there could be no question of socio-economic equality, let alone frugality. Depending on which set of figures one chooses to believe, and which starting point one selects, socio-political gaps have remained largely unchanged. In 2008 the top quintile owned 89 percent of the country's wealth. The other four made do with 11 percent.[31] The Constitution itself can be interpreted, and often has been interpreted, as a document deliberately designed to enable the rich to retain their property while keeping the poor firmly in their place.[32]

The American version of equality, combined with democracy, also brought other benefits. Unable to extend citizenship, in other words give the people of its subject-cities rights equal to those its own citizens enjoyed, Athens had to rule them by force. Incorporating foreigners as they did, other historical empires, however much they differed from Athens in other respects, also used force. The situation of the U.S. was, and is, entirely different. Thanks largely to the principle of representation, throughout its history it has only governed very few people who were not citizens. Over time, even the Indians have somehow been incorporated. It speaks volumes in favor of the system that the vast majority of people would not exchange their U.S. citizenship for any other. Conversely, in over two centuries since 1783 many millions have done what they could to obtain it. This success was by no means self-evident. Like Thucydides, both Locke and Montesquieu had worried lest democracy, and the equality on which it was based, would lead to instability and sought to avoid it. Montesquieu even doubted whether a democracy larger than the Athenian one was possible at all. The example he and many of his contemporaries had in mind was Republican Rome. As it grew it lost any democratic elements it had ever had, turning into an empire ruled by despots instead.

In response, Jefferson wrote that "the principles of compact and equality" would enable the U.S. to expand far beyond the ancient democracies.[33] His prediction turned out to be more correct than he could ever have foreseen. The American version of equality has made possible a very large Republic indeed. The major, major exception of the Civil War apart, in domestic policy at any rate that Republic has also been a model of political stability. In almost twenty-five decades there have been no coups, not even attempted ones. Even the assassination of a few presidents and the impeachment of one of them have not prevented power from being transferred in an orderly manner. The Constitution itself has been modified several times. Much of this is due to "equality," meaning that no part of the population was able to lord it over the rest.

The U.S. did, however, fully meet Plato's description of democracy as "feverish." The more it grew, the more it turned into perhaps the most competitive, dynamic, fastest-changing, society the world has ever seen. The more it grew, too, the stronger its tendency to engage in foreign adventures or, as George Washington called them, "entanglements." Since at least the early 1960s, most of these adventures have been foolish indeed. Not one did anything to advance America's interests, and several have ended in resounding defeats.

*

Though the countries of the Old World also moved towards equality, with them the process took very different forms. The major reason for that was the existence of centuries-old "feudal" privileges which could not be abolished without a struggle. By and large, the further east one went the greater the obstacles and the longer it took to remove them.

Initially the country most affected was France, home to many of the most vociferous Enlightenment thinkers. Here as elsewhere, the gap between the prevailing conditions and those Rousseau had envisaged was enormous. The National Assembly, consisting of the representatives of the French people, in their 1789 Declaration of the Rights of Men only went so far in its attempt to correct the problem.[34] Article 1 said that "men are born and remain free and equal in rights. Social distinctions can be based only on public utility." Article 6 explained that "all citizens have the right to participate personally, or through their representatives, in [the law's] formation. It must be the same for all, whether it protects or punishes. All citizens, being equal in its eyes, are equally admissible to all public dignities, positions, and employments, according to their ability, and on the basis of no other distinction than that of their virtues and talents." As in the U.S., though, there were limits. "The aim of every political association is the preservation of the natural and imprescriptible rights of man. These rights are liberty, property, security, and resistance to oppression" (Article 2). Article 17 put the icing on the cake: Property being "an inviolable and sacred right, no one can be deprived of it, unless legally established public necessity obviously demands it, and upon condition of a just and prior indemnity."

Jefferson's Declaration of Independence had nothing to say about property. In this it differed from its French equivalent. By promising to protect both equality *and* property, the latter contradicted itself. The contradiction, left-wing critics would say, was inherent in "liberal" equality. The subsequent history of equality in France was much more tortuous than in the U.S. First came the Reign of Terror. Robespierre, who more than anyone else initiated it and was responsible for it, saw himself as a disciple of Rousseau. In his diary he called the latter "a divine man."[35] It was from Rousseau, that he took the idea that anybody suspected of opposing the general will—in reality, Robespierre' own—at a time when the *patrie* was in danger deserved to be put to death. The outcome was that an estimated 30,000 people lost their lives, many of them for no other reason but that they had "aristocratic" blood flowing in their veins.

Having appointed himself emperor, Napoleon left revolutionary civic and political equality intact. He also retained the system whereby people voted for parliament; however, so many deputies were nominated by the government that it did not matter very much. Acting on the centuries-old theory that aristocracy formed a natural bulwark against popular revolution, the restored Bourbons tried to reintroduce some aspects of "feudalism." Those included a bicameral parliamentary system with a hereditary upper chamber, modeled on the British one across the Channel, and a lower one elected on the basis of a very narrow franchise indeed. Their efforts did not work very well.[36] In 1830 Charles X was deposed. The

"July Monarchy," which lasted until 1848 and was headed by Louis Philippe, in some respects followed in Napoleon's footsteps. That was even more true of Napoleon's nephew, Napoleon III. Having been elected president, he followed his uncle in mounting a coup and making himself emperor. Yet it is important to note that both Napoleons always maintained the principle of one man, one vote. To that extent, political equality persisted.

The Third Republic upheld both the principle of one man (but not one woman), one vote and that of equality in front of the law. Yet the 1871 Constitution was not the last word. Under the Vichy Regime "work, family, fatherland" took the place of "liberty, equality, fraternity." Both democracy and elections were abolished. Officials started drafting a new Constitution. However, the German withdrawal of 1944 brought the regime to an inglorious end before it could be completed. Aside from the Vichy years, the above-mentioned principles were never seriously questioned. Under the Fourth and Fifth Republics they remained intact. Each year on 14 July, Bastille Day, they continued to be celebrated.

The French Revolutions of 1793–1794 and 1871 (though not those of 1830 and 1848) were accompanied by massive bloodshed. In Britain things were different. While the nineteenth-century movement towards civic and political equality was as complicated as in France, it was practically bloodless. The main reason for this was that the Glorious Revolution of 1688 had already done away with many, though by no means all, forms of civic inequality. The Reform Act of 1832 expanded the electorate but fell far short of establishing political equality in the sense of universal suffrage. The Chartists between 1837 and 1842 demanded universal male suffrage, electoral districts of equal size, and the abolition of property qualifications for members of Parliament. To put rich and poor on a more equal footing, they also wanted MPs to be paid.

Eventually all these reforms were realized, but only long after the Chartists themselves had disappeared from the stage. In 1867 the Second Reform Act again expanded the electorate. In 1908, David Lloyd George, acting as secretary of the treasury and wishing to pass a liberal budget, threatened to pack the hereditary House of Lords with large numbers of new peers. The House gave way and lost much of its power, thus marking another step towards equality. However, political equality in the form of universal suffrage had to wait until after World War I. As in the U.S. and France, none of this did much to increase economic equality which remained about as pronounced as it had ever been. Britain has also remained famous for maintaining a kind of social inequality based not just on wealth but on education, manners and pronunciation.

Germany during the eighteenth century was divided into over three hundred petty principalities. Most were "feudal" and hered-itary. Others, though no less "feudal," were governed by officials of the Catholic Church. Either way, of equality, civic or political, there could be no question whatsoever. To make matters worse, the small size of many principalities made it harder than usual to distin-guish between political government and the rulers' private affairs. The outcome was a peculiarly stifling atmosphere characterized by obsequiousness and groveling servility. As the Jewish-German poet Heinrich Heine later wrote, it was as if people had swallowed the stick their superiors used to beat them with.[37] Starting in 1794, the revolutionary and Napoleonic wars brought some change to the western parts of the country. But east of the Elbe, absolutism and "feudalism" continued to reign almost undisturbed.

In Prussia, which apart from the Habsburg Monarchy was the largest German state, change only got under way during the so-called Era of Reform that started in 1807. It did not originate from within, but was forced on the country by the smashing defeat it had recently suffered at Napoleon's hands. Some, though not all, of the aristocracy's privileges were abolished, as was serfdom. Henceforward all Prussian subjects were free, and a considerable degree of civic equality was instituted. After 1808 Prussian towns, which previously had possessed no independence whatsoever, started administering themselves with the aid of magistrates elected by all taxpaying citizens. Yet an effort to set up a country-wide parliament, however restricted the electorate on which it was based and however high the barriers that prevented all but the members of the highest classes from serving in it, did not succeed. In this respect Prussia fell behind the German states farther to the west which never quite undid the French-induced reforms.

Thus the situation remained until 1848 when another revolution broke out. Eventually it was suppressed, but not before King Friedrich Wilhelm IV was forced to grant a Constitution. Even so, political equality remained a pipedream. True, every adult male Prussian was now entitled to vote. However, the electorate was divided into three classes according to the taxes each person paid. Each class was entitled to fill one third of the seats in parliament. The way it was done, an upper-class voter was worth almost twenty lower-class ones. Only in 1867 did the North German Bund adopt equal universal manhood suffrage, and only in 1871 was the latter extended to the rest of Germany. To that extent, the dream of the 1848 German revolutionaries was realized. In Prussia itself the principle of one man, one vote, had to wait until after the fall of the monarchy and the establishment of the Republic in 1919. As in other countries the Prussian/German nobility during the nineteenth century, and to some extent even later, also continued to enjoy some other privileges. Perhaps the most important one was easy access to desirable positions in the military and the state bureaucracy.

In Russia a large part of the population was literally owned by a relatively small number of aristocrats. Even after Tsar Alexander II finally liberated the serfs in 1861, inequality among different classes remained as great as in any other country. However, the nineteenth-century drive towards equality went beyond the political and the civic spheres. Education was just as important. From the time of Plato on, many authors had seen it as the only possible foundation on which everything else could be built. On both sides of the Atlantic, throughout the century universal, compulsory and free education was greatly expanded.[38] Much, though not all, of this was occasioned by the demand for equality. Not everybody could be a university professor; but at any rate it was possible to give everyone some kind of foundation on which he could later build. To use a phrase coined much later by an aide to U.S. President George W. Bush, no child was to be left behind. The outcome was a virtuous cycle. Educated people demanded equality with their betters. Equal people demanded even more education for themselves and their children. All this was well and good, so far as it went.

One of the most interesting aspects of the post-1776 drive towards liberal equality was the emancipation of the Jews. Throughout the centuries of the Diaspora the Jews were regarded as less than equal. However, since the concept of equality itself was unknown or only played a minor role in social affairs, this fact did not create undue difficulties. Jews were just one of many groups to which special laws, favorable or unfavorable, were attached. The advent of the Enlightenment with its atheism and emphasis on equality caused things to change. Jews ceased to be simply the devilish enemies of a God who was Himself losing importance day by day.

Instead, and precisely because their basic humanity was granted, they became a blot on the landscape and a glaring eyesore. Their very existence put in question the anticipated progress of man towards equality.[39] Hence the idea, the beginnings of which can be discerned during the last decades before 1800, that they should be freed from discrimination and educated. As one would-be reformer put it, having once overcome their "clannish religious opinions," the Jews would cease to be Jews and become citizens instead.[40] At the age of twenty-five Karl Marx, the son of a converted Prussian Jew, penned a paper in which he expressed the hope that in a re-formed socialist state, Jews would be emancipated from their own "objective" nature and disappear. Famous anti-Semites such as the writer Paul de Lagarde (1827–1891) and the historian Heinrich von Treitschke (1834–1896) agreed with him on this point.[41]

In one country after another, Jews received full civic and political rights. Legally speaking, they were put on an equal footing with other citizens. France emancipated its Jews in 1791. That did not prove the end of the story. In 1806 Napoleon emancipated the Jews for the second time.[42] Naturally he took the opportunity to make a little propaganda for himself. Paintings showed him graciously handing over the relevant document as Jewish men and women, flanked by the appropriate Jewish symbols, thanked him profusely. Later still the reform gave rise to some difficulties because Jews could hardly speak favorably of Napoleon without offending the Bourbons who succeeded him. The Netherlands, which at that time were known as the Batavian Republic, followed the French example in 1796. Many German states did so between then and 1815. Later a reaction set in and full equality was only reached in 1869 (the North German Bund) and 1871 (Germany as a whole). Even so, Prussian Jews were not allowed to become officers.

In Britain emancipation did not take place at once but took decades to accomplish. Not until 1858 did the first Jew, Lionel Rothschild, take his seat in parliament. Not until 1890 were the last remaining restrictions on Jews (and Catholics) removed. In the U.S. Jewish emancipation was carried out not by the Federal Government but state by state. It was only completed in 1877 when Vermont finally ceased demanding that office-holders take their oath in the name of the Christian God, thus ending all forms of official discrimination. In Russia as late as 1912 a law was passed that prohibited even the grandchildren of Jews from serving as officers in the Tsar's army. Emancipation had to wait for the Revolution of February 1917.

Again it is important to emphasize that civic and political emancipation did not necessarily mean that, socially speaking, Jews were really accepted as equals. Even in the U.S. in the 1950s, employers looking for workers sometimes specified that they did not want Jews.[43] Many country clubs did not accept Jews, and many universities had quotas for them. In the case of the former it was probably simple anti-Semitism. In that of the latter, it was because Jewish students were so numerous and so good that faculties felt overwhelmed by them. It is said that nowadays, the same kind of reverse affirmative action is being applied to Asian students.[44] The persistence, even in the most "advanced" liberal-democratic countries, of unofficial discrimination caused many Jews to turn to socialism. Only the latter, they hoped, would *really* remove the obstacles under which they labored and put them on an equal basis with everyone else.

✳

The move towards Jewish emancipation was anything but smooth, and in any case it only affected a relatively small minority.

Nevertheless, in many ways it both typified liberal equality and represented the latter's logical culmination. Paradoxical as it sounds, the origins of this particular form of equality are to be sought in Thomas Hobbes' absolutist vision. By inventing the abstract state, the Leviathan, as he called it, Hobbes conceived of government without the various relationships between superiors and inferiors on which, except in the ancient city-states, all previous regimes had been constructed. From then on neither any special link with the divine, nor ancestry, nor wealth, meant that some people could claim greater rights than, or power over, others. By the second half of the eighteenth century equality had become one of the principal rallying-cries of the Enlightenment. Some thinkers, notably Rousseau, sought to take it to the point where it not only resulted in the abolition of all institutions inside the community but led to the total loss of liberty. Much later, this came to be known as "totalitarian democracy."

Starting with Locke, most thinkers took a different path. Their goal was to combine equality with freedom. At the same time they looked for ways to adapt it to the needs of the modern territorial state. Hitting upon representation, a system that strangely enough had been carried over from the detested "feudal" Middle Ages, they laid the theoretical foundations of liberal democracy. The first states specifically designed to uphold that ideal made their appearance in 1776 and 1789. Much blood was shed and setbacks were not lacking. However, throughout the nineteenth century progress in this direction continued. This happened first in Europe and then, gradually and hesitantly, in other parts of the world too. Such was its impetus that even Jews, who for over a thousand years had been despised minority, were officially emancipated. The process culminated in 1948 when liberal equality was extended to "everyone" and formally enshrined in the United Nations Universal Declaration of Human Rights.[45] Yet as considerable as the achievements of liberalism and democracy were, they did little to reduce socio-economic inequality. So little, in fact, that many came to regard liberalism and democracy as mere fig leaves to cover its absence.

Chapter 6

Socialist Equality

The idea of equality goes back to ancient Athens, and that of liberalism to the ancient Roman *libertas*. By contrast, the term socialism is less than two centuries old. Apparently it was first used in 1832 by a disciple of two contemporary "socialists," Robert Owen and Henri Saint-Simon.[1] Eight year later it was followed by "communism." Both terms have in common that they refer to ideologies intended to combat the kind of socio-economic inequality which democracy and liberalism barely touched.

Man is the animal that invents its own past. Never was that more true than in the nineteenth century; and never more than at the hands of socialist and communist writers. Like so many other modern ideologues, they discarded God and looked to history to make their case. Within a few years of the two terms' first appearance they started being projected backward. As socialists and communists saw it, the first and possibly the most important communist was Plato, from whom everyone else took his cue. The Spartan kings Cleomenes and Nabis were communists. The brothers Gracchus were socialists. By some interpretations Jesus was a communist and the early Christian communities adopted a communist lifestyle. The list, compiled by countless post-1840 socialist and communist writers, kept growing. Some of history's alleged socialists/communists had risen in rebellion against their oppressors. To quote Luther again, most previous historians had treated them like "mad dogs." Now they were transformed into forerunners, martyrs, and heroes. Others wrote "utopian" books in which they explained how socialist/communist societies could be established and made to function, whereas others still actually tried to set up real socialist or communist settlements.

Equality in the early Christian communities as well as monasteries has already been addressed. Monasteries still exist in many countries and are as egalitarian, or inegalitarian, as they have ever been. Towards the end of the English Civil War in 1648–1649, a group known as the Diggers made its appearance. As so often, the background was formed by the extreme contrast between rich and poor. To this was added the War itself. The dawn of the Commonwealth created messianic hopes concerning a new kind of government and, perhaps, a different kind of society. The Diggers' direct inspiration came from Gerrard Winstanley, a failed Manchester merchant who dealt in cloth.[2] Previously he had belonged to another group, known as the Levelers, a name that speaks for itself. He believed in republican government as well as political and economic equality for all. Production was to be carried out in common and the products equitably distributed among the members. However, the family was to be kept intact. The Diggers never numbered more than a few dozen. Still their attempts to set up communal settlements on uncultivated land at several places around London led to much controversy and fear. In the end, the authorities intervened and forced them to disperse, although there appear to have been no casualties. Winstanley himself went on to sum up his experience, and his hopes, in several books and pamphlets. He is known to have been alive in 1660, and may even have survived until 1676.

Extremely small in size, the Diggers' efforts only lasted a few weeks. Early in the nineteenth century several other attempts were made to set up communal settlements. Particularly interesting are those associated with the name of Charles Fourier (1772–1832).[3] The background was formed by the early stages of the industrial revolution and the immense amount of human misery it created among those who had been forced to leave the countryside and take up work in the mines and the factories. Fourier's most important work, *La Phalansterie*, from the Greek phalanx, was published in 1832. In it he proposed the creation of settlements known as *phalansteries*. A drawing showed a huge building modeled upon a royal palace, probably Versailles, but larger and more grandiose.

Like Versailles, the palace would offer every sort of comfort contemporaries could think of. It would be home to approximately 1,800–2,000 people divided into 400 families. Working the surrounding land in common, they would produce most of their own needs. What they could not make for themselves they would obtain by means of exchange with similar communities nearby. Distribution was to be based on the amount of work each person had done, his or her natural skill, and the amount of capital he (not she, because married women were not supposed to have capital) had put at the community's disposal. Private property was not abolished. People could even leave what they owned to their children. Since everybody would live harmoniously with everybody else, there would be little need for government. Essentially its task would consist of administration. With so many excellent amenities freely available, the outcome would be a fairly egalitarian lifestyle. In this way Fourier hoped to square the circle, making possible a socialist community without forcing everybody into the same mold.

Where Fourier differed from run-of-the-mill utopian writers was that some people tried to put parts of his vision into practice. At the time, perhaps more than at other since the first centuries after Jesus, such attempts were "in the air." Most were made in the United States. There, in contrast to Europe, land was plentiful and cheap. During the 1840s about a hundred phalansteries were established, many of them on the initiative of Albert Brisbane (1809–1890). He hoped that they would help complete what the Revolution of 1776 had done by extending equality from the civic and political fields into the socio-economic one. The best-known community, Brook Farm near Boston, lasted for seven years before it fell apart.[4] Seeking to combine the principles of Fourierism with those of Unitarian Christianity, originally it was located in a large farmhouse together with the surrounding outbuildings. Later work was started on a larger structure meant to house up to four hundred people, but it was never completed.

Members, who were also stockholders, received equal pay on the basis of the number of days each of them had worked per year. Things were organized, or were supposed to be organized, in such a way as to give everybody an equal chance for social, intellectual, and spiritual development. In practice it turned out that many of the seventy or so adults who made up the community preferred play to work. Some visitors claimed they had never seen a group of grownups so addicted to games of every kind. The experiment excited much interest. Famous and later-to-be-famous persons such as author Ralph Waldo Emerson and journalist Horace Greeley came to see how it was done and stayed for a while.

Brook Farm and the other phalansteries were not alone. All over the U.S. during this period, dozens of "utopian" communities were founded in places as far apart as Pennsylvania, Illinois, Indiana, Utah and California. Some followed Brook Farm in that the land, buildings and equipment were paid for by the members who formed a joint-stock company. Others were set up by rich industrialists such as the Scot, Robert Owen.[5] Most probably had philanthropic motives in mind. Then as now, some tycoons felt the need to justify their wealth by helping build a better world. Others, such as the railway-car manufacturer George Pullman, hoped to turn a profit as well. He did so by renting out houses to his workers and introducing the truck system whereby the latter received their pay in company money. The coupons in question could only be spent at the company's shops. Equality through semi-slavery, one might say.

Typically, in each community, production, both agricultural and industrial, was carried out by all the members in common. Products were either consumed by the members and their families or sold on the open market. Different communities worked out different systems for sharing products among their members. Generally, though, the leading principle was "from everybody as much as he can, to everybody as much as he needs." Many communities had some kind of affiliation with dissident Protestant groups. Particularly important in this respect were Shakers, Mennonites and Hutterites. All of these shared a belief in a rather unforgiving, rather awesome, personal God before whom everyone, from the highest to the lowest, was supposed to tremble. Others, to the contrary, were secular-minded and hoped to pursue the communal life so as to emancipate their members from religious superstition among other things.

Some communities abolished private housing along with the family, banning marriage as well as sexual intercourse. Male and female members were to live together in a single large building as if they were all brothers and sisters. Continuity was to be assured by taking children from orphanages and raising them.[6] Others did away with monogamy in favor of larger, but also apparently less stable, family units. One such was the Oneida Community in New York where older women were supposed to initiate young men to sex and the other way around.[7] Almost all tried to put all their members on an equal basis, socially and economically, so as to keep them united, prevent tensions among them, enable them to lead a decent human life, and permit them to develop themselves in the direction the originator had pointed out. Normally he was a man, but here and there a community was led by an enterprising woman.

To save money, many communities were set up in relatively un-inviting places and led a fairly frugal life. Nevertheless, maintaining equality proved harder than many had expected. Even administering a relatively small community consisting of a few dozen members takes some skill and charisma. Not everybody was a Lycurgus or a Solon who, having carried out their reforms, exiled themselves from their native cities. Instead, leaders who had those skills and that charisma often translated them into privileges of every kind. In the case of Mormon communities, those included not just money and comforts but sexual access to many of the community's female members.[8] Some leaders, the most important of whom was John Noyes of Oneida, even tried to pass their status, and of course their privileges, to their offspring. At the other extreme were members who, far from contributing as much as they could, had joined specifically because they were unwilling or unable to make it on their own in the outside world.

Some of these communities held out for two or three generations, even reaching into the early years of the twentieth century.

However, most were dissolved after only a few years. Often the break-up took place amidst acrimonious disputes among members and former members who could not agree which of them would get what share of the community's assets. Still the utopian tradition has never quite died out. Both in the U.S. and elsewhere, islands of communal life still exist. They are most numerous in California, followed by Michigan and Washington. Their total number is estimated at 20,000.[9] Some continue to be built around religion. Others try to promote an ecological approach to life.[10] At least one is devoted to exploring orgasm in all its possible and impossible varieties.[11] Both in the nineteenth century and today, communities have always been fairly small. A few had as many as 1,000 members, but most had less than one hundred. Many only counted twenty or thirty people at any one time. To make things worse, often the strict regulations, both those that were obeyed and those that were not, caused the members to be regarded as weirdos by their neighbors. This fact limited their impact on society at large.

The situation of those other twentieth-century communal settlements, the Israeli kibbutzim, could not have been more different. The kibbutzim, too, were born under the auspices of an ideology, i.e. Zionism. Soon after 1900 small groups of young men and women started emigrating from Europe, mainly of what were then the western districts of the Russian Empire, to what is now Israel. Arriving penniless in a foreign and rather strange country, they were supported by the Jewish Agency. It bought land and provided capital for buildings, agricultural machinery and tools, and seed. Settlers lived in tents or shacks. Some did not even own the clothes on their backs. The combination of communal life with extreme poverty led to equally extreme socio-economic egalitarianism.

A number of years having passed, the Jewish Agency would for-

mally transfer ownership over the means of production to the kibbutz. Either the latter had repaid its debt or else it received the
land and everything on it as an outright gift. After Israel's 1948
War of Independence, acting with or without government permission, many kibbutzim also annexed abandoned Arab land. Production was carried out in common by all the members. Some
pocket-money apart, they did not receive pay but obtained what
they needed for free out of the communal store. Meals were taken
in common, and indeed the completion of the communal dining
hall always acted as visible proof of the fact that the kibbutz had
become firmly established. Some kibbutzim tried to go further still
and abolish the family. Regular meetings were held in which everybody was expected to confess everything to everybody else. Most
did not go quite so far. While many couples dispensed with formal marriage, they did form unions in individual "rooms" meaning
small flats. On the whole such unions were as stable, or unstable, as
anywhere else.[12] Children, even small ones, did not live with their
families. They were brought up in children's homes where kibbutz
women took turns in looking after them. They saw their parents for
an hour or two during the late afternoon and on weekends.

Early kibbutzim only had a few dozen members, sometimes less.
This in itself meant a democratic regime. Regular assemblies were
held, and everybody participated in them on an equal basis. Committees looked after different kinds of agricultural production, education, and housing. The central figure in each kibbutz was an
elected secretary who, however, had little formal authority over the
members. Some kibbutzim also took in non-members. Either living
in the kibbutz or commuting, they got paid for their work but did
not vote in the assembly. At peak, in the early 1950s, four percent
of the entire Jewish population of Israel lived in kibbutzim.

Compared to similar communities elsewhere, what distinguished the kibbutzim most of all was the fact that, far from being
treated as weirdos by society at large, they were upheld as models of
what Zionism were able to achieve. Had they not been "pioneers"
who settled the land and turned it from a desert into a garden? Had
some of them not paid a heavy toll in blood while trying to stop the
Arab invasion in 1948? Did not their sons serve in disproportionate
numbers in every kind of élite unit? And did not their very presence
secure Israel's borders and make infiltration harder? Too, kibbutz
members naturally tended to give their votes to the left-wing parties. That included Prime Minister David Ben Gurion's Mapai, the
largest among them, which governed Israel for many years. Those
parties in turn pampered them and extolled them.

All this caused kibbutzniks to see themselves, and to be seen by
others, as the salt of the earth. During the 1960s, some kibbutzim
working for the government of Israel, and indirectly for the U.S.
as part of the attempt to win hearts and minds, even sent personnel to several African countries to help set up similar communities
there. Nevertheless, in the long run the kibbutzniks were swamped
by the rest of Israeli society. As the latter became better off economically, living standards rose. Kibbutz members wanted a piece of the
action even if it meant, as it almost always did, greater inequality
among them. The outcome was transformation.[13] Some kibbutzim
did away with common meals and children's houses so that members came to live in their own, considerably enlarged apartments and
even bungalows. Others started paying their members differential
salaries based on the skills their work demanded and their performance. Almost all ended the free distribution of clothes and other
household items. Some transferred houses and the land on which
they stood to private ownership. Since some of the land in question

is enormously valuable, the process often gave rise to the most acrimonious disputes imaginable. As the saying goes, "small place, big hell."

Rather like most monasteries, past and present, all of the different kinds of communities discussed in this section formed islands within much larger societies. Especially in the early Middle Ages, and also in the Middle East, some monasteries were heavily fortified to withstand Norse or Arab marauders. On the whole, though, they were unconcerned with what is usually the most important single function of any government, i.e. the use of armed force for offense and defense. The same applied to the various utopian communities, the kibbutzim included. Although in the early days, kibbutz members sometimes had to fight off bands of Arab marauders, their defense needs were mainly provided by the British Mandatory Government with its troops, armored cars, and aircraft. After the establishment of the state the Israel Defense Force took over. To prevent theft and vandalism male kibbutzniks, armed with leftover weapons they were given by the military, sometimes stood guard at night. But that was all. Thus their kind of socio-economic equality developed under a protective umbrella. In this sense, it was a sort of luxury others could ill afford.

Within the various communities democracy and equality did indeed prevail, but only up to a point. This may have been even more true of the Israeli kibbutzim than of America's "utopian" communities. The latter were always small and without any political influence on society at large. Not so the former. Not only did some of them grow to the point where they had many hundreds of members, but they acted as the spearhead of Israel's ruling left-wing parties. Larger kibbutzim required a more sophisticated administration. As time went on and they switched from agriculture to industry and tourism, this became even more the case. Generally those in charge also liaised with the politicians in Jerusalem and Tel Aviv. Over time, this enabled them to acquire important privileges; if not in the form of better pay, than in that of comfortable jobs, expenses, superior transportation, better opportunities for travel, and opportunities for hobnobbing with the great and powerful of the land.[14] The figure of the kibbutz leader who maintained, at kibbutz expense, a room or flat in some town and used it for entertaining his mistresses, has become a literary stock in trade.

As of the second decade of the twenty-first century the kibbutzim, and the special kind of egalitarianism they introduced, seem to be fading out slowly but surely. A shame, some would say: it was nice try.

*

"Utopian" communities and kibbutzim have always been protected communities inside much larger societies. By contrast, socialist and communist parties have aimed at taking over entire countries, even the world. At first the two terms were used more or less interchangeably. It was only around 1900 that the German socialist leader Eduard Bernstein and the Russian communist one Vladimir Ilyich Lenin drew a clear line between socialism and communism.[15] Socialists hoped to achieve their goals gradually, peacefully, and by democratic means as more and more people voted for them. Not so communists, who believed they could only do so by setting up a tight body of disciplined party members, engaging in bloody revolution, and imposing the dictatorship of the proletariat. Between them, at their peak socialists and communists governed about one-third of humanity, and even more if India during the first few decades of its independence is included. Communism ruled supreme from the Elbe to Pyong Yang and Hanoi. Many countries in Western Europe and Australasia adopted a democratic form of socialism. Others, located in Asia and Africa, claimed to combine socialism with dictatorship or, as they preferred to call it, one-party rule. Yet they were not strictly communist. Whatever the precise form, there was no continent and hardly a country where communists, socialists, or both were not present and active. Some of them are still around and continue to make their impact felt.

Socialists raised the same old questions as Plato had: is a system that grants civic equality but leaves socio-economic inequality intact really egalitarian? How just is a justice system that imposes the same fine for the same offense on rich and poor alike? Isn't it true that economic power can be, and often has been, translated into political power as well? And isn't it true that the "voluntary" submission of the poor in all liberal systems is often not voluntary at all? By far the best-known document that sought to undermine belief in liberal equality was the Communist Manifesto.[16] Its authors, Karl Marx and his associate, Friedrich Engels, were aged 29 and 27 respectively when they wrote it in 1848. In thunderous prose, they denounced every form of oppression by one class of another from the beginning of history on. At the same time they called on the proletariat to cast off its chains and rise against the bourgeoisie and the "liberal" ideology it had invented for itself. "Crying inequality" in the distribution of products, in other words the contrast between rich and poor, had to be abolished. The outcome would be an altogether different kind of society, the first in history to do without classes.

The two authors well understood that any measures aimed at achieving this goal could not be the same everywhere but would have to take a somewhat different form from one country to another. "Nevertheless," they wrote, "in most advanced countries, the following will be pretty generally applicable. 1. Abolition of property in land and application of all rents of land to public purposes. 2. A heavy progressive or graduated income tax. 3. Abolition of all rights of inheritance. ... 5. Centralization of credit in the banks of the state, by means of a national bank with state capital and an exclusive monopoly. 6. Centralization of the means of communication and transport in the hands of the state. ... 8. Equal obligation of all to work. ... 10. Free education for all children in public schools. Abolition of children's factory labor in its present form."

Had Marx and Engels risen from the grave around 1970, no doubt they would have been surprised to see how many countries had implemented these measures to one extent or another. Communist countries put Marx in particular on the sort of pedestal previously reserved for God and His prophets. But even in the United States, the self-declared bastion of capitalism, numbers 2 and 10 had been enacted. Instead of working, almost all children attended school. Number 3 had been enacted decades earlier, albeit in a considerably less extreme form that taxed large estates but did not abolish inheritance itself. Number 6, in the form of Nixon's nationalization of the railways and the creation of Amtrak, was on the way. It is true that, in the U.S., the call for socio-economic equality was muted. As Terence Powderly (1849–1924), leader of the Knights of Labor, once commented, American workers dreamt of becoming capitalists, not of eliminating them. Nevertheless, as far as the various measures went, the outcome was the same.

Other "advanced" countries had gone much further. For example, Britain in 1974 raised its top marginal income-tax rate to 83 percent, no less.[17] Some corporations were established by the state *ex novo*. Others were taken away from their private owners and na-

tionalized. Among them were British Aircraft Industries, British
Airways, British Coal, British Electricity, British Gas, British Rail,
British Shipbuilding, and British Telecom. Health too was nationalized, although private physicians were still allowed to practice. All
these joined older state-monopolies such as the Royal Mail Service.
Politicians waged fierce battles over the question whether all education should be nationalized or whether at least some parts of it
should be allowed to remain independent. Much of this was done
in the name of equality or rather, several different kinds of equality.
First, the gap between employers and workers was to be reduced,
though not eliminated. Second, all children were to receive a similar "comprehensive" education and thus a more equal chance of
advancing in life. Third, the country's principal natural resources,
industries and services were supposed to belong to, and benefit, all
citizens rather than just a privileged minority of stockholders.[18]

In Britain and in other countries, the U.S. included, socialism
seems to have done something to reduce socio-economic equality.
Taking 1945 as the starting point, the share of those in the top income decile declined, sometimes by as much as one half. At the
same time, those at the bottom were able to increase theirs.[19] The
problem of poverty was also alleviated, though it never disappeared.
Still, equality did not come for free. First, many of the nationalized
industries proved to be monuments of inefficiency. Operating at a
loss, they swallowed huge sums in subsidies and soon came to hang
like albatrosses around governments' necks. Second, taxation, and
with it the share of the state in GDP, went up, sometimes dramati-
cally so. So heavy was the burden that, during the 1970s, almost all
the countries in question suffered from chronic underinvestment.
With underinvestment came massive unemployment. Unemployment led to transfer payments, which led to taxation (or, if it did

not, to inflation), which led to underinvestment, and so on in a vicious cycle few countries escaped.

In addition, the kind of equality that was established, to the extent that it was established, was problematic. First it is not at all obvious that progressive taxation of the kind Marx and Engels proposed, and most states later implemented, is in fact as egalitarian as it is said to be. To speak with Aristotle and many present-day political scientists, there may be good reasons for trying to reduce the gap between rich and poor in a polity; for example, to increase the size of the middle class on which stability depends. However, and precisely if one looks at things from the point of view of equality, they may well appear in a different light. If equal rights is our objective, why should those whose income and/or property are high pay proportionally more than those whose income is low? Since when is making money, provided it is legally done, an offense that requires the intervention of the law so as to punish those who are good at it?

Second, much of what equality socialism was able to achieve was due to a series of measures the *Communist Manifesto* never mentioned: namely, transfer payments, or entitlements, as they are often called. In Britain during the same period, they amounted to fully one quarter of GDP.[20] Even in the U.S., by 1977 almost half of the population was receiving them—at the expense of the other half, needless to say. Early in the twenty-first century they accounted for the largest part of the current-account deficit by far. The situation in other developed countries was similar. Speaking of equality, is there really any reason why some should be entitled to something regardless of work, merit, or accomplishment? Should one receive more money from the state merely because one is young, or old, or divorced, or homeless, or sick, or shiftless? Or because one has more children to look after? Or for any number of similar reasons? Perhaps so; as Saint Thomas Aquinas wrote, the reason why God has created the poor is to encourage the rest us to give to charity.[21] By doing so we preserve our humanity. A society that does not help its weaker members does not deserve to be called a society at all. However, the desire for equality before the law can hardly justify such measures. Nor was the "Angelic Doctor," as he was called, thinking in such terms. To the contrary, the whole objective of charity was to enable people to live with their conscience amidst inequality.

Reducing some kinds of inequality, in other words, could only be carried out at the expense of increasing others. Not that this was the first time in history such a thing had happened. As we saw, instituting the liberal version of equality meant giving the green light for an indefinite growth of socio-economic gaps. As Plato and the rest knew very well, such problems were hard enough to solve in the relatively small ancient city-states. They were even harder to address in large, complex, industrial societies with their extensive specialization, division of labor, exchange, and the level of sophisticated organization required to cope with all of these complications.

Third, Marx and Engels looked down on "utopian" socialists, a term they themselves had coined. Their own views, they claimed, were based on "scientific materialism" and historical processes whose laws they had mastered and whose general direction they could foresee. Objective facts, not wishful thinking, should rule supreme. Yet this approach did not prevent them from sharing the idea that the end of exploitation of inferiors by superiors and the establishment of socialism/communism would make government unnecessary. Instead of government, whose sole purpose was to enforce inequality between the classes, there would be administration. Marx even quarreled with the anarchist leader Bakunin over precisely this question. The idea itself was common at the time. Among its adherents were Saint Simon and, in the 1880s, the famous American socialist Edward Bellamy.[22] The latter, incidentally, could equally well be understood as a proto-fascist. The society he envisaged depended less on voluntary cooperation and more on firm authority exercised from above.[23]

As it turned out, nothing could be more mistaken. Socialism did not mean that managers took the place of politicians and that politics, meaning the process whereby society determines who gets how much of what, waned away. Instead, the opposite happened. Managers became politicians and politicians, managers. Far from losing power, politicians increased it. They took over a whole range of fields that they had previously been content to leave more or less alone, reaching deep into society's guts. To return to Britain as our example, politicians, or else political appointees, now ran every one of the industries listed above. This meant that, in addition to democratically ruling over their fellow citizens, they also wielded direct economic control over millions of workers. With power came privilege, in other words inequality. The new class of politicians/managers may not have owned the corporations they managed as stockholders did. They were employees like the rest. However, they certainly awarded themselves "appropriate" salaries. To both accentuate and disguise the gap that separated them from their workers and from other citizens, they also took every kind of perk, including houses, cars, extended holidays, membership in exclusive clubs, and mistresses disguised as secretaries.

Living under this new kind of privileged class, people in social-democratic countries, of which Britain was one, at any rate had one consolation: come elections, they had the right and the opportunity to throw out the scoundrels and replace them with a new lot. That was by no means the case in most developing countries that

claimed to have adopted socialism. The last thing the numerous
tin-pot dictators who ruled in the name of "Arab" and "African"
Socialism had in mind was to allow themselves to be unseated by
democratic means. The same was even more true of so-called East
Bloc countries. Instead, all the regimes claiming to be built on the
doctrines of Marx and Engels did was create inequalities of an altogether unprecedented and often particularly vicious sort

*

The first, and, until 1945, practically the only Communist
country was the Soviet Union or, to call it by its official name, the
Union of Soviet Socialist Republics. As Marx had predicted, it was
brought about through revolution and a bloody civil war. In the
process countless aristocrats, wealthy people, and senior civil servants who had served the previous regime were killed and had their
property confiscated. The same fate overtook anybody identified as
"an enemy of the people" or, to quote Lenin, whose existence was
considered "inexpedient." If there were any trials at all, they were
of the kind where the accused is not permitted to defend him- or
herself. As Marx had also predicted, these events led to the creation
of the dictatorship of the proletariat or, to be precise, of a small
clique of determined leaders who claimed to represent it. Representation itself, incidentally, was not based on open competition
among several parties with equal rights before the law, as in bourgeois and socialist democracies. Instead it was based on inequality
as the communist party prohibited all others.

Once they felt themselves firmly in the saddle Lenin and his
comrades in arms lost no time establishing the kind of socio-
economic equality they had been planning for perhaps two decades
past. At the top of the pyramid stood Lenin himself and, after

his death, Stalin. The latter liked to say that "nobody was indispensable." Coming from *that* mouth, under *that* moustache, that was equality with a vengeance. No sooner had the new communist government been established than it launched some of the most comprehensive reforms in the whole of history. All mines, factories and buildings of any size were nationalized, i.e. confiscated without compensation. So were banks, insurance companies, every kind of financial institution, transportation, communications, and telecommunications. Initially much of the land, its owners having been killed or driven abroad, was left alone. Later, though, it too was formally confiscated. The *mujiks*, or peasants, who worked it were either incorporated into cooperatives or simply turned into state employees. The process was nothing if not barbaric. As it unfolded several million "*kulaks*," i.e. relatively well-to-do farmers, lost their lives.[24]

Compared with advanced countries Russia had always been quite poor. In 1914 per capita income only stood at about eleven percent of that of the United States.[25] Following the destruction caused first by World War I, then by the Civil War, and finally by the Communists' forcible reforms it was turned into a land of beggars. Millions died of malnutrition and disease. During the 1930s much of the damage was repaired and the economic situation improved somewhat. However, the 1941 German invasion, which was only finally thrown back in 1944, once again left in its wake a country so devastated as to almost defy the imagination.[26] After 1945 it was the Eastern European countries' turn. They, too, had suffered badly from the war. They, too, were captured by the communists, either local ones such as had survived the German occupation or such as had earlier escaped to Moscow and were put in place by the victorious Red Army. By 1948 the whole of Eastern Europe had adopted, or more often had been forced to adopt, the Soviet system. To quote Winston Churchill, an Iron Curtain had come down, reaching from the Baltic to the Adriatic.

In seeking to re-organize China from 1949, one of the very few native egalitarian doctrines Mao Tze Dong could possibly draw on was the one initiated by Mo Tzu (470–391 BC). In fact, some attempt was made to study him. Partly because it was backward, partly because of years of warfare both international and internecine, China was poorer than any other country that adopted the red flag. Before the Communists seized power tens of millions died. After they had done so, additional tens of millions died. Many lost their lives during the Party's initial efforts to impose equality. Others did so during the so-called Great Leap Forward and the Cultural Revolution which Mao called in an attempt to restore equality among other things. In China, too, nationalization proceeded on a huge scale. However, since industry was under-developed, land aside there was relatively less to nationalize. In the countryside from 1953 on, people were forced to give up all land, farm animals and larger agricultural implements. Next they were herded into teams numbering some 200 people each. The teams were formed into larger units, which from 1958 on were grouped in communes.[27]

Most communes numbered 4,000–5,000 households though some were larger than that. Each was a kind of cage to which people were bound by a system of household registration, work units, and terror over themselves and others. Production was carried out in common as each member was assigned his or her task every morning. Private cooking was banned and meals were taken in dining halls. Some communes even tried to prohibit the use of money. Ostensibly the entire structure, having done away with both landowners (who were often simply killed) and hired labor, was democratic and egalitarian. In reality it was tightly run by appointed Communist Party officials who called the shots. The officials obeyed, or were supposed to obey, instructions they received from their superiors. Any attempt to differ from the latter could easily lead to dire consequences. Towering over the country was the usual communist system of one-party dictatorship. It came complete with bogus elections and a central "people's assembly." In China it was known as the flower vase—beautiful to watch, but totally useless.

In no country did the communist party enroll more than a few percent of the population. Everywhere members, depending on their party rank, were privileged.[28] Senior officials were better paid, but that was the least of their benefits. The latter included homes and vacation homes; superior access to transportation in the form of private cars and chauffeurs; superior access to educational facilities for themselves and their children; superior access to cultural, entertainment, and leisure facilities; superior access to information, both domestic and foreign; and superior access to hospitals, clinics, etc. Others were better food and luxuries such as cigarettes, alcohol, and fancy clothing, cosmetics and perfumes for their wives and mistresses. Many of these luxuries could only be had at special shops that sold Western goods at amazingly low prices. In Warsaw in 1989, just before communism collapsed, a bottle of whiskey at the so-called PEVEX shop cost perhaps one quarter of what it did at a Western duty-free one. To buy at these shops one had to have either special coupons or else hard currency. The latter being found in the possession of ordinary citizens would quickly land them in jail.

Every communist regime maintained lists of offices only party members could occupy. In East Germany there existed a so-called *Reisekader*. They were a select group of trusted people, often techni-

cians and academics, who had special permission to travel abroad in
order to represent the country or acquire useful knowledge.[29] Returning home they could bring along some goods which they then
went on to sell on the black market. One East German professor I
knew secured his future by bringing back thirteen Black & Decker
electric drills and stashing them away! Other countries had similar arrangements. Yet for ordinary citizens to apply for a permit
to travel abroad could be dangerous, inducing many to refrain from
doing so in the first place. Unless some superior official had ordered
it to be used against them, members of the elite were also largely free
from police harassment. That in turn meant they could break the
law as they saw fit.

Given how powerful officialdom was, it is hardly surprising that
bribery was rife. In 1969, to purchase an appointment as head of a
Kolchoz, or cooperative farm, one had to pay 50,000 rubles. Head-
ing a Sovchoz, a state-owned farm, cost 100,000. A post as second
secretary of a party district in Azerbaijan cost 100,000 rubles, while
a post as first secretary went for twice that figure. For a factory
worker that amounted to no less than 160 years of income.[30] In
economies where money meant little and some items were always
in short supply, hoarding was omnipresent. An appropriate "consideration" could make better food, clothing, medicines, household
goods, and tickets for all kinds of events appear as if by magic.[31] In
China, so pervasive was corruption that, if you wanted to sell your
blood, you had to share the sum you got for it with the doctor in
charge.[32] Ordinary citizens detested the system, hated it, and told
jokes about it. But life for the more equal could be sweet. It certainly was so in comparison with that of the broad masses whose
condition they said their rule has been designed to improve.

The "cadres'" wives and offspring also enjoyed these privileges.

Members of the Communist *jeunesse d'orée* tended to meet at the universities, at exclusive leisure facilities, and in the often equally secluded neighborhoods where the leaders lived. Often they married each other, giving birth to something like a hereditary aristocracy. Had communism not collapsed in 1989–1891, very likely it would have developed even further. At and near the top stood the most privileged men (and very few women, except in so far as they were related to the men) of all. Originally the Bolshevik leaders lived in the Metropole, the most sumptuous hotel in Moscow. As hundreds of thousands of Muscovites hungered, froze, and tried to make ends meet by buying and selling on the black market, this was no small privilege.

From the Metropole the Bolsheviks moved into the nearby Kremlin where they took over all of the Tsar's magnificence and all of his amenities. They had servants and maids who did everything from keeping the gardens trim to cooking, laundering, and polishing shoes. They traveled by special railway carriages or even by private aircraft. Stalin himself had several planes at his disposal, courtesy of President Roosevelt during World War II. They also enjoyed the use of any number of splendid villas, or dachas, that had been confiscated from their former owners. Some of the villas were located in a wood not far from Moscow that was reserved for their use. Others were scattered in the most desirable regions in the country; the Black Sea Coast was a particular favorite. Stalin and other members of the Politburo used to spend long vacations there.[33]

Other Communist leaders followed Stalin's example even when they set themselves up in opposition to him, as some did. Consider Yugoslavia's Josip Broz Tito. Before the Germans invaded his country in 1941, he had served as the secretary-general of the illegal Communist Party and was jailed several times. During World

War II he led partisans. With his men he moved about the forests and mountains, sometimes taking up residence in ruined castles, at other times living undercover in towns. Many times he had to run for his life as the Germans tried to kill or capture him. Western offices who were parachuted into the country described his life as austere and often harsh.[34] Yet no sooner did he come to power then his demeanor underwent a complete change. Former royal palaces built for members of the exiled Karadjordjević dynasty were confiscated. Following restoration they were provided with the finest furniture taken from the museums and put at Tito's exclusive disposal. Parks were landscaped, zoos installed. He traveled in a Rolls-Royce, hunted as keenly as any of the "feudal" aristocrats whom he had spent half his life attacking, and maintained a large stable of horses.

Milovan Djilas was Tito's comrade-in-arms during World War II and occupied a senior position in the regime before he turned against it. Here is his description of the leader: "[Tito's] uniforms were edged with gold. Everything he used had to be just right and very special. His belt buckle was made of pure gold, and was so heavy that it kept slipping down. He wrote with a heavy gold pen. His chair was impressive and always placed at the center of the room. He changed his clothes as often as four times a day, according to the impressions he wished to create. ... He used a sunlamp regularly to maintain a tan. His hair was dyed, his teeth were false and gleaming white."[35]

During the years he spent in the remote province of Shaanxi, Mao lived in a cave. His comrades also worked in caves or, when the weather permitted, in the open.[36] Having seized power, at his public appearances he always took care to wear the so-called Mao jacket, a simple but comfortable piece of clothing originally devised by Sun Yat Sen. Under Mao the jacket became almost obligatory for everybody. Behind the scenes, however, things were quite different. In the words of his Australian-trained physician, Li Zishui, who looked after him from 1954 on: "It was only when I started traveling with Mao that I began to understand the lavish and wasteful arrangements that were always made on his behalf. No measure to protect his comfort and his safety were too great. His comfort and happiness were paramount. ... He traveled ordinarily in his own private, elegantly appointed train, eleven cars in all. ... Mao and [his fourth wife] Jiang Qing each had a separate car...." Provincial officials through whose territory the train passed would line up thousands of peasants and have them transplant crops along miles of the track, creating the impression of a bumper harvest.[37]

In Beijing, Mao occupied the palace of the Qianlong emperor (reigned 1736–1779). Like Tito, he also had at his disposal any number of other sumptuous residences his underlings requisitioned for him throughout China. Others were built from the foundation up. Since Mao liked swimming each was provided with a pool. Some retreats were provided with shelters designed to withstand a nuclear explosion. At least one, located in the mountains of Hunan near the farmhouse where he was born, has since been turned into a museum. There hundreds of thousands of Chinese who come to visit each year can listen as the very stones sing the praise of the Great Helmsman amidst thunderous cheers. Erich Honecker, the East German dictator, was said to have kept an entire collection of prohibited Western pornographic movies at home.[38] He hunted in the same game-reserve on the Schorfheide that had once been used by Herman Goering and Emperor Wilhelm II. So many animals did he kill that the reserve had to be restocked with new ones from other friendly socialist countries. Whenever he traveled, traffic on the *Autobahn* was closed. At Berlin's Schoenefeld Airport there was a special terminal that served him, his minions, and foreign guests he wanted to honor. It looked quite different from the grimy structure ordinary citizens had to use for the few trips they were allowed to make.

Nicolai Ceaușescu, the Romanian dictator who governed his countrymen with an iron fist, built the biggest palace in the world. In the process he demolished a large part of central Bucharest. Communist North Korea actually saw the establishment of a dynasty that is currently headed by the founder's grandson. All these men also made certain that the women with whom they associated should have the finest clothes, the most precious perfumes, the most expensive jewelry, the best available cars, and so on. The functionaries who worked with, and for, them imitated them. They took up residence near the chief and set up their own courts. If some of them did not line their pockets at the state's expense, then it was only because the state and all its resources were at their disposal anyhow. Meanwhile, in some cases, all around them the people they had supposedly come to liberate from oppression were literally starving.

For half a century after 1848 Socialism and Communism were all but indistinguishable. It was only around 1900 that they clearly separated. Once that had happened they often fought one another tooth and nail as, for example, happened in Germany immediately after World War I. Yet in all that regards equality, the way they understood it and the wish to achieve it, they still had quite a lot in common. Both focused on socio-economic equality, opposed capitalism, and nationalized many if not all of the more important instruments of production. Both, far from doing away with politics, created a situation where politics became more important than ever.

Here, however, the similarities stop. Socialists, at any rate those who governed advanced democratic countries, compensated owners whose property they nationalized. Property-owners in communist countries were lucky if they escaped with their lives. Socialists imposed heavy progressive taxes. Communists used police methods and simply imprisoned or killed anybody they disliked. Advanced socialist countries continued to hold elections where parties competed on a more or less equal a basis as before. Communist ones came under strict one-party rule. Considerable as the privileges of socialist leaders were, they paled in comparison with those communist ones enjoyed.

In both socialist and communist countries, the attempt to create and maintain socio-economic equality led to economic stagnation and decline. In many of the latter it also led to immense bloodshed, mass starvation, and some of the worst totalitarian regimes in history. By 1980 most Western socialist countries were approaching bankruptcy. They only saved themselves by a radical change of course. Hats off to Western-style democracy; it enabled both the process of nationalization and the privatization that followed to go ahead without civil war. Even Sweden, long one of the most socialistically-minded countries of all, was finally forced to follow suit. China, though anything but democratic, also successfully changed its system. In all cases, the outcome was the re-opening of socio-economic gaps.[39] So large have they become that, in the West, some believe they are threatening their societies with disintegration.

By contrast, the Soviet Union and east-European satellites refused to look bankruptcy in the face. With little but police power to back them up, they kept their peculiar kind of equality for another decade. When the crash came it was spectacular indeed. In 1991, after two tumultuous though largely bloodless years, the Soviet experiment in equality, one of the largest ever attempted, collapsed. May it never rise again.

Chapter 7

The Rise and Fall of Racism

Liberalism aimed at instituting a kind of equality that would enable everyone to compete with everyone else on a legally equal basis. Socialism sought a world in which everyone would be so equal that competition itself would become superfluous and fade away. Despite their differences, proponents of both doctrines agreed with Hobbes that nature, or God as the case might be, had created all men equal. Liberals thought inequality grew out of competition and attempted to organize things in such a way that everyone should be allowed to compete under equal conditions. Socialists thought it grew out of private property, and the more extreme of them tried to eliminate it.

In reality, Hobbes was breaking revolutionary ground. In all of history, nothing could be *less* self-evident than the idea that everybody was, or ought to be, equal. Proud as they were of their ancestry, not even the Athenians of Pericles' day would have subscribed to it. *A fortiori*, neither would any other people at any other time or place before the middle of the seventeenth century. Nor were the words of Hobbes, Locke, Montesquieu, Rousseau, Paine, Jefferson,

Marx, Engels, and the rest the final ones on the subject. Starting during the first half of the nineteenth century, powerful voices began asserting that inequality, this time not between individuals but between different human "races," was a biological fact. Far from wasting their efforts in a vain attempt to fight it and eradicate it, men and women should do what they could to protect and foster it. Failure to do so was tantamount to declaring war on their own "blood"—and, in the end, bringing about a situation where human civilization itself might collapse.

To deny that that different groups of human beings have different physical characteristics is sheer hypocrisy. Anyone who has ever visited some inland Chinese town or village knows the score. All around big-eyed toddlers stare at those strange, rather large, pale, big-nosed apparitions that have emerged out of nowhere. They have round eyes of several unusual colors—not just black and brown like normal people, but blue, green, and grey. They also have lots of facial hair. Some are actually blond! True racism consists of three elements. First, there is the notion that the groups in question differ not only physically but mentally, i.e. in intelligence, emotional makeup, criminal tendencies, etc. Second, those characteristics are said to be inherent and heritable so that they pass from one generation to the next. Third, the people of some races are superior to others and are entitled to rule over them, if not to enslave them, exploit them, and even exterminate them in pursuit of their own objectives.

There probably has never been a society that did *not* hold at least one of these beliefs. The ancient Greeks considered themselves as freedom-loving by nature and thus superior to everybody else. The Romans were prepared to grant that others excelled them in some fields, but only as long as those others allowed them, the Romans, to rule over them.[1] Supposedly in Islam everybody regardless of status, wealth or race was equal in front of God. But this did not prevent medieval Islamic scholars from claiming that black Africans were the sons of Ham. They had been put under his curse and were condemned to perpetual slavery because of the way their ancestor had exposed the genitals of his father, Noah.[2] Blacks could rise in Moslem society, but only if they had first been turned into eunuchs.[3] The Chinese considered themselves superior to anybody who was not Han. The Japanese took the same view in respect to anybody who was not Yamato. Sixteenth-century Spaniards were enormously, almost desperately, interested in *Limpieza de Sangre*, purity of blood. Jewish blood in particular was considered to be contaminated. Mixing with it should be avoided at all costs. So strong was this prejudice that the Inquisition, one of whose missions was to look after the spiritual welfare of *conversos*, disliked it and tried to combat it.[4]

Spanish priests of the same period often debated the question of whether the Indians who populated America were possessed of reason. If they did, they were human and equal in the eyes of God. If not, then they could reasonably be treated like animals.[5] The question was of great practical importance because a negative answer was used to justify the most iniquitous form of inequality, slavery. Seventeenth-century English settlers in North America resorted to similar reasoning to defend black slavery.[6] Many present-day orthodox Jews are similarly convinced that they are the most intelligent people in the world and look down on *goyim*. In the Old Testament, *goy*, singular of *goyim*, simply means people, the People of Israel specifically included.[7] Later, the term was only applied to non-Jewish people and acquired a negative connotation it still retains. Some orthodox Jews go much further still. They claim that, since they alone are of the right stock and practice the right faith, everybody else is duty-bound to support them. That even includes their fellow Jews. Many of these societies also placed restrictions on the freedom to marry. Moslem men could marry Christian women (if the latter converted), but Moslem women could not marry Christian men. Jews were supposed to marry only within their own group.

Though the list of precedents could be extended *ad infinitum* if not *ad nauseam*, the invention of modern racism is generally linked with the name of the aforementioned Gobineau.[8] Gobineau was a close contemporary of Marx. Marx certainly read Gobineau, but the opposite may not have been true.[9] Both men were characterized by enormous erudition. Both also followed Hegel in that they saw history as the clue to understanding human society in all its complexity. A diplomat by trade, Gobineau spent time living in several non-European countries, including Iran and Brazil. There he had the opportunity to observe many different peoples at first hand.

Humanity, Gobineau claimed, was divided into three great races, i.e. the white, the yellow, and the black. They formed a hierarchy with whites at the top, yellows in the middle, and blacks at the bottom. Gobineau even thought it possible that, contrary to what the Old Testament says, all living peoples did not have the same ancestor but were created separately. While this claim was long denied, and even presented as wicked and intolerable and "racist," it has been revived, though not finally confirmed, by recent discoveries in paleontology and genetics.[10] Of the three, the white race was the only one capable of building an orderly, sophisticated, civilization. That civilization, in turn, went back through the Germanic tribes, Rome, and Greece all the way to the "Aryans" of ancient India. The Aryan's existence had first been postulated sixty years earlier by another remarkable geographer, ethnographer and linguist by the name of William Jones. While it was true that advanced civilizations had also developed in other regions Gobineau reasoned that was only because their ruling classes were of Aryan stock.[11]

Since some races were superior to others, the greatest sin of all was miscegenation. Mixing blood could only lead to chaos and degeneration. The countries of Eastern Europe, Southern Europe, North Africa, the Middle East, and Central Asia were all populated by racially mixed people. So were Austria and Switzerland. Even Gobineau's own country, France, was not immune. The French nation was made up of three sub-races. They were, in descending order of excellence, Nordics, Alpines, and Mediterraneans. The first two were clearly white but the last-named had been tainted by an infusion of black and Semitic blood. The Nordics were in danger of being swamped. It was almost enough to make one give up on the future of the white race. As the barriers that separated them from the rest broke down, the higher forms of culture the Nordics had created would surely collapse. There was only one way to save the white race: namely, to make its members cease mixing their blood with that of their inferiors.

All of this made Gobineau draw the logical conclusion that the colonial empires many European countries were building for themselves were harmful. Later in life he changed his view on this particular point. The vigorous expansion of Britain and the United States, he wrote, proved that whites still had plenty of life in them. The message was well timed. From the beginning of European overseas expansion around 1500 on, much of the work on the spot had been done not by governments but by missionaries on one hand and commercial companies on the other. During the nineteenth century things changed. Increasingly national governments started ruling their colonies directly without, of course, giving the natives any say in the matter. Yet wherever one looked, more and more of those governments themselves came to be based on the idea of equality. Nowhere was this more true than in the greatest colonial Powers of all, Britain and France. The solution to the dilemma was obvious. One had to find proof that non-Europeans, belonging as they did to different races, were *not* their rulers' equals. Gobineau, who specified that "strict despotism" was the only way to govern "the Negro," was the perfect man for the job.

From that time on, racism was on the rise. Gobineau's work was translated into several languages. It became particularly popular in the United States. Not that racism was new to America as none other than Thomas Jefferson had led the way: "Comparing them by their faculties of memory, reason, and imagination, it appears to me that in memory they [blacks] are equal to whites; in reason, much inferior as I think one could scarcely be found capable of tracing and comprehending the investigations of Euclid; and that in imagination they are dull, tasteless and anomalous."[12] Before 1865 racism provided a rationale for slavery. After that date it did the same for segregation and Jim Crow. Being based on sheer hypocrisy, a doctrine such as "separate but equal," which the U.S. Supreme Court upheld in the 1896 case of *Plessy v. Ferguson*, did nothing to help. America being a country of immigrants, blacks were not the only victims of racism. At various times Germans, Irish, Italians, Mexicans, and of course Chinese and Japanese were all looked down upon and discriminated against. Visiting foreigners often made Americans uncomfortable by their comments on this contradiction. Nowhere else was the eugenics movement as strong as precisely in the land of the free.

When Japan proposed that a paragraph concerning the equality of all races be included in the Charter of the League of Nations, its demand was rejected. Much worse was to follow. Bismarck's Second Reich had acquired some colonies in Africa and Asia. However, they never amounted to much and in 1919 they were lost. Inside Germany proper there were very few non-whites. Hence interest in that subject was limited to men such as the philosopher-biologist Ernst Haeckel (1834–1919) who compared blacks to "four-handed apes."[13] Following the Allied occupation of the Rhineland in 1919–1920 and the Franco-Belgian one of the Ruhr in 1923–1925, German propagandists, including those working for the fledgling National Socialist Party, had a field day. They hammered home the "shame" of having French black colonial troops stationed in the regions in question. The degenerate French were consciously trying to debase the superior race! Some German women had been raped and, it was claimed, had later atoned for their sins by committing suicide. Worse still, a few had so far forgotten themselves as to sleep with black members of the occupation forces out of their own free will. But these particular episodes neither affected a large part of the country nor lasted for very long. Hence there were limits to how much could be made of them.[14]

Instead, racism was directed primarily against two groups. Austrian Germans, of whom Hitler was one, very much feared being swamped by the Slav, mainly Czech, populations of the Empire since the latter's birth rate far exceeded their own. Using "equality" as their rallying-cry, the Slavs demanded reforms that would mean the end of German primacy.[15] Both on the Austrian and German side of the border many people directed their hatred against the Jews. Traditionally they had been a small and despised minority. During the nineteenth century emancipation caused their number to grow very rapidly, and they gradually started occupying leading positions in society to boot. Beginning around 1870, i.e. the very time when German Jews had finally been put on an equal basis with everybody else, legally speaking, modern, race-based anti-Semitism raised its ugly head.

By the last years of the nineteenth century and the early one of the twentieth at least one politician, the popular Mayor of Vienna Karl Lueger, was showing the world how to use anti-Semitism in order to gain power and wield it for years. Theodor Herzl, who lived in Vienna, wrote that things were getting worse by the day.[16] Ironically enough, Gobineau himself believed Jews were Aryans and rather admired them.[17] Haeckel, in an illustration that accompanied the first edition of his book, *Natuerliche Schoepfungsgeschichte* (The Natural History of Creation) placed them near the top of the evolutionary tree and within the same species as the Germans. He thought they were on a par with the latter and, curiously enough, with the Berbers of North Africa.[18] In an interview he gave in the early 1890s he spoke of "refined and noble Jews" who, forming an important part of German culture, fought for enlightenment against reaction.[19]

In the minds of both men, as also in that of Friedrich Nietzsche and the anonymous author of *The Protocols of the Elders of Zion*, admiration was not unmixed with fear. They also saw Jews as being uncanny. Having survived countless persecutions from ancient times on, the Jews had offered ample proof of their racial fitness. Where might they turn their attention next? Others turned this argument around. If Jews were persecuted so often, this proved they were inferior and deserved being thoroughly detested by everyone else. Even before 1914 Jews were often blamed for being socialists (*and* capitalists, but that is another story). After the Russian Revolution of October 1917 many Germans started combining Jews with Slavs under the rubric of "Jewish Bolshevism." Throughout the 1920s Hitler, Goebbels and other German propagandists never ceased harping on these themes. Now they put the emphasis on one group, now on another. But always they came back to the idea that both Jews and Slavs were alien, inferior, and mortal enemies of everything "German." On 30 January 1933 President Paul von Hindenburg made Hitler Germany's Chancellor. Then everything changed.

✳

At first glance, National Socialism and the Third Reich may seem to be strange places in which to look for equality. In the words of prominent political scientist and Hitler supporter Carl Schmitt (1888–1985), was not the Nazis' central message that not everyone with a human face was, in fact, human?[20] And isn't it true that Hitler always presented life as a harsh social-Darwinist struggle in which "the strongest," meaning himself, came out on top whereas "the weakest" had to perish? How about the *Fuehrerprinzip* and the requirement that inferiors blindly obey their superiors? How about the strict hierarchical organization of society on quasi-military lines? After all, Hitler never ceased shouting that Aryans were and should be high on top, Slavs and Jews low near the ground or, if possible and necessary, under it. Furthermore, gradation was a question of race, not religion or wealth or anything of that kind. No mere human hands could alter what nature in her wisdom had determined. Attempts to do so could only lead to bastardization, degeneration, and, ultimately, the demise of the superior race. Hans Globke, co-author of the 1935 Nuremberg Laws that regularized the persecution of the Jews, wrote that "National Socialism opposes the theories based on the equality of all men."[21]

Yet National Socialism also had a different face. The way many Germans saw it, the industrial revolution had caused the nation—all "civilized" (as the phrase used to run) nations, but the German nation in particular—to be divided between capitalists and proletarians. In the process, the "organic" unity of the countryside had been broken apart and destroyed. Each in its own way, liberalism and socialism had tried to cope with this situation. Germany had as many socialists, and perhaps only a few less liberals, than other countries did. Where it differed from at least some other countries was that it also had a third group whose adherents designated themselves as *voelkisch*. The noun *Volk* can mean either people or nation. "Volkswagen" simply means the People's Car. The adjective *voelkisch* is harder to translate. Depending on the context it can mean either "originating in the people" or "folksy." *Volk* is a very old word, but *voelkisch* is not. Apparently it was coined very late in the eighteenth century when the Romantic Movement, opposing rationalism in general and "French" rationalism in particular, started using it. It carried connotations such as "deeply-rooted" and "authentic" as opposed to "newly invented" and "artificial."

With *voelkisch* came *Volksgemeinschaft*, "folk-community." The implication was that the entire *Volk* was, or should be, a single community. What held the community together was not merely a single government but common ancestry, language, traditions, beliefs, and attitudes. Initially there was nothing particularly chauvinist in any of this. The philosopher Johann Gottfried Herder (1744–1804) taught that humanity was divided into *Voelker*, plural of *Volk*. Each had its own characteristics and intrinsic worth.[22] Late in the nineteenth century things began to change. Ancestry was equated with race, race with the alleged superiority of Germanic people over all the rest. World War I, which saw Germany fighting practically the entire world, added the idea of a common fate—one everybody shared "in prosperity and in ruin," as Germans say. If a common fate was to have any meaning at all, it could only be based on some kind of equality among all the community's members.[23]

The Nazis took up this idea and developed it further. Right from the beginning, *National* Socialism rejected socialism and fought the "Red Menace" tooth and nail. Right from the beginning, its leaders sought a way to combine socialism with nationalism. Doing so was a revolutionary idea indeed. Had not Marx and Engels in the *Manifesto* claimed that workers have no fatherland and called on them to unite? Did not Lenin and his successors declare themselves to be "internationalists"? Entire libraries have been written to explain how National Socialism was the lackey of German capitalism and thus an instrument for maintaining the existing inequality between the classes. The claim may or may not have been true; but there can be no doubt that both the Nazis and those who voted for them did advocate a certain kind of equality, known as *Gleichheit*. The appeal of *Gleichheit* was exactly what distinguished the Nazis from the old German right. In it lay a good part of their appeal.

Nazi *Gleichheit* had many faces. Hitler himself was, or was presented as, a living example of what it was about. On one hand he was the exalted Fuehrer, almost divine in his courage, wisdom, industry, and love for his *Volk*. On the other he was a man of the people, though perhaps not quite to the extent he pretended to be in *Mein Kampf*. It was as a "simple soldier" that he spent four years fighting in the trenches. Right down to the end, propaganda minister Goebbels often called him "our Hitler." He usually wore simple clothes or uniform. In the open cars he favored, he did not sit in the rear seat but sat or stood near the driver. His Hohenzollern predecessors owned no less than 167 palaces while Hitler made do with a comparatively modest villa in the Bavarian Alps. During his stays there he was sometimes mobbed by crowds of visitors. The resulting scenes, which under any previous German regime would have been inconceivable, were regularly shown in the newsreels. Visiting the front during the early years of World War II, Hitler was photographed eating food from the so-called goulash-cannon while sitting on a bench along with everybody else. Some of his collaborators did the same. As he himself liked to put it in his speeches, he was the German people and the German people were him.

As important as the Fuehrer's personality and public image was *Gleichschaltung*, another one of those hard-to translate German/Nazi concepts. The verb *schalten* means to shift, or engage. *Gleichschaltung* derives from the field of electrical engineering where it stands for the equalization of phases between circuits. The Nazis applied it to the process whereby, starting soon after they came to power, they "equalized" all parties and other political organizations so as to either demolish them or render them impotent. The outcome was a certain *Gleichheit* in that everybody was made equally subject to the Nazis' own unquestioned authority. As a German novelist, Hans Carossa (1878–1956) told a friend in 1933, "There is a lot going on here in Germany. We are being laundered, purified, scrubbed, disinfected, separated, nordicized, toughened up, and, I caught myself almost saying, alienated."[24]

Not all of it was done by order. There was also something called "*Selbstgleichschaltung*," i.e. *gleichschalting* oneself. Some organizations started purging their Jewish members even before the regime told them to do so. In the words of one famous slogan, "you are nothing, your *Volk* is everything." In face of the people or nation, all individuals were equally insignificant. Something has already been said about traditional German obsequiousness and submissiveness to authority. In pre-1933 Germany, class divisions, based on partly on ancestry and partly on wealth, had run as deep as anywhere else. To this should be added the reverence for *Bildung*, or education. It may have been stronger than in other countries. The outcome was extremely, some would say ludicrously, tall barriers separating *Herr Professor Doktor* from ordinary human beings. This again was something the Nazis set out to change, not entirely without success. On one hand, all trade unions were prohibited and their officials dismissed, arrested, or killed. On the other, functionaries of the Deutsche Arbeitsfront, German Workers' Front, a state-sponsored organization of which all workers had to be members, went to see employers. The latter were asked to improve working conditions by providing better lighting, better ventilation, better meals, and so on. There was also something known as *Schoenheit der Arbeit*, "the beauty of work." By this was meant an attempt to make the factories aesthetically more appealing. To some extent it worked; in the National Socialist State, being asked to do this kind of thing almost amounted to an order.

The objective was to create a community, or at any rate the feeling of a community. Within it everyone would contribute equally, each according to his or her abilities, to the welfare of the *Volk*. Wasn't that what socialism was all about? For those who could not make it, economically, there was the so-called *Eintopf*. It was a festive meal consumed by all Germans on the same day and at the same hour and consisting of a single dish. The resulting savings were supposed to be used for helping indigent *Volksgenosse*, comrades. There was also *Winterhilfe*, "Winter-Help." It assisted the poor by the free distribution of clothing, coal, toys, etc. Posters and movies criticized class-differences and emphasized the bond between white-collar workers and manual ones. Others showed SA and SS men shaking the hands of Wehrmacht soldiers. These and other measures were intended to create, and to some extent probably did create, a sense of common destiny. In the words of the educational theorist Ernst Krieck, the aim was "to standardize the inner education of all members of the nation, to produce uniformity of bearing, attitude, identity, and task."[25] Teachers were told to drop Prussian discipline and come closer to their students. School excursions organized by the schools, the Hitler Jugend, and even the universities provided lessons in collective living. Young people had to spend a year in the Arbeitsdienst, or Labor Service, which took in all lads and lasses regardless of origins or class. Educational institutions such as the Nationalpolitische Erziehungsanstalten, or NAPOLA, were part of the design. Ignoring social classes, they accepted students on the basis of physical and mental exams, thus providing them with equal opportunities to get ahead. Inside the schools, too, students were treated as equals. In a country where the sons of the well to do and those of ordinary workers and peasants had seldom shared the same bench this was an innovation. Former scholars in their memoirs mentioned it with profound gratitude. At least one called it "the joy of my youth."[26]

The system the SS, and even more so the Waffen SS, used to select officer-candidates worked in the same direction. Until the time when heavy losses brought on change, Wehrmacht officers had to have the high school graduation diploma. Thus only a small fraction of all German youths qualified. The SS also allowed youngsters who had not taken the examinations to apply, thus attracting the scions of lower-class families. The highest-ranking officer who made it in this way was General Sepp Dietrich, the Panzer commander who was later tried as a war criminal. Another was Adolf Eichmann who, however, only rose to lieutenant-colonel.

Another peculiar Nazi institution working in the same direction was Lebensborn. Both during the days of the Third Reich and later, Lebensborn was surrounded by many legends. Some claimed it was a stud-farm where unattached German women could meet some SS stalwart and be impregnated by him. Alas for those who want to see some psycho-sexual complex inside every Nazi, the truth was much more prosaic. The head of the SS, Heinrich Himmler, was concerned about the discrimination to which unwed mothers and their illegitimate offspring were subjected because it might result in precious German blood being lost. To prevent this from happening, he set up the Lebensborn, "Born Alive." There pregnant women, first German ones and then "Germanic" ones from the occupied territories in the west and north, could stay during the last weeks before giving birth, deliver, and recuperate. In his capacity as Minister of the Interior he even provided them with the appropriate papers so they would not be stigmatized later on. This too was a form of equality, albeit one that was quite unusual and, in the eyes of many contemporaries, bizarre.[27]

German media during the Third Reich never tired of trumpeting the virtues of the Nazi version of *Gleicheit*, contrasting it with the way these things were handled in other countries, England in particular. Some foreign observers agreed. Visitors, including journalists and even some diplomats, to the annual Nazi Party Rally in Nuremberg regularly returned home full of tales about the equality and national solidarity they had witnessed.[28] During the halcyon days of June 1940, when the Germans were overrunning France, American radio correspondent William Shirer commented on the healthy-looking German troops with their bodies bronzed by years of hiking in the countryside. Their relationship with their officers was also surprisingly egalitarian. The contrast between them and their English opponents, many of whom were slum-dwellers with poor physiques and rotten teeth, could hardly be greater.[29]

Briefly, the Nazis had their own ideas about equality. While they differed from those of other modern societies, probably they worked as well as any. Certainly during the early years of the regime they were enthusiastically welcomed. But all this only applied to racially pure members of the *Volksgemeinschaft*. The Nazis were neither the first nor the last who insisted on keeping the blood of their own group "pure." Like others, they put a special emphasis on female chastity. They claimed any woman who slept with an *Untermensch*, or subhuman, even once would spoil her blood forever and could no longer have healthy Aryan offspring. Articles and drawings in the *Stuermer*, the semi-pornographic anti-Semitic weekly tabloid published by Julius Streicher, drove home the message. Never mind that a racial "expert" by the name of Walter Gross at one point told Hitler himself that there was no scientific foundation for this claim. Never mind, too, that years of attempts to discover some biological characteristic by which Jews could be "objectively" distinguished from other people ended in failure.[30] Apparently these facts caused Hitler to tone down his racism for a while. But it would not have been characteristic for him to allow them to deter him.

Starting with Solon, most communities in quest of equality sought to achieve it by placing some kinds of limits on the more equal. From the Hellenistic city-states all the way to the French, Russian and Chinese Revolutions, often doing so meant killing the people in question. The Nazis took the opposite road. To impose their particular brand of *Gleichheit* they started from the bottom, not the top. The least the "racially unfit" could expect was compulsory sterilization. Take the case of a sixteen-year old *Mischling*, or mixed-race person, born to a German mother and a black French soldier. In the late 1930s, while employed on a barge that plied the rivers Rhine and Meuse, this individual became the subject of a vast correspondence among Nazi bureaucrats. Over two hundred letters were exchanged dealing with the question as to whether he should be sterilized, on the authority of which law or decree the sterilization would take place, how it would be done, when, by whom, and, not least, at whose expense.

Another category of *Untermenschen* comprised those afflicted by incurable hereditary diseases. Such diseases included some forms of deafness and blindness as well as chronic alcoholism; but not, interestingly enough, drug addiction, which German doctors, many of whom themselves took drugs, considered curable.[31] The total number of those who were sterilized was probably in the low hundreds of thousands. Had the Third Reich not collapsed, it might have reached into the millions. The policy was not unique. Quite a few other countries, including Sweden and the United States, had similar, though smaller, programs, some of which continued for decades after 1945.[32] Where the Nazis really stood out was in two respects. First, using either gas or lethal injections, they put to death some two hundred thousand people, mainly mentally deficient and badly deformed.[33] Second, they took aim not just at individual "lives unworthy of living" but at entire races. First, Niagaras of propaganda were organized to prove that Jews and Gypsies in particular were strange, wicked, and dangerous to the *Volksgemeinschaft*. Next they were discriminated against, compelled to wear special identification badges, segregated from the rest of society, and expelled. In the end they were exterminated like vermin.

Like the Roman god Janus, the Third Reich had two faces. On one hand it was nothing if not hierarchical. On the other it emphasized the Golden Rule: "Treat your comrade as you would like him to treat you."[34] What distinguished the Nazis was the fact that, instead of referring to humanity as a whole, they only meant healthy members of their own "racial community." Nazi crimes against the supposedly less than equal were committed in the name of a certain kind of equality, or homogeneity (from the Greek *homos*, meaning equal, similar, one and the same). Perhaps, having seen so many other historical attempts to establish equality lead to horrible results, we should not be too surprised.

World War II, the war crimes trials that followed it, and the vast literature that grew up around Nazi crimes and the Holocaust have given racism a bad name. In 1950, a number of geneticists and physical anthropologists were asked to endorse a UNESCO document on the subject. It confirmed what the Nazis themselves already knew: that there were no mental and psychological differences among people of different races and that race-crossing carried no disadvantages.[35] In the words of one German philosopher, Juergen Habermas, the death camps pulled the rug from under any ideology that did not at least pay lip-service to the equality of all men (and, later, women too).[36]

Yet the centuries-old idea that non-white was inferior did not disappear all at once. The September 1945 cover of the U.S. Marine Corps magazine *Leatherneck* showed a drawing of a laughing Marine. On his arm he was carrying a Japanese officer in the form of a monkey, albeit a fairly cute one. British officials and soldiers serving in Palestine called the Jews "towels," after the prayer-veils they wore. French ones serving in Algeria spoke of *fellaghas*, peasants. (The term has the added connotations of simple-minded, ignorant, and dirty.) Americans in Vietnam called both their enemies and their allies "gooks". The term was coined by an earlier generation of U.S. soldiers who, serving in the Philippines during and after the Spanish-American War of 1898, used it to mean "low prostitute."[37] Later they applied it to various non-Caucasian peoples. Not to be outdone, Israelis invented the term *Arabush*. A strange combination of Arabic with the Russian diminutive *ush*, it is best translated as "dirty little Arab."

Sooner or later, all of these peoples, and many others as well, learned the lesson that the people whom they despised so much were at least their equals in the place where it mattered most of all, i.e. the battlefield. The Jews in Palestine threw out their British masters, for which the latter have never quite forgiven them. The *fellaghas* went through the torture-rooms of the French *paras* and emerged victorious. The gooks sent the Americans packing, and the *Arabushim* (plural of *Arabush*) are still courageously fighting for their own independent state. Yet inside many countries, both Western and other, things hardly changed. Some Americans continue to use the centuries-old term nigger, ultimately derived from the Latin *niger*, black. Both South Africans and Arabs called blacks *kaffirs*, from the Hebrew word *kofer*, heretic. All these, and a great many more, terms imply that those to whom they are applied are *not* equal.

Much more seriously, quite some countries also retained racial discrimination in their official codes of law. Often it was a question of keeping out undesirable immigrants. Starting in the 1950s, Australia had a "whites only" immigration policy. It was only brought to an end in 1975. For forty years before 1965 the U.S. took in immigrants on the basis of racial quotas expressly designed to discriminate among people from different parts from the world. To this day many European countries do whatever they can to prevent

immigrants from Asia and Africa from entering. Japan has an exceptionally rigid immigration policy. So, for different reasons, does
Israel. As a rule, the higher the per-capita income inside the borders of a given country the more that country's government tries to
ensure that foreigners will not cross them—often without success.
Poor countries may be more permissive, but only because few people want to enter them anyhow. Both rich and poor pay lip-service
to the idea that all men are equal. Yet their laws and day-to-day behavior shows that they do not believe in it any more than the ancient
Athenians, who rigidly excluded other Greeks from citizenship, did.

The question of immigration apart, for a long time the most
interesting countries in which racism held sway were the U.S. and
South Africa. In the case of the former this was because of the sharp
contrast between declared values and the prevailing reality. Another
reason is because it is, after all, the strongest Power on earth. In
many ways it has long acted, indeed claimed to act, as a model for
the rest to follow. In the case of the latter it was because nowhere else
were policy and the law so expressly designed to maintain inequality
between the races. Each in its own way, these countries offer lessons
in what the struggle against inequality has achieved. Each also offers
lessons in what that struggle has not achieved and very probably will
not achieve.

American discrimination against blacks, as well as the struggle
against it, goes back several centuries. It persisted long after slavery
was finally abolished in 1865. Blacks accused of committing crimes
often could not obtain equal justice if they were not lynched before obtaining any justice at all. Black victims of crime could not
get equal justice either. In many places blacks were not allowed to
vote. They were discriminated against in pay, in housing, in public
transportation, in education, in welfare, and in not being allowed

to join professional associations. They were refused entry into all kinds of facilities, could not join certain arms of the military and/or be promoted in them, and were not even able to order a meal in many restaurants. Many States also had laws against mixed marriages. Only in 1967 did the Supreme Court proclaim the last of these laws unconstitutional. As late as 2000, one university, Bob Jones in South Carolina, still had a rule forbidding students to date people of other races. One high school in Georgia waited until 2007 to hold its first mixed prom.[38] It might be argued that, since the laws and rules in question applied equally to whites and blacks alike, they were not discriminatory. If that is not hypocrisy, one is hard put to think what is.

South African racism resembled that of America in some respects but differed from it in others. As in the U.S., blacks, who in this case formed the majority of the population, were discriminated against in countless ways. As in many American States, miscegenation was officially prohibited, though this did not prevent many white males from crossing into neighboring countries in order to taste the forbidden pleasures of black prostitutes. Where South Africa differed from the U.S. was in that a far larger part of the discriminatory practices, including black participation in elections, were not simply rooted in State law or in people's private behavior. Instead, they were officially anchored in the law of the land. Fearful of being swamped by their black neighbors, the white government in South Africa went further than the U.S. in that it put in place a system of internal passports that prevented blacks from living in white areas. It also put a ban on black political parties which was only finally rescinded in 1990.

In both countries the systems, official or unofficial, that had been designed to keep the members of the "inferior race" in their proper place were ultimately dismantled. In the U.S. this was the work of the Civil Rights Movement. It started making its impact felt during the late 1950s, operated in the name of equality and equity, and was joined by many whites as well. In Alabama, Mississippi and elsewhere, demonstrators were killed, and others injured, beaten up, and imprisoned. The late 1960s also witnessed riots in numerous black ghettoes with some loss of life. Still, considering what was at stake, the level of violence remained fairly limited. Some Americans were aware of the cost that racism entailed in terms of foreign policy. However, on the whole, such considerations played a relatively small role in the process of emancipation. The years since 1970 have seen a great many laws passed by Congress in an effort to ban discrimination not only against blacks but against many other groups as well. They covered such things as housing, education, jobs, etc. The laws probably had some success in limiting the more blatant public forms of discrimination. However, they are far from having altered everyone's thoughts and behaviors, let alone managed to place everyone on an equal footing.

In South Africa things developed in a different way. Thanks to extensive legislation, throughout the years from 1948 to 1990 the country was probably the most segregated in the world. Two communities, white and black, existed side by side. As in had earlier been the case in the U.S., there was some talk about "separate but equal."[39] Yet nobody had any doubt as to which one of the two communities was more equal and which one less so. Black political parties being banned, some of the victims of Apartheid resorted to terrorism. Over the years, thousands were killed, the great majority of them blacks. Often they were targeted not only by the police but by their own people in all kinds of internecine conflicts. The implications for stability were serious, though the situation never got to the point where the country sank into anarchy. Yet South Africa was not the USA. Its economy was almost entirely dependent on the export of foodstuffs and raw materials, so in the long run it was in no position to ignore external pressures and U.N.-imposed sanctions. During the early 1990s the government and the African National Congress, the most important black party, started negotiations. An agreement was finally reached and Apartheid went the way of all flesh. But that of course does not mean that there is no discrimination. Today, especially when it comes to government work, instead of whites discriminating against blacks, blacks in power often discriminate against whites. Socially the two communities remain almost as separate as they used to be before 1995.[40]

Elsewhere in the world not much has changed. As of the beginning of the twenty-first century there is hardly a single government or country left that will not profess its support for equality while claiming that its policy is as free from racism as anything can be. Many will also assert that distinguishing people by race is not justified by science.[41] Yet they still continue to base their immigration policies on racial prejudices as they did in the past. Mass migration and the existence of many mixed couples have probably caused fears that miscegenation may result in biological deterioration to fade. There is even some evidence that mixed-race people are considered the most attractive of all.[42]

On the other hand, everywhere there are great masses of people who believe that foreigners adhere to ideas, customs, attitudes, and forms of behavior that are not only very different from their own, but to a large extent remain resistant to change. The polite way to express this belief is to say that it is not based on race, which heaven forbid, but on "ethnicity" and "socio-cultural" circumstances. In practice, the results are often the same. In many places Japanese,

Chinese, and even Jewish people have been "emancipated." Instead
of being seen as inferior, they are now regarded as equal with, or
even superior to, numerous others. It has been claimed that Jews in
America, members of a people that so many throughout history have
regarded as inferior, actually have a higher average IQ than non-
Jewish whites. In China, too, Jews are highly regarded.[43] That does
not necessarily mean that anti-Semitism has disappeared; only that
it has taken on new forms. Others, especially blacks, are still more
or less where they have long been, i.e. at the bottom of the racial
ladder. Whenever black people move into a neighborhood others
move out. Until not so long ago Moslems, almost all of whom lived
in countries far away about which most people knew nothing, were
perceived mainly as dirty, poor and ignorant. Now that many of
them have come to live in Europe and North America they are often
seen not only as dirty, poor and ignorant and but also as dangerous,
fanatic, and, in not a few cases, half-mad.[44]

Some countries, especially EU ones, spend heavily in an effort
to change attitudes towards immigrants and integrate them. So far
success has been elusive, and some even believe that the effort is
counterproductive. Many countries have worked hard to abolish
the most blatant legal forms of racial discrimination. Other forms
were pushed underground where they are less exposed to the eye.
However, almost everywhere, prejudices and stereotypes, many of
them very negative indeed, persist. When it comes to accepting immigrants, often all that has changed is the terminology. As a character in the French comic series *Asterix* puts it, people don't mind
foreigners as long as they stay in their own foreign places. On the
whole, the world is probably not much closer to equality than it has
ever been.

*

As practically all of us have known from 1945 on, racism, as well as the form of inequality on which it claims to be based and to which it leads, is bad, bad, very bad. So it is, but that does not change the fact that some forms of racism have almost certainly been around ever since the first humans lost their tails and came down from the trees, perhaps even longer. Did Cro-Magnons live peacefully with Neanderthals, or did they exterminate them?[45] It is true that most scientists deny the existence of any but physical differences between present-day human races. Most social scientists argue that any other differences between them are purely psychological, social, and cultural. Yet dissenters do exist. In 1994 *The Bell Curve* was published.[46] Citing hundreds of studies, the authors argued that there are some IQ differences between East Asians, whites, and blacks. To be sure, they were careful to point out that statistics tell us nothing about the abilities of individuals. Still it is not hard to see how their work could be used to justify discrimination. Nor was there a shortage of voices accusing the authors of racism. Here the question is not whether they were right or wrong. Rather, it is their right to do research and express their views regardless of present dogma. Or is the quest for equality going to force all of us to shut up and salute?

South Africa apart, since 1945 no country has sought to impose the kind of systematic racial legislation so pervasive in Nazi Germany. However, especially in the so-called developing world, often this may have had more to do with administrative incapacity and political chaos than with any lack of murderous intent. As the Nazis also found out, in some ways it is easier to kill hundreds of thousands or even millions of people than to decide exactly who should, and should not, be killed. Mass-murders of people perceived as belonging to a different race or group—definitions vary endlessly—have not been rare. Hindis massacred Moslems. Sinhalese massacred Tamils. Serbs massacred Bosnians (whom they call "Turks"). In all these cases things also worked in reverse when the opportunity presented itself. Indonesians massacred East Timorese. Hutu massacred Tutsi. Sudanese Arabs from the north of the country massacred Sudanese blacks in its southern half. In the Congo, everyone seems to be slaughtering everyone else much of the time. There is something strange about this. Even as people of one group hate and despise those of another, they insist on sharing the same polity with them. Often they have equality on their lips and weapons of mass murder in their hands. If this will ever change, if it can ever change, remains to be seen.

Chapter 8

Minorities Into Majorities

In many ways, the most interesting modern experiment with equality is the feminist-instigated one concerning men and women. Nothing similar has ever been tried before. In all historically known societies, women have always been subordinated to men. That was true both inside the family and in public life. A century-and-a-half of contact with civilization has made it impossible to say whether women of the Andamanese, the simplest society of all, were permitted to be shamans. But there is no doubt that male shamans outnumbered female ones.[1] That is not necessarily to say women were oppressed. Some women dominated their husbands, as they still do. For every disadvantage under which women labored there were almost always was, and still is, some privileges they alone enjoyed.[2]

The most important privileges were the right to be supported by their husbands (often, in case they had no husbands, their brothers) and the right *not* to go to war, *not* to fight, and *not* to die for their dearly beloved rulers, polities, and countries. In many modern societies, the advent of feminism has caused men and women to be placed on a more equal footing than ever before. The catch is that, in most of the societies in question, women, desperately trying to achieve what they see as equality, no longer bear enough children to maintain the population. Some countries, such as the U.S., are making up for the deficit by importing millions of foreigners. Others, such as Japan, seem resigned to gradual demographic decline and hope that robots will make up the difference. If demographics count for anything, the future of patriarchy—not the comparatively mild form of patriarchy that is said to have characterized the West, but the more rigorous Islamic variety—seems assured.[3] Primatologists agree that, among chimpanzees, all adult males dominate all females. Females have their own separate hierarchies. However, in case of a male-versus female encounter the latter do hold a trump card. It is their rump, which they present to the males.[4] With bonobos the situation is more complicated. According to de Waal, captive colonies are ruled by an older female. In the wild, things are different. Individual males, being larger than females and having larger canines, may push individual females aside. But collectively females always contrive to dominate males.

Thus the two species that are closest to us present a mixed picture. How about humans? According to de Waal and others our ancestors lost their tails, started walking upright, and left the forest for the savanna. As they did so they became prey. They lived in constant fear of pack-hunting hyenas, ten different kinds of big cats, and other dangerous animals. Females with young were the most vulnerable and could only exist thanks to male protection. "The size-difference between the sexes," he adds, "combined with excellent cooperation among males makes it likely that male dominance has always characterized our lineage." The result was "the typical human pattern by far is a sex-for-food deal between a man and a woman with children attached."[5] Many tribal societies around the world have stories concerning some long-past period when women ruled until, at some point, the men rebelled and took over. Doing so, they appropriated certain magic powers that had originally belonged to women. Supposing there is any truth in these myths, they represent another argument in favor of the belief that the earliest source of inequality was some sort of supposed proximity to the supernatural world. In the Old Testament, the subordination of women ("thy desire shall be to thy husband, and he shall rule over thee") was part of a punishment that God had inflicted on Eve for sinning in the Garden of Eden. Others attributed the emergence of male superiority to men's greater physical force or to the invention of private property which led to inheritance and monogamy. Somewhat like *Genesis*, Freud thought it was women's own doing. In his view male dominance resulted from penis envy which is always causing women to emulate men as best they can.

Over the ages there have been many "utopian" schemes for putting men and women on an equal basis. Plato wanted his male and female guardians to receive a similar education and engage in similar work on behalf of the city. He could not change the natural inequality that results from pregnancy, childbirth and childcare. But he did propose to take children away from their mothers (and fathers) and have them raised by the community. Starting with the Stoics Zeno (334–262 BC) and Chrysippus (279–206 BC), many other utopian writers, including not least some modern feminist utopias, have followed his suggestion.[6] Other authors sought to maintain the family, and with it, women's traditional position, as did Thomas More. Some even proposed an end to sex, as in some medieval utopias and a few American utopian communities, or suggested that the link between sex and procreation be cut, as in *Brave New World*. To date, the only place where any of these schemes have been realized, even partly, for any length of time is the kibbutz. Reader, wait. You will find out what happened there soon enough.

Thomas Hobbes believed that men and women in the original state of nature had been equal. However, since his main concern was with order, he had little to say about the position of women in society.[7] Neither Locke nor Rousseau nor Montesquieu extended the kind of equality they envisaged to women. When Abigail, wife of John Adams, asked that the Declaration of Independence be modified to read "all men and women" he ignored her.[8] One of the few, and most interesting, voices calling for gender equality was that of the Marquis de Sade (1740–1814).[9] Today Sade is remembered mainly for his name which gave rise to the term sadism. In reality, though, he was a radical thinker and a good writer who deliberately moved from the banal to the sublime and back again. To Sade the quest for liberty, which at the time stood at the center of public discussion, could not be complete until men *and* women were put on an equal basis, sexually speaking. Each person, limited only by his or her power, should have the right to do anything with and to anyone he or she liked. Only by carnal knowledge could they learn who they really were and realize their full potential for good and evil alike. In the event, the realization of Sade's dream had to wait until the invention of the pill in the 1960s. Instead of execrating him, as many of them do, feminists should erect a statue in his honor.

The mother of the present-day drive for women's equality is often said to be Mary Wollstonecraft (1759–1797). Wollstonecraft was a disciple of Rousseau whose "sensibility" she greatly admired and whose grave she visited. She was, however, disappointed by his failure to make women equal to men. In her 1792 volume, *A*

Vindication of the Rights of Women, she demanded women's social, professional, economic and political emancipation. Born to a father who did not, as she saw it, carry out his duty to feed his family in a satisfactory way, Wollstonecraft did her modest best to live by her pen without male support. Where she differed from many subsequent feminists was in that she did not blame women's allegedly sad condition on men alone. Reviewing books for the *Analytical Review*, she claimed that "lady authors" were "timid sheep." In their work, "weakness too often is exalted into an excellence."[10] The problem persists—mainly among feminists who, even as they demand "equality," often present women as foolish, psychologically vulnerable, and unable to stand up to the machinations of wicked men who somehow succeed in misleading them and subjugating them.

The problem, Wollstonecraft thought, was not natural ability but education. From the beginning of history on, women had been made into "little, smooth, delicate, fair creatures." They were taught "to lisp and totter" so they could "inspire love." She felt little but contempt for them. To help them develop "courage and resolution" they should be subject to a "masculine system of education." As the ancient Spartan *agoge* demonstrates, though, such a system was likely to be rather harsh, physically and mentally. Probably few women would have chosen to enter it, let alone successfully completed it. In one modern Canadian experiment, out of 100 women who joined a full infantry training course just one graduated. Conversely, no sooner are women admitted to any field then it starts losing much of its rigor, as has happened to basic training in the U.S. armed services from about 1980 on.[11] Mary Wollstonecraft herself was well aware of these problems. Having joined her sister in running a school for girls, she believed that most women were only too happy to accept the privileges that men, seeking sex and love, were offering them.[12] Never mind that the price of privilege was subordination.

Generations of subsequent feminists have seen *A Vindication of the Rights of Women* as the starting-shot for a quest of equality that is still going on. Like so much else in the modern world, feminism—the term, incidentally, was invented by Charles Fourier whom we have already met—started in what is now known the West.[13] From there it spread to the rest of the world, with very mixed success. Nineteenth-century European and North American feminists focused on questions such as property rights, divorce, and child-custody. They also demanded admission to educational facilities and the professions, the vote, and the right to serve in public office. By the end of World War I many of these fights had been won, more or less. Even so, the number of women who did paid work outside the home remained much smaller than that of men. Unless they were members of the lowest classes, few married women worked at all. Female politicians did exist, but very few of them rose to the first rank.

During World War II the proportion of working women went up. Still, except in the Soviet Union where they formed a majority even in the mines, they were greatly outnumbered by men. The vast number of casualties their country had suffered forced Soviet women to keep on working even after 1945. Elsewhere, most female workers and soldiers were happy to go home.[14] Communist countries had their own separate version of women's equality. The *Communist Manifesto* denied that there was any intention of abolishing the family and instituting a commonality of wives. The leader who took the greatest interest in the question was August Bebel (1840–1913), one of the founders of the German Social Democratic Party. His *Women and Socialism* (1879) remained a bestseller for decades and was translated into some fifty languages. To Bebel, history was a sad tale in which woman had been prevented from participating in society's productive labor. That in turn forced her into an inferior position inside the family as well as in society. Accordingly, he suggested making men and women equal in respect to family law as well as granting women the vote. Child-raising and cooking would be taken over by the community. As women's economic dependence came to an end, for the first time in history people of both sexes would be free to choose their partners and live with them for love alone.

In many ways, Bebel's work formed the basis for the policies adopted in the Soviet Union from 1918 on. Having seized power in a country ruined by war and revolution, the Bolsheviks' most immediate concern was to restore production. They believed the fastest way to achieve this goal was to draw upon what they saw as the country's chief untapped source of manpower, i.e. the vast number of women who did not do paid work. It was primarily to enable, not to say compel, them to do so that the nascent communist state carried out some of the most thorough reforms in the situation of women in history.[15] Men's position as the heads of households was terminated. With it went the distinction between legitimate and illegitimate children. Expecting women to work for a living on equal terms with men, the government made divorce so easy that the family itself was all but abolished. Two prominent women, Alexandra Kollontai and Lenin's wife Nadezha Krupskaya, drew up utopian plans for communities in which private housing and domestic life would be abolished. Children were to be taken away from their families and raised in dormitories.[16] As we saw, some of those plans were later put in action in Mao's China, with disastrous results.

However, Soviet women refused to give up their children as Kollontai and Krupskaya, neither having children of their own, wanted them to. If only for that reason, little came of the plans. Even so, the results of communist-style equality between the sexes were not slow to make themselves felt. The number of divorces exploded. That of deserted wives and children desperately trying to survive without male support rose into the millions.[17] Poverty bred crime as a generation of youngsters was thrown into the streets and forced to live by theft or prostitution. In the late twenties the authorities performed an about-turn. Family law was re-tightened. Kollontai's works were banned and she herself banished to Sweden where she served as Soviet ambassador. She may have owed her life to Stalin whose mistress she was reputed to have been; several of her collaborators were arrested and shot.

The most important part of the original program to survive this turn-about was the one that sought to take women out of the household and make them take up paid work. Under Stalin the percentage of female workers in the factories skyrocketed. Whereas, under the Tsarist regime, women had not been permitted to enter the universities, now hundreds of thousands of them did so. To make all this possible, free kindergartens were provided. These efforts notwithstanding, the Soviet Union was like all other countries in that women remained over-represented at the bottom of the political and economic hierarchy and greatly underrepresented at the top.[18] The same thing happened later in the Soviet-satellite countries of Eastern Europe.

Meanwhile cramped housing, the need to spend hours queuing for even the simplest consumer goods, and the continued burden of housework made the lives of many women all but intolerable. In the 1930s, women began to respond to the burden equality had imposed on them by having fewer children. Around 1900, the average Russian woman lived in the countryside, looking after the household as well as doing the less onerous kinds of agricultural work. During her lifetime she would have six to eight children, of whom four usually survived. Under the equality regime, the typical Soviet family was urban, with two working parents, one child, and a grandmother to look after him or her became the norm. Around 1980, the regime realized it had a problem on its hands. It tried to put back the clock, but it was too little, too late. The dearth of children affected the urbanized parts of the USSR where the Slavs lived much more than it did the outlying Moslem ones where patriarchy and inequality still reigned. This contradiction, as Marx would have called it, led straight to the breakup of the Soviet Union in 1989–1991.

In 1963 Betty Friedan, author of the *Feminine Mystique*, jumpstarted the so-called Second Feminist Wave. During an interview she told me that what really got her going was the fact that, working as a journalist, she was twice fired because she was pregnant. Friedan's main point was that women who stayed at home were likely to suffer from depression, or take to drink, or have an extramarital affair. To retain their sanity they should leave their homes, work like men, and earn money like men. Exercising a hobby, or doing voluntary works of the kind many upper class women had always done and still do, was not good enough. Conversely, nonworking women were responsible for many of society's ills. If, at the time, the Soviets were ahead of the U.S. in the space race that was because more Soviet women worked. If many American men were homosexual, that was because, in their youth, they had been spoiled by bored stay-at-home mothers with too much time and not enough to do. In the view of Friedan, Simone de Beauvoir, and many of their followers, *Arbeit macht frei* and non-working women scarcely deserved to live.[19]

Since then, so relentless has the quest for women's equality been that a google.com search on 30 October 2013 yielded 152,000,000 hits. The movement has even brought some change to many Moslem countries. Slowly, and often screaming at the top of their lungs, they are being dragged into the twenty-first century as their women demand equal rights with men. As millions of women took jobs they discovered two things. First, the road ahead was often much harder than they had thought. Men, with good reason as it turned out, feared that their own work would be devalued. Almost always they resisted. Quite often male resistance could be overcome and some sort of equality attained, only through the aid of the courts. Second, working closely with men in an environment originally created by and for men exposed women to "sexual harassment." The precise meaning of the term has never been clarified. In practice, it meant any attempt to communicate with a woman that she, for whatever reason, did not like and decided to report to her superiors and to the justice system.

At this point a Catch-22 situation emerged. Success in the workplace requires drive, aggression, and a tendency towards dominance. Getting mileage, and often enough money, out of sexual harassment suits presupposes presenting to the world a certain kind of helplessness and vulnerability, real or make-believe. As Wollstonecraft might have written, in such cases weakness, even stupidity as women claim not to understand what men want of them, is exalted into excellence. The two sets of attitudes are contradictory. How can a woman who suffers, or claims to suffer, a life-long psychological trauma because somebody at work tried to make a pass at her be trusted to withstand the pressures that business life very often involves? Perhaps even worse, a woman who complains and fails will never again be approached by any man. A woman who wins her case will be seen as dangerous and men will avoid her as if she were a leper. However one looks at it, the price of equality at the workplace is a truly high one indeed. No wonder many, probably most, women do not complain. Of those who do complain, quite a few are persuaded, if not coerced, into doing so by their feminist sisters.[20]

Of course, women who wanted to work needed someone else to raise their children for them. That was how the Israeli kibbutzim used to operate. Early on, kibbutz women worked in the fields along with men, though it goes without saying that men always did the harder kinds of labor. Later, as children were born, they increasingly found themselves relegated to a life in which they were endlessly rotated between children's home, kitchen, and launderette. Kibbutz women participated in the kibbutz general assembly and voted in it. However, as in the rest of Jewish-Israeli society, practically all important public positions were occupied by men. In the 1970s, kibbutz women raised the standard of revolt. Some took jobs outside the kibbutz where they did work they found more interesting. They also started demanding to have their children back at home. Once that demand was granted couples again turned into families. Families needed larger houses with kitchens and other amenities to live in. As differential salaries based on performance rather than needs were introduced, communal life started falling apart.[21] As it declined economic inequality between members grew, threatening the kibbutzim's very existence. Whether they will survive remains to be seen. In all societies, the vast majority of those hired to mind children and do housework were themselves women. The traditional gap between mistresses and maids (paid or unpaid as in the case of grandmothers), continues to exist. More equality for some led to less equality for others. Much worse still, in all known societies since the world was created practically all new discoveries and innovations have been made by men. By adopting men's life-patterns women mounted a treadmill where they were forever running behind, trying to catch up.[22]

Once they were on the treadmill another problem emerged. For men, money, fame and power have always been the strongest aphrodisiacs of all. For women things do not work in the same way. As Rousseau once put it: "the more you become like us, *Mesdames*, the less we shall like you." Almost the only exceptions are women, especially the exceptionally attractive, who succeed in fields where they only compete with other women; such as dancers, singers, actresses, models, women in some kinds of sports, etc.

Women's quest for equality has even led them into fields for which they are simply not suited; principally to war and the military. There are many physical reasons why women are less suited for war than men. While women may forge ahead and ignore those reasons, experience shows that doing so is dangerous to their health.[23] Judging by the fact that among veterans of the war in Iraq, women are more likely to suffer from post-traumatic stress syndrome than men, war is also dangerous to their mental health as well. Some psychological studies reported such a large difference between the sexes that a new kind of disorder, "military-sexual trauma," had to be invented to explain it away.[24]

In any case, not every woman may feel that attaining the sort of equality that the military in particular offers is worth being made to travel seven or eight thousand miles from home, spending months or years in a foreign, mostly underdeveloped, country, and risking death in combat. For many, perhaps most, women the attempt to gain equality by doing as men do has caused more harm than good. It is even now causing the difference in life expectancy between them and men to decline.[25] The point has been reached where many women, by focusing on their careers and refusing to have children, are literally waging war against their own genes. The better educated they are, the more true this is. As has been said, the feminist movements' cathedrals are the abortion clinics on one hand and the adoption agencies on the other; neither of which enjoy a particularly good reputation.

Throughout all this, the quest for equality has hardly caused the basic relationship between men and women to change. Today, as ever, men protect women and feed them, which itself entails a certain kind of inequality. Today, as ever, the higher one climbs, the fewer women one meets. And some of those one meets are there to create the illusion of equality, not the reality. Many feminists who demand equality do so primarily because they despise women and admire men. Others, by suggesting that women not have children, are bent on making the human race commit suicide. If present trends continue, the societies in which the movement towards women's equality is strongest are simply doomed to disappear. In fact, as Plato wrote, men and women are similar in some ways but differ in others. The differences are as important as the similarities. Furthermore, a good deal of the attraction between the sexes rests on both the similarities *and* the differences. Women who try to gain equality with men by acting like men, living like men, and being like men will end up by becoming (second rate) men.

Women who try to exploit the advantages nature has given them to obtain the protection of men and be fed by them cannot and will not be equal with men. Women who are equal with men will in many ways cease to be women at all. The see-saw between equality and protection is as old as human history and is unlikely to ever come to an end. Each of the two approaches, when taken to extremes, has the potential to inflict endless misery on both women *and* men.

As complex as the question of equality between men and women is that of homosexuality. The ancient Greeks appear to have been bisexual. Not even pederasty, let alone homosexuality, was considered a crime. Still, Athenian law did penalize men who had prostituted themselves by denying them political rights. In Rome, too, for a youth to have taken the passive role in intercourse with another man was not exactly an honor. The historian Suetonius speaks contemptuously of those who had been so "polluted".[26] Rome was also one of the few historical societies where men could sue for rape, thus putting them in an equal position with women. With the spread of Christianity things changed. Starting from the late fourth century AD many Christian rulers, acting on behalf of the Church, persecuted homosexuals, though the intensity with which they did so varied. At this point a distinction must be drawn between male homosexuals and lesbians. The former were often persecuted with the full force of the law, the latter hardly ever. Even the Nazis, who sent 10,000 male homosexuals to the concentration camps where many of them died, did not bother to extend the same policy to women too.[27] Why this should have been the case is anything but clear.

With the exception of the ancient Greeks, none of the polities of which we are talking here had much use for equality. Either homosexuality was a crime, or it was not. In the modern world the first country to decriminalize homosexuality between consenting adults was France in 1791. I have not been able to discover the immediate background for this measure. Even so, the age of consent for homosexual relations was fixed at twenty-one years. For heterosexual relations it was eleven, later raised to thirteen, where it remained until 1984. French homosexuals often suffered police harassment. Nor did the police always respond to homosexuals' request for help when they were being harassed by ordinary people. In 1942, the Vichy Regime, taking a leaf from Fascist Italy and National Socialist Germany, reversed course and re-criminalized homosexual behavior. The laws it passed were seldom enforced after 1945, but they were not finally taken off the books until 1981.[28]

Most other Western countries also waited until the last decades of the twentieth century before following suit. Meanwhile, homosexual preferences and practices were regarded as a sort of disease, biological or mental. Physicians and psychiatrists made many strenuous attempts to "cure" them. Either they used dubious hormonal preparations or else they resorted to psychotherapy. Homosexuals continued to be discriminated against in countless ways. Depending on the country in question, these included not being allowed to join certain organizations such as the military and the police. Other homosexuals were refused jobs, housing, and admission to all kinds of posts, including the priesthood. The U.S. Federal Government not only refused to employ homosexuals but demanded that contactors ferret them out and fire them. Many U.S. State governments passed legislation that prohibited gays from working in bars and restaurants. Many municipalities organized regular campaigns to suppress gay life. Engaging in public homosexual behavior, such as kissing or even hand-holding, all but invited being lynched. In Hollywood, gay and lesbian characters were taboo in films and all discussion of homosexual issues was likewise forbidden.

Even today, two characters on the children's show *Sesame Street*,

Bert and Ernie, still give rise to fierce controversy. Some suspect they are supposed to be gay and would like nothing better than to see them and their creators crucified. Others suggest that they should openly proclaim their homosexuality.[29] Either way, there can be no question of simple equality with everyone else. To avoid the various forms of discrimination, many if not most, homosexuals chose to remain in the closet, as the saying went. They did their best to pretend they were like anyone else. In 1993, the U.S. military, which previously had refused to take on known homosexuals, institutionalized the closet by adopting the "don't ask, don't tell" policy. Doing so, it opened the door to endless prying into people's private life as well as blackmail.[30] Given the way most militaries operate, concealing one's sexual preferences was more difficult than doing the same in civilian society. Both inside and outside the military it was very hard, psychologically speaking. Often it translated into loneliness at work, parties, excursions, family events, and the like. Conversely, anyone who did not have a family tended to fall under suspicion of being gay. Nor was concealment of any help in avoiding various other forms of discrimination. Unable to marry their partners, homosexuals were denied many of the rights mixed-sex couples enjoyed. Again depending on the country in question those might include tax breaks, pensions, the right to adopt a child, and much more. A homosexual couple could not even rent a room at a hotel.

Other civilizations had their own ways of dealing with homosexuality. Hinduism does not seem to take a firm stance on the matter. Some sects are opposed to it, and a few have even gone so far as to advocate the execution of homosexuals. Surprisingly, the *Kama Sutra* has nothing to say about anal intercourse between males. Men who fellate their fellows are compared to dogs, but the practice is not prohibited. In any case women who perform fellatio on men are seen as being no better.[31] But not all Hindus saw things in this light. Some temple sculptures even show men and women engaged in homoerotic activities. Recently, more favorable attitudes appear to have prevailed. In 2009, India's Supreme Court, reacting against the British set of laws that made homosexuality a crime, prohibited discrimination against homosexuals.[32] That of course is proof, that such discrimination did exist in the past. Buddhism strongly opposes homosexuality among monks who are prohibited from having any kind of sexual contact whatsoever. However, it does not have much to say about the way laymen should behave. As long as sex is non-compulsory and pleasant it seems to be OK.[33]

Neither Confucianism nor Daoism has much to say about homosexuality. To the extent that they do have an attitude to it is one of mild dislike. In the case of the former this is because of man's duty to beget children, especially males that can take part in ancestor worship. In the case of the latter it is due to the need to maintain a balance between *yin* and *yang*, the female and male principles in general.[34] In contemporary China homosexuals are not persecuted, but they do give rise to some concern owing to the spread of HIV and AIDS.[35]

Finally, Moslems have long taken it for granted that homoerotic tendencies are widespread and hard to control. That was why, in the middle ages, not only those in charge of the harems but also those responsible for the casernes where young boys were trained as soldiers had to be eunuchs.[36] The *Quran* reproaches men who practice homosexuality but does not specifically say they should be punished. However, in the *Hadith*, which purports to be collection of Mohammed's sayings, it is treated as a capital offense against God.[37] Many present-day Moslem countries have taken this approach, forcing gays to lead a furtive underground existence. Moslems living in Western countries have often drawn attention to themselves by bringing their anti-gay (and anti-women) attitudes with them.[38] In the former Soviet Union, homosexuality was decriminalized after the Revolution but re-criminalized by Stalin in 1933s. The law was later used to get rid of unwanted personalities. One such victim was Nikolai Yezov, chief of the secret police from 1936 to 1938, who was probably bisexual.

Today the country least friendly to homosexuals is Kenya, where only one percent of those polled consider it to be acceptable. Other poor developing countries, especially Moslem ones, also tend to be intolerant. Russian President Vladimir Putin has launched an ongoing campaign against homosexuals, although its objective is not clear. Incidents where homosexuals are attacked, or else arrested, tried and punished are quite frequent. Homosexuality, real or alleged, is also used to get rid of political opponents. In the countries of Latin America, as well as the richer ones of East Asia, the number of people who accept homosexuality is usually somewhere between 40 and 60 percent. Globally speaking, there is no doubt that the road to equality is likely to be long and hard.

In the West, however, the homosexuals' fight for their rights has been one of the most successful on record. To a large extent, that is because someone had the brilliant idea of campaigning under the standard of equality. After all, equality was an idea the West itself had invented and claimed to spread all over the world. Having done, so, it could hardly retreat from it. In Europe, growing secularization also helped. One indication of success is the fact that Moslem homosexuals do what they can to enter Western countries where they feel less at risk than at home. To be sure, some problems remain. Legal equality is not the same as social equality, let alone a complete end to discrimination. Hate crimes up to and including, murder are not rare. In the U.S. in 2009, 1,220 were reported, and they are not unknown in other countries either.[39]

Still, compared with the situation only a few decades ago the change is momentous. Since 1980, Canada, Germany, Britain, Japan, Spain, Sweden, and the U.S. have all witnessed sharp declines in the number of people who believe that homosexuality is "never acceptable." Conversely, surveys show that 91 percent of Spaniards consider homosexuality acceptable. The corresponding German figure is 87 percent, the French 86, the British 81, the American 60. Due to its strong Puritan tradition, the U.S. is the most anti-homosexual Western country of all. It is also the only one where the number of those who disapprove of homosexuality, though considerably smaller than it was some decades ago, has risen in recent years. Perhaps surprisingly, most Americans polled prefer to have Moslems or foreign workers as neighbors rather than homosexuals. Yet even in the U.S., such attitudes are less common among the young than the old.[40] As it is said, it is not old opinions that die but those who hold them.

In 2012 Tel Aviv was voted the world's most gay-friendly city.[41] There is a paradox here. In Israel, unlike most Western countries, state and religion are not separate. Judaism is as strongly opposed to male homosexuality as the two other monotheistic religions to which it gave birth. The book of *Leviticus* commands that men who engage in it should be burnt. Many Israeli cities and neighborhoods are inhabited mainly or even exclusively by orthodox Jews. In those areas, anti-gay fanaticism reigns, and equality for homosexuals is inconceivable. It is different in Tel Aviv, although there have been some isolated incidents, including a murder that was never cleared up. The city was founded out of nothing in 1909. Located on the Mediterranean coast, right from the beginning it had a strong commercial orientation. This caused it to be more tolerant and open to the world. In Tel Aviv, as in other cities around the world, gays' relentless quest for equality has created a situation where kindergarten children are subjected to "sex education," including explicit references to homosexual and lesbian sex, long before they have the slightest idea as to what sex is. Whether that will result in a more equitable society, as the exponents of gay rights claim, or merely lead to a generation of thoroughly confused and disturbed young people, as many parents fear, remains to be seen.

*

A third important group that has taken up the quest for equality in recent years, or in whose name it has been taken up, consists of the handicapped, disabled, or whatever they may be called. From the beginning of history on there have always been people who were physically or mentally below some vaguely defined norm. Methods—if that is the right word in a situation where government was often decentralized and uniformity lacking—for coping with them varied. The physically disabled might be sent begging or, if they could not do that, were kept at home. Often they were excluded from employment even if they were capable of filling it.

Usually such sequestration was done by individuals on an instinctual basis, but here and there it is possible to find written laws to that effect. For example, the Old Testament book of *Leviticus* specifies that no one who had any blemish on his body could serve in the Temple of the Lord.[42] This law seems to have been rigidly observed. In 40 BC the Hasmonean pretender Aristobulus had the ear of his brother, Yohanan Hyrcanus, cut off so as to prevent him from serving as High Priest. Provided they were harmless, mentally disabled people would probably be treated much like those with

physical disabilities. Those considered dangerous either to themselves or to society were likely to be restrained. At most times and
places this was done at home. In much of the developing world cases
when families imprison members at home for years on end are not
rare even today. The first hospitals specifically designed to house the
invalids and the mentally disabled seem to have been established in
Europe during the last decades of the seventeenth century.[43] In an
age whose overriding interest was order, the objective was to isolate
them and keep them away from the public view so that only visitors
could see them.

Originally people were referred to the hospitals either by the
authority of the towns in which they lived or by their own relatives
who got tired of looking after them. During the nineteenth century
states started appointing physicians and psychiatrists who assumed
this responsibility. Many such institutions still exist all over the
world. Their very existence is a tacit admission that some people
are not up to the demands equality places on them. Horror stories
about the way both those who remained free and those who were
hospitalized were treated abound. Probably such cases are no less
numerous today than they have always been. The free disabled were
often ridiculed, beaten, tormented, and driven away to some other
place where the process would repeat itself. They were also discriminated against in many ways. The fate of the unfree was in some ways
even worse. Once committed, usually for an unspecified time, they
lost every civic right they ever had. They found themselves totally
dependent on staff whose job was to look after them and cure them
if possible.[44]

Some of those responsible used rather peculiar methods for the
purpose, to say the least. In the past they have included immo-
bilization, silence, cold baths, insulin therapy, electroshock and

lobotomy, to name but a few.[45] Today, treatments are more likely to consist of drugs that turn those who take them into zombies and often have severe physical effects. The declared objective was to make patients sufficiently equal to resume their place in society. Among the worst sinners in this regard were the Nazis. They simply killed many of those who could not look after themselves and whom they perceived as inferior. That, too is a way to impose equality.

Like the Women's Liberation Movement, and the Gay Liberation Movement, the campaign to end discrimination against the disabled seems to have taken a leaf from the Civil Rights Movement. Women, gays and the disabled all presented themselves as the victims of discrimination. All three focused on "equality" as the magic key with which to end that discrimination and gain what they saw as their proper position in society. All have made considerable headway in bringing about legal changes. All also keep complaining, no doubt with reason, that much remains to be done. In many ways their struggles have been similar to each other.

In one country after another the law prohibited landlords from refusing to sell or let their property on the basis of race, sex, sexual orientation, and, as far as possible, physical and mental disability. The same applied to clubs, employers, shopkeepers, and other providers of public services from catering to travel to medical services. All these may also be prohibited from discriminating among their members or clients or users on the base of their employment, trade, business, occupation, profession, and level of education. In some cases the necessary reforms were relatively easy to carry out. For example, by taking away "whites only" shields from buses, restaurants, toilets, etc. In others it was much more complicated. Expensive computer programs might have to be rewritten. To participate in government tenders, firms beyond a certain size

had to prove that they employed a "proper" mix of different people. Jobs had to be redesigned so that women, who are physically
weaker on the average, could do them. Often physical facilities such
as buildings and public transportation vehicles had to be modified
so that the disabled could reach them or use them.

Probably the most difficult demands were those made on the
schools. Children, after all, represent the future. Reaching adult-
hood, hopefully they will do as they have been taught. Often text-
books had to be re-written, and teachers re-trained, in order to make
sure that any kind of discrimination would disappear and equality
reign supreme. Instead of presenting the world as it is, they described it as the authors, often assisted by whole armies of supervisors, psychologists, sociologists, and similar experts would like it
to be. That, however, was only the beginning. In the adult world,
where life is serious and where there is keen competition for money
and power, there have been few attempts to make up for all kinds of
mental deficiencies, or disabilities as they are politely known. Whatever the regulations in other fields may say, apparently no government or private employer has been obliged to take on office workers
who suffered from attention deficit hyperactivity disorder (ADHD),
dyslexic lawyers, dysnumeric accountants, dysnomic lobbyists, or
terminally shy salespeople.

When it comes to the young, the situation is entirely different.
The first reason for this is that parents demand it. The second is that
the government mandates it. The most extreme cases are usually referred to institutions that cater to students with "special needs." In
the U.S., this group numbers about ten percent of the total. In Germany the figure is just over five percent, in Canada just four percent.
Assuming U.S. students are no less bright than others on the average, how such vast gaps originated is by no means clear. Possibly

it has something to do with the huge number of psychotherapists and social workers of every kind, all of whom have to justify their existence.[46] Yet the name "special" does not mean that these students are not supposed to achieve the same academic standards, and pass the same tests, as everybody else. To the contrary, by the provisions of the 2001 No Child Left behind Act they *must* do so. Should they fail, then the schools they attend may be taken to account.

The upshot is that, both in special and ordinary schools, the quest for equality is causing students with disabilities of every kind to be given any number of privileges. Shy students may not be required to speak up in class or may be given written examinations instead of oral ones. Conversely, dyslectic students may be given oral examinations instead of written ones. Slow students may be given additional coaching or more time to do their assignments and submit their exams. To make this look as if it never happened, another *1984*-like euphemism, "flexible hours," has been introduced. Based on the assumption that substituting other people's work for one's own requires a certain amount of intelligence, some students are permitted, even encouraged, to do exactly that.[47]

Both students and teachers have internalized the new rules. Students may claim to have ADHD in order to get all kinds of privileges. They or their parents may even have paid a psychiatrist or psychologist to certify them as suffering from the syndrome.[48] Pressed by administrators, who in turn are being pressed by their superiors, some teachers have developed pretending that slow students are as good as the rest into a fine art. Based on the principle that everybody deserves the carrot and nobody the stick, originally such privileges were meant for, and limited to, young students in kindergarten and elementary school. Later they spread upward, becoming common even in college where a growing number of students started demanding them as a matter of right. As long ago as 1995, it was claimed that about fifty thousand substandard students, constituting nearly three percent of all new entrants, were entering U.S. colleges each year.[49] Even graduate school is no longer immune. Faculty and administrators are exhorted to provide "adjustments, such as the possibility of flexible work hours and other accommodations" to those suffering from LDs (learning disabilities).[50]

In Imperial China and other countries that adopted examinations early in the nineteenth century, the objective of the system was to find out who was better than the others. To do so, all students were treated equally by being given the same questionnaires to fill in or answer in the same time under the same conditions.[51] Today's Western societies do exactly the opposite. Some students are given unequal learning opportunities and exams so that they may somehow achieve equality with all the rest. The quest for equality and the campaign against "bias" has caused not only physical but verbal behavior to be regulated and penalized. It is no longer "acceptable" to mock or denigrate anybody on the basis race, sex, sexual orientation, appearance, etc.

To say that some kind of behavior is "unacceptable" or "inappropriate" means that, though there is as yet no law against the behavior, people can nevertheless be punished for engaging in it. Perhaps the change is for the good. Who knows how much misery the world might have been spared if Goebbels had not been called club-foot and former Iranian President Ahmadinejad "the monkey"? However that may be, in today's "advanced" countries, the drive towards equality has reached the point where almost anybody who says anything about a member of a "disadvantaged" group can be, and quite often is, accused of being offensive. To avoid committing what George Orwell in *1984* calls thoughtcrime, many of us

engage in Newspeak. For example, in the EU one cannot say anything against Moslems who, as everybody knows, are a minority.
However, the faith they profess, i.e. Islam, may be freely attacked
(or, depending on prosecutors' whims, the other way around). In
other countries one may be prohibited from believing that women
are different, or that homosexuality is unnatural, and many other
things.

Social science is an inexact science and presumably will always
remain so. Definitions capable both of expressing an idea or concept in an unambiguous way and of surviving ongoing change are
very rare, perhaps nonexistent. In their absence, what constitutes
"offensive behavior" and "offensive speech" is very much a question of individual decision as well as political power. The quest for
equality is causing them to expand all the time. Countless acts and
words that were acceptable yesterday no longer are so today. Simply by being performed or used, those that are acceptable today almost certainly will acquire an offensive connotation tomorrow and
will have to be dropped. People who used to be called first cripples
and then handicapped—physically or mentally—are now referred
to as disabled. Other euphemisms will almost certainly follow. Not
that it makes much difference, say, to somebody who is bound to a
wheelchair.

The combination of vague definitions and constant change has
given plenty of scope to litigation. A restaurant owner is not allowed to exclude anyone on the basis of race, sex, sexual orientation, or age. Does that mean he has to admit a person who stinks to
high heaven? If the odor results from the fact that the individual in
question has been wearing the same clothes for several months, the
answer is probably negative. After all, such a client may very well
drive away many of the rest so the decision not to admit is based

on relevant business considerations. But what if the odor is the re
sult of the fact that the individual happens to come from a different
country, one that is hot and poor, where the main food is garlic, and
people feel no obligation to shower or use deodorants? Or what if
the odor originates in some medical condition the individual har-
bors through no fault of his own? How is the restaurant owner to
know? Should he call on an ethnographic expert or a physician before making a hiring decision? Far from being jokes, these are serious
questions that have been debated in the legal literature.[52] An entire
class of lawyers has specialized in such cases. They surf the law in an
attempt to locate such questionable cases and capitalize on them.

While the quest to impose equality and do away with discrimination has greatly expanded some industries, it has limited or even
eliminated others. Consider customer profiling, where banks, insurance companies, and other corporations have long used it to divide
their clients into various categories. Often those categories included
such factors as race, sex, sexual orientation, and others. The same
applies to genetic information concerning a person's likelihood to
contract certain diseases. In most advanced countries today, the
law no longer allows this kind of information to be used to profile,
or in other words, to discriminate between, different groups of people. That is equality, but equality comes at a price. For example,
are policemen in many countries really going to ignore the fact that
most immigrants belong to certain groups and ask everyone for his
or her papers all the time?

Another very good example of the problem is found in the field
of civil aviation. Here profiling is used in order to subject the members of groups who, on the basis of previous experience, are considered statistically more likely to pose a security risk, to more careful
examinations than others. Today the group most likely to be tar-

geted is Moslems. In the past, some airlines also included single women, because several were apprehended unknowingly carrying bombs, courtesy of their lovers.[53] Whatever else profiling may be, it is definitely not egalitarian. It discriminates, it humiliates, and in many cases, it delays. Opinions concerning whether it works are divided.[54] In the U.S., some attempts have been made to ban it. However, the Israeli airline EL Al, whose security is widely believed to be the best in the world, swears by it and uses it all the time. The process starts even before people enter the airport proper.

Supposing it does work, does that mean that, in the name of equality, we should not do whatever we can in order to prevent another 9/11? Or that we are going to pass everybody through the same exhaustive checks, making airport queues grow even longer than they are and possibly destroying the industry we are trying to protect? Former Homeland Security Undersecretary Asa Hutchinson's statement that profiling is based not on race but on country of origin did not help.[55] Even if accepted at face value, all it really meant was that discrimination is applied to one group rather than to another.

Paradoxically, but perhaps not surprisingly, in many ways the quest for equality is taking us back to times and places where people did not believe in it and may not have even heard of it or known what it meant. In some of those places they were prohibited from believing that there was no God. Now, in many of the self-proclaimed advanced countries, equality itself has been turned into the most jealous, and most vindictive, god of all. He may not demand bloody sacrifices and prayer, but he certainly requires certain forms of decorum and acceptance of dogma as well as an endless capacity for simulation, dissimulation, hypocrisy, and embracing one euphemism after another. Like the old one whose place he has taken he has his priests, his acolytes, and his executioners. Anyone who doubts Equality and thinks or speaks or writes or acts in ways that are perceived as contrary to his Holy Writ had better beware.

✳

The stated reason for many of the aforementioned anti-discrimination measures is to obtain equal rights for minorities. In the U.S., at any rate, blacks were originally meant. Later the term was broadened to cover many other groups. They now include women, homosexuals, Hispanics, the handicapped or disabled, the aged, and more. Hardly a month goes by without some other group demanding, and often receiving, recognition of its "minority" status. Other countries have targeted other groups. In Europe they are often Moslems, in India the Untouchables, in Japan the Eta who number three million and who until very recently were discriminated against in various ways.[56] In Australia, it is Asians, especially those coming from Moslem countries such as Pakistan, Afghanistan, and Bangladesh. The potential for expansion is near infinite. Simply doing one's best to avoid discriminating against this or that group is no longer enough. Some people are actually made to defend themselves, in court, for allegedly harboring a "subconscious bias."[57] As more groups joined the bandwagon, the numerical balance started tilting. All over the "advanced" world women now form the majority of the population, and with every passing day more countries are added to the list.[58] Since there are very few countries left in which women do not outlive men, the direction in which things are moving is beyond doubt. Add the other groups, and it is clear that "minorities" have turned into the majority.

The outcome is a new phenomenon known as reverse discrimination. Its targets are groups, usually white males, whose members were, at one time or another, perceived as the "dominant" ones. As the law has turned against them, with every passing day they are being made less equal than the rest.[59] Some countries, notably Britain, even have a "minister for equality." As of 2012 the portfolio was held by a woman. Her real job, taken straight out of *1984*, is to make sure men in general and able-bodied heterosexual ones in particular are discriminated against as much as possible. A brave new world is rapidly being built. Like it or not, it is the one in which our children and grandchildren will have to live.

Chapter 9

Brave New World

As of the second decade of the twenty-first century, much has changed on the equality front. Research into the possibility that people of different groups may have different mental qualities, and that these qualities may be due not to environmental factors but to genes and heredity, has been all but brought to an end.[1] Paradoxically this has happened exactly at the time when a new gene purported to govern some aspect of human behavior is being discovered almost every day. Many social scientists are now obliged to submit their projects to "ethics committees." Hence those who still dare to ask the relevant questions will run into difficulties even before they start. Research into the differences, biological and social, between the sexes is still permitted, but only on condition that the results favor women. Those whose findings indicate the opposite will find the road ahead filled with obstacles. One German author who tried to show the advantages that society afforded to women had his work rejected by no fewer than hundred-thirty-five publishers before it finally saw the light of print. Had we been living in a fair world, this should have earned him a place in the *Guinness Book of Records*. Research on homosexuals is as restricted as that on other groups. Woe the scientist who says they are different or that being gay is a disease! In many places looking for answers other than those dictated by current public opinion, or at any rate its self-styled "liberal" and "progressive" components, is prohibited. The intentions behind the prohibitions may often have been good, but we all know where they can lead.

The main difference remains the one between poor countries and rich. People in poor countries are usually too busy trying to survive and provide their children with some kind of future to worry about discrimination against this or that group. Often, too, there are so many groups that the term itself becomes meaningless. Where the state is weak and people belong to twenty different tribes speaking twenty different languages, who is equal to whom? Not so the citizens of rich countries. Right or wrong, most of them seem to believe that imposing equality is cheaper, economically and socially, than trying to maintain its opposite. To do so they have passed extensive legislation against discrimination. Additionally, there is affirmative action and reverse discrimination. Merriam-Webster defines affirmative action as "an active effort to improve the employment or educational opportunities of members of minority groups and women; also, a similar effort to promote the rights or progress of other disadvantaged persons." Dictionary.com defines reverse discrimination as "the unfair treatment of members of majority groups, resulting from preferential policies, as in college admissions or employment, intended to remedy earlier discrimination against minorities."[2] Affirmative action is utilized even when the groups in question have long ceased to be minorities.

The modern idea of equality is now almost four centuries old. By contrast, the notion that some classes of "disadvantaged" people should be treated equally with everybody else *and* be given special rights seems to be quite recent. Apparently the first group to which it was applied was American blacks. In June 1965 President Lyndon B. Johnson made his famous freedom speech. First he used statistics to show how "the great majority of Negro Americans" were "poor," "unemployed," "uprooted," and "dispossessed." In spite of recent court orders, laws and legislative victories, "for them the walls are rising and the gulf is widening." To fix things, "equal opportunity is essential, but not enough…. You do not take a man who for years has been hobbled by chains, liberate him, bring him to the starting line of a race, saying, 'you are free to compete with all the others,' and still justly believe you have been completely fair. … We seek not just freedom but opportunity—not just legal equity but human ability—not just equality as a right and a theory, but equality as a fact and as a result."[3]

The speech was part of the President's plan, announced thirteen months earlier, to create a "Great Society." In that society "every citizen," "Negroes" specifically included, would enjoy "the full equality which God enjoins and the law requires, whatever his belief, or race, or the color of his skin" as well as be helped to find "an escape from the crushing weight of poverty."[4] To the old idea of civic and political equality was added that of equal opportunity—one that in many ways is unprecedented in history. The timing appeared as propitious as it could be. The U.S. was flourishing like no nation before or since. Economic growth was steady, inflation moderate, unemployment way down. The War in Southeast Asia was already under way, but it had not yet developed into the all-devouring cancer it was to become during the next few years. To quote a visiting German journalist, "utopia and reality seemed to coincide."[5] Taking a minority of about eleven percent of the population by the hand so as to enable each person to "become whatever his qualities of mind and spirit would permit" did not seem impossible either economically, socially, or politically.

The signal having been given by the single most powerful person on earth, equality of opportunity began its march of conquest. As has so often been the case, one of the first groups to which the policy was applied was children. Often this was not because parents wanted it but because the government had mandated it; also, because children have few rights and could not resist. That in turn enabled all sorts of educators, supervisors, consultants, politicians and legislators to experiment with them and have a field day at their expense. To create a proper racial mixture at school, students were bused around for hours each day. Sometimes students of different races were compelled to sit next to one another. This was equality with a vengeance, except that it did not work. It did not work because forcing students to attend schools they did not want to attend was seen as degrading by those at the top and those at the bottom alike. It did not work because, in most cases, instead of those at the top pulling the bottom-most upwards, the opposite happened. It also did not work because the parents of those at the top, realizing what was happening, moved their children from public schools into private ones. Since doing was expensive, often it made the more equal more equal still.

For good or ill, adults could not be treated as the children were. But they could be, and often were, subjected to many other forms of reverse discrimination. Often this was done in the name of "diversity." The invention of the term itself reflected the fact that, instead of one group demanding special rights for itself, there were now many. In deciding whom to enroll, universities started imposing admission-quotas on some and giving extra points to others. Either out of their own free will or, perhaps more often, because the government had ordered them to, some employers started doing the same. Traditionally those who held a disproportionate number of good positions and run the country had been white, male and heterosexual. Now, being white, male and heterosexual gradually became a handicap. It meant being pushed to the back of the queue behind blacks, Hispanics, women, homosexuals, and if at all practical, the disabled as well. To achieve equality in the future, what equality existed in the present was sacrificed. As Supreme Justice Harry Blackmun put it in *Regents of the University of California vs. Bakke* (1978), "in order to get beyond racism we must first take account of race."

Like Blackmun himself, those responsible for enacting the relevant laws and supervising the process were, almost without exception, members of the upper or at least upper-middle classes. They were well educated, lived in expensive neighborhoods, and had their children attend good schools. They had good jobs and good incomes. Their positions were safely beyond the reach of most minority groups, ethnic ones in particular, whom they claimed to be helping improve their condition. Thus the burden of achieving diversity was not uniformly, or at least widely, distributed over society as a whole. Instead it was thrust primarily onto the shoulders of one particular group. Its members were elderly, blue collar, and male. In the recession that started in 2008, one out of six blue collar jobs disappeared.[6] With union membership much lower than in previous decades, the men had no one to represent them. To cite George Orwell once again, people who fall into any of these three categories have been turned into unpersons.

Taking their cue from the U.S., many other countries have followed suit. While the details differ from one place to another, everywhere growing numbers of people are being screened for such things as race, sex, sexual orientation, and age. Quotas have been established and must be filled. Now equality was manipulated to favor the less equal, now the more equal. An excellent case in point is the Universities of Sweden, a country famous for its high principles as well as the omnipresent and often fatuous bureaucracy that implements them.[7] Years ago, to ensure that women could enroll in equal numbers with men, Sweden imposed gender quotas on many programs. This caused many men with high grades to be denied places because the courses were filled with women. The system worked in both directions. Men received priority in fields where they were under-represented such as veterinary medicine, dentistry, medicine and psychology; as a result, women with high grades were denied places already occupied by men. How intolerable! Following a suit by thirty-one women, the system was abolished in order to enable more women to enter those fields. Does this sound confusing? It most certainly is! The one certain fact is that, as soon as gender equality begins to favor men in some regard, it is rapidly modified in order to favor women again and things are thus made unequal once again.

Another example is Germany. By law, at least a third of the Bundestag seats must be filled by women, but there is no provision against the possibility, which was actually realized in Swedish universities, that more women than men will be elected. Thus a woman who wants to run for one of those seats operates in a less crowded field than men who, if they want to fill one of the remaining two-thirds of seats open to them, must compete against both women *and* men. This is one reason why female politicians in Germany, Chancellor Angela Merkel herself included, tend to reach the Bundestag faster than their male colleagues. In other words, being a woman

automatically means being put on the fast track—with all the ad
vantages and disadvantages, such as less time for one's own life, that
such a track entails.[8] German political parties also have quotas for
women. An exception to the rule is the Free Democratic Party.
Liberal in outlook, it opposes quotas as a matter of principle and
prefers to reach gender equity by different methods. The result has
been that women started leaving the Party in unprecedented numbers. And quite rightly so: anybody who prefers a Party in which
she is equal to one in which she is more so must be out of her mind.

Among the latest to join the bandwagon is Brazil.[9] The country
has had anti-discrimination legislation since the 1950s. The Constitution of 1988 criminalized both racial abuse and racism. The rum-
blings that have been heard in recent years probably have something
to do with the country's growing prosperity and rising per capita income. They are making people think about problems they had previously ignored. In the census of 2010 just over half of Brazilians
defined themselves as black or brown. As in most other countries
outside Africa, blacks are relatively disadvantaged when it comes to
such things as access to education and health services. Whereas over
half of the people who live in the slums of Rio de Janeiro are black,
only seven percent of those who live in the city's richer districts are.
Black and brown incomes lag far behind white ones.[10] Brazilians
have long known these facts perfectly well. However, they explained
them away by saying that it was a question of class, not race, and
that unlike North Americans, Brazilians are not and never have been
racist. Though slavery was only abolished in 1888, many of Brazil's
blacks had already been free. Nor did Brazil ever pass Jim Crow
legislation of the kind so prevalent in the U.S. The absence of segregation, at any rate legal segregation, explains why there is so much
mixing of the races.

Understandably, people at the bottom of the social heap tend to be less convinced by this argument than those at the top. Opinions as to what should be done about the gap, if anything, also differ. Some worry that putting in place affirmative action programs, by requiring that each person define himself as belonging to one race or another, will do more to foster racism than to end discrimination. Others respond that pretending the problem does not exist is no way to solve it. As usual, the first to feel the impact is the education system, in this case the universities. As in other countries this may have something to do with the feeling that, compared with government on one hand and business on the other, the universities do not matter much. Whatever wild experiments are made will only affect the young who are still in a liminal stage and have not yet become full members of society.

Starting in 2001 more than seventy public universities have introduced admission standards designed to make the less equal more so and the more equal, less so. For example, at Rio de Janeiro's state university twenty percent of slots are reserved for blacks and another twenty-five percent for the scions of families whose income is less than twice the minimum wage. Of the latter many, though not all, are black. Never mind that, since nobody knows exactly what "black" means, the kind of equality that is aimed at is often meaningless. In one notorious case involving two identical twins, one was classified as white, the other as black.

Again as in other countries, the next target is the labor market. Both public and private employers are starting to move in this direction by instituting quotas and other measures intended to promote "diversity." Compared to the U.S., Brazil has the great advantage that it is less centralized. Most pressure for affirmative action comes from below, not from above. That means that those who are being subject to reverse discrimination can often, though of course not always, find ways to buck the system. In other words, there exist in that system some safety-valves that the U.S. does not have. Another advantage is that many judges seem to think that the penalties for racism are much too harsh. As a result, to adapt a German proverb, the soup is not eaten as hot as it is cooked.

For good or ill, it is clear that the old meaning of equality no longer applies. In many ways the quest for it is causing it to be turned into its opposite. To make some people more equal others are systematically being made less so. This process has given rise to many new questions no previous society has ever had to confront. In the past decisions as to what to study, which university to choose, and what kind of work to do were based on one's free preference while taking into consideration the available means. Do we really want a different kind of society in which such decisions will reflect the need, and ability, to suit all kinds of regulations many of which are so complex that even those who made them do not understand them? One in which politics, which ultimately govern the regulations, will weasel their way into the most individual and most everyday decisions? And isn't there a danger that, as diversity causes peoples and nations to break up into their component groups, each of which only thinks about how to obtain its own privileges at the expense of all the rest, equality will become as meaningless as it has been during most of history and still is in many developing countries?

The largest "minority" consists of women. As a result, "gender equality" may well represent the most difficult problem of all. At stake are not some marginal adjustments but the creation of an entirely new society with no historical precedent whatsoever. It used to be said that, to get ahead, a woman must be much better than

any man (some added that, fortunately, that was not very difficult).
Now in many cases things work the other way around. In many
countries, the advanced ones in particular, men are being systematically discriminated against from infancy on.[11] Again, the worst
offender is Sweden. The life of Swedish men is being made intolerable by whole series of laws specifically designed to put them in their
"proper" place.[12]

In large part this is probably because, certainly as far as Western
countries are concerned, ours is the most peaceful period in history.
One's chances of dying in war have become very small indeed. Under such conditions women no longer need men to protect them
as they always have. Men, a minority, are finding themselves with
their backs up against the wall. But how long will men's lamb-like
acquiescence with their new status in which women have all the
privileges and they bear all the burdens last? Will they go on strike,
refusing to study, work, marry, and have children, as some already
do?[13] Will they rise in rebellion? May some of them not feel compelled to use the one quality in which their superiority over women
is undisputed, namely, physical force?

There are signs that this is beginning to happen. A Google.com
search for "rape on the rise" yielded 435,000 hits. Another one
for "domestic violence" yielded no fewer than 41,000,000. Every country from Argentina to Zimbabwe is on the list. Even in a
peaceful country such as Norway, according to the responsible minister, "more women are affected by domestic violence ... than are
affected by cancer, motor accidents, war and malaria."[14] In fact, a
woman who suffers nothing worse than rape and domestic violence
may count herself fortunate. Among some categories of American
women, being murdered by a man with whom they have been ac-
quainted is now the leading cause of death.[15] In Sweden, which

considers itself a world leader in all that pertains to gender equality, one out of three women who meets a violent end is killed by her past or present male partner. Some men have turned women-bashing into a cult. They actually prefer to have sex with animals than with Swedish women—a practice sufficiently common to given rise to legislation aimed at banning it.[16]

Feminists claim that violence against women is due the persistent "fundamental inequality" between the sexes and to their being "dehumanized" by those bad, bad, men (many of whom they had earlier chosen as their partners in life and in bed). In doing so they are following the ideas of Konrad Lorenz (1903–1989), an Austrian Nobel-Prize winning ethologist who earlier in life had been a Nazi Party member and a Hitler supporter. He theorized that, to kill others of their own species, people must "dehumanize" them first. Is it possible that, to the contrary, it is men who have begun to be "dehumanized" and suffer from "fundamental inequality"? That recent trends reflect growing male resentment against the countless privileges women have been given and are still being given every day? One thing appears certain: if this trend continues and intensifies, as it well may, then surely we shall have changed the Devil for Beelzebub.

✳

Throughout history, success has usually gone to those who were motivated, energetic, intelligent, and, truth to be said, not entirely without means. In 1989–1991, the communist attempt to put everyone on the same basis with respect to their means collapsed under its own weight. Yet this failure, colossal as it was, has not deterred some from continuing to advocate it and experiment with it. We live in an age where no regime is deemed legitimate unless it is democratic. That is why even many of those that are nothing of the kind call themselves "Peoples' Republics." Putting the poor aside, why should not the dumb, the lazy, and the lackadaisical succeed like anyone else? After all, no one is to blame for the qualities he or she was born with. If we are going to iron out, as far as we can, differences of race and gender, why should we not do the same with respect to other personal qualities too?

In a sense, people have always tried to improve on whatever qualities nature had given them. To hide their physical defects they invented clothes. To improve their looks they modified their hairstyles or, if they did not have hair, put on wigs. They applied cosmetics, wore tons of jewelry, and much more. Nero's wife Poppaea Sabina used to take a daily bath in she-asses' milk. Success was limited and she ended up dead after he kicked her in her pregnant belly.[17] Somewhat later, the encyclopedist Pliny accused Roman women of bankrupting the empire by spending 100,000,000 sesterces a year to import choice perfumes from as far away as Arabia, India, and China.[18] Countless other women of all ages, especially those married to the powerful and the rich, spent fortunes trying to improve themselves so as to fend off younger and better-looking competitors.

Overall men may not have used cosmetics as often as women did. However, at least until the first half of the nineteenth century, when the drab business suit started its triumphant march of conquest, they were in no way behind women in other respects. Kings and emperors spent fortunes on jewelry. Louis XIV's wardrobe was at least as expensive as that of any of his mistresses. People of both sexes also did what they could to improve their personal qualities such as strength, stamina, memory, and the like. To overcome his congenital speaking defect, the Athenian orator Demosthenes practiced with pebbles in his mouth. The number of self-help books on the market must run into the thousands if not more. Currently the field is being computerized and made "interactive."[19] To this long list modern medicine has added plastic surgery. Had Oliver Cromwell been alive today, then instead of reminding his painter not to omit his warts he might have asked a dermatologist to excise them. Fat can be removed from many parts of the body. Breasts can be enlarged or reduced. Hairlines can be moved back so that foreheads appear larger. Noses can be re-sculpted, lips made larger or smaller, faces lifted. Eyelids can be lifted and the shape of the eyes themselves changed, as in the case of Asian women who want to look more Western.[20] There is hardly any part of the body the scalpel cannot improve.

Much of this is done in the name of inequality. Some people want not only to be more equal than others but to look it, too. One author speaks of enhancing what she calls "erotic capital."[21] Erotic capital, she explains, is what makes some people, especially women, so much more attractive than others. It gives those who have it a huge advantage in life. Much of the erotic capital one has, like most other forms of capital, is congenital. If the above methods can be used to help some people become more equal than they were, why not also use them to make those who are less than equal more so? During most of history being able to purchase fine clothes, or wear jewelry, or apply cosmetics, or go for all kinds of aesthetic surgery, was a question of wealth above all. As far as the first three are concerned this remains the case today. Nobody in his or her sound mind proposes that "unattractive" people be subsidized so they can buy themselves better and more expensive clothing. But come to think of it, why not?

Already today many people believe they have the right to cosmetic surgery so as to improve their "erotic capital." The U.S. apart, most modern countries have state-run, compulsory, medical insurance schemes. They will pick up the tab of all "medically necessary" procedures. That includes the repair of congenital physiological defects. But where should one draw the line between medically necessary procedures and pure cosmetic surgery? Is elective eye surgery that will remove a person's cataract, thus enabling him to do without glasses and become more attractive, "medically necessary"? How about women who, having given birth, are left with protruding inner vulva lips which they feel makes them unattractive and diminishes their self-confidence and erotic capital? How about a person born with a cleft palate and harelip?

A medical problem of this sort will certainly not lead to a person's death nor even cause him or her to be sick. To that extent, fixing it is not strictly "necessary." Yet when people meet strangers the first thing they look for is symmetry in the face.[22] A cleft palate can also make it almost impossible to speak clearly. Such a person will be at a disadvantage in forging social ties, finding work, attracting a mate, and so on. Probably women will be at an even greater disadvantage than men with the same deformity, thus making the problem even more complicated. How many corrective operations and hours of speech therapy should he or she be entitled to? Should men and women receive the same amount, or should women be entitled to special privileges? At what point does the problem cease to be physiological and start being psychological? And don't those who, owing to the psychological problems from which they suffer, find it hard to accumulate "erotic capital," deserve to be treated just as physically unwell people are?

Patients and bureaucrats will likely dispute the extent to which people are entitled to be made less unequal by such methods. If the bureaucrats do not give way, patients may, and quite often do, sue them in order to obtain the services they have been denied. This seemingly absurd future is already here. In Ontario, Canada, Medicare will not only cover the cost of correcting a harelip but also that of operating upon children whose ears stick out "too much."[23] Once some patients have got their foot in the door of corrective surgery, others will surely follow. Why not fix other aesthetic blemishes as well, and why only those of children? In Denmark, cosmetic surgery is so popular that one in eight people have undergone it. At least twice as many are actively considering it. One reason for this is that the public system pays. The most common procedures are eyelid surgery, breast reduction, and obesity surgery. The figures are growing all the time. Sooner or later a halt will have to be called. Until that happens, both surgeons and patients are having a ball.[24]

Taking Britain as our example, both men and women, but more women than men, are persuading doctors to perform free cosmetic surgery by explaining how unhappy they are with their looks and how much improving those looks could contribute to their psychic welfare. Common operations include tummy tucks, breast implants and nose jobs. Patients refuse to accept no for an answer and dramatize their problems. Please help me, Sir, or else my husband will no longer consider me attractive! Surgeons respond by operating without waiting for psychologists and psychiatrists to give the green light as the regulations of the National Health Service require. Later, filling in the necessary forms, they describe the job they did in such a way that will make the authorities happy. All this causes the number of "unnecessary" procedures to soar. There are no official figures on the sums spent or, depending on one's point of view, misspent, in this way. Clearly, however, they must be very considerable.[25]

If drawing the line in the case of physical handicaps is hard, doing the same in respect to mental ones is much more difficult still. In any society there will be large numbers of people who suffer from various mental problems that will render them less able to compete than others. Such problems are as likely to turn "equal opportunity" into a mockery as physical disabilities and socio-economic differences are, perhaps more. Do they deserve to be treated at the expense of the state? Precisely which mental problems are incapacitating, which ones are not, and what does "incapacitating" mean? And how should one factor in the effort the patient does or does not make? After all, the strongest will in the world cannot correct a problem such as ears that stick out and, by making their owner look foolish, prevent him or her from getting ahead in life. However, in treating some other dysfunction, such as drug addiction or alcoholism, the situation is different. Willpower is certain to play some role even though doctors cannot agree among themselves just how important it is in relation to other factors. Does that mean uncooperative patients deserve less treatment than cooperative ones? Or perhaps things should be organized the other way around?

Even that is not the end of the matter. For several decades now some people, especially schizophrenics and manic-depressives, have been given compulsory psycho-pharmaceutical medication. Others are injected with hormones to increase this drive or decrease that. Some people are treated inside the institutions to which they have been committed. Others must take it as a condition for being released from them. The objective is to prevent them from harming themselves and others. Is it possible to imagine a policy that will also compel people to take such products in order to make them more able to compete in society, in other words put them in a position where equal opportunity, instead of being a mere illusion, will be real? A policy, for example, that will oblige a person to increase his powers of concentration by swallowing a pill to prevent him from becoming a burden on society?

At first sight the question appears to be preposterous. However, the fact is that children, the most vulnerable group of all, have been subjected to this kind of thing for years. I am referring to the cocaine-related drug Ritalin. A stimulant sometimes known as "the chemical cosh," it is used to treat children who supposedly suffer from ADHD. Some see it as simply as a method which bad teachers have enlisted to make their bored students sit still. Legally speaking, schools in most countries cannot force a child's parents to have their child take it. In practice, on pain of being re-classified and sent to "special education" schools, hundreds of thousands if not millions of children in many countries are being compelled to do so. The authorities in Orwell's own country have even given serious consideration to imprisoning parents who did not comply.[26]

What comes next? Compulsory hormonal treatment for those who have more testosterone than others and are perceived as aggressive and/or sexually dangerous, perhaps? That is old hat. In Kuwait some years ago, officials said that two dozen men arrested at a homosexual party during which some of them dressed as women might have to undergo such a procedure. What became of the matter is not clear.[27] Nazi-style sterilization may have gone out of fashion. However, a number of countries have resorted to chemical castration, at least on an experimental basis. The side effects may be severe, but the procedure has the advantage that it is said to be reversible.[28] Obligatory abortions? Recent advances in medicine have made available dozens of so-called pregnancy screening tests that can be applied to fetuses to discover possible abnormalities. They range from cleft palates to Down's Syndrome and from spina bifida to various chromosomal abnormalities.[29]

Once a problem has been diagnosed it is up to the women themselves to decide whether or not to terminate the pregnancy. Again
with the exception of the U.S., most advanced countries offer both
the tests and the abortion itself for free. But what about women
who, for religious or other reasons, refuse to take them? And what
happens to a fetus that is found to be severely abnormal but which
the mother, for whatever reason, refuses to abort? Should she be
coerced? *E chi paga*, as the Italians say? Who pays? When such an
abnormal child is born, who will pay for the necessary corrective
medical procedures, the years of special education required, and the
institution in which it may have to spend its life? How severe must
an abnormality be to justify an abortion? How severe must it be to
justify a compulsory one? Who decides, and on the basis of what
procedures? To date no country seems to have made abortions obligatory. Yet insurers, both public and private, clearly have an interest
in the matter. Considering the magnitude of recent social changes,
the possibility is far from unimaginable.

The decision to "take care" of those considered too inferior to
serve the *Volksgemeinschaft* was made by Hitler personally in con-
sultation with the chief of his chancellery, Philip Bouhler, and his
favorite physician, Dr. Karl Brandt.[30] Reluctant though they are to
admit the fact, many modern societies are confronted with the same
problem. Now that they are able to judge the fitness of the unborn
some of them may well end up by adopting the same solution, if
they have not secretly done so already. Officially, though, they have
moved in the opposite direction. Instead of improving the community by getting rid of its "inferior" members, they try mandatory
treatment to enable those members to join the community. In some
societies, and for some of the unequal, this is not utopia but everyday reality. The number of those involved is growing very rapidly.

In Britain, according to the government's own statistics, the number of prescribed Ritalin pills rose from 2.5 billion in 2001 to 19.2 billion in 2006.[31] Once again, what we are talking about is forcing those whom society regards as less than equal to become more so.

At present, most of those affected are children. Yet as attempts to add fluoride to drinking water shows, in principle no man and no woman is safe from the clutches of teachers, administrators, physicians, drug-manufacturers, and insurers. Each for their own reasons, they have a vested interest in making all of us conform to certain, often extremely ill-defined, mental and physical standards. Many are doing their utmost to achieve that goal. How far this kind of thing will be taken in the future remains to be seen.

※

In principle, from repairing people or testing them for various defects and discarding those who do not measure up to designing them *ex novo* it is a relatively short step. From Plato on, many utopian writers have suggested breeding people on eugenic lines just as we do with horses and dogs. But humans are more complex than animals. The mix of desirable qualities is more difficult to define. Except in places like Plato's Republic, where they were made to disappear "in darkness and unmentionability," and in Nazi Germany, where they were killed, getting rid of undesirables is also a little harder.[32]

Instead of selective breeding, may it one day become possible to design people by directly interfering with their genes? Among the first to consider this possibility was Aldous Huxley in *Brave New World*. Huxley planned to become a physician, but a disease that made him half blind forced him to switch careers. That did not prevent him from keeping abreast with the medical science of his day. In the book, design was used not to make everybody equal but, on the contrary, to make them unequal. The objective was to make them fit smoothly into the roles society had destined them for. For example, those destined to repair rockets in outer space might be so conditioned that they would feel really comfortable only when standing on their heads. Round pegs into round holes, was the motto. Yet as a character in the novel says, in principle it was perfectly possible to use the same techniques to make everybody equal. In fact the experiment was tried. The outcome was a war of all against all in which most participants were killed.[33] Had Hobbes been able to read the book, he would not have been surprised.

Producing babies to order on assembly-lines without a human mother remains a distant dream, or perhaps a nightmare. But modifying them genetically to achieve this or that objective is becoming a distinct possibility. It is being done with many kinds of farm-animals, and the potential seems limitless. Scientists have produced worms that lived six times as long as their unmodified comrades. Others have engineered mice with formidable powers of learning and memory. Some years ago, a fertilized rabbit-egg had a gene from a jellyfish injected into it. The resulting rabbit gave off a green-ish glow and was called, appropriately enough, Alba (Dawn).[34] So why not use a similar procedure to make the less equal equal? Genetic manipulation might produce individuals who are immune to certain diseases. As with Huxley, they would be more suitable for living and working in certain regions and climates, thus overcoming any handicaps they may have. It might also make people stronger, or more intelligent, or increase their memory and their ability to concentrate, or make them live longer. Since the goal is equality, surely everybody deserves a shot at it?

Conversely, would-be parents, if there are still any left, will be able to choose a son or daughter who is as wise as Plato, or as mathematically gifted as Albert Einstein, or as strong as Arnold Schwarzenegger, or as sexy as Marilyn Monroe. They might even—who can foresee the limits of human folly?—go for one as wicked as Adolf Hitler. After all, there are plenty of people who worship the Fuehrer. They would like nothing better than having him around and putting him in charge. Though he could not fully imagine the achievements of modern technology, Ira Levin in his 1976 novel, *The Boys from Brazil*, described just such an effort. Insofar as the DNA of dead cows has been used to clone new ones, in principle at any rate even that age-old dream, physical immortality, no longer appears out of reach.[35] Many animals, including sheep, cows, and dogs, have been cloned already. An individual could be cloned and the fertilized egg placed inside the womb of a surrogate mother. Next he or she would be born for the second time. The process could be repeated as often as desired.

Suppose treatments of this kind become feasible and somewhat affordable, who receives them? Who decides? On the basis of what rules? To date, the first tourists in space were chosen from among the rich and the powerful. The former are able to pay for privilege. The latter will find some reason why those in charge should allow them to jump the queue. The same is almost certain to happen in the case of genetic manipulation. In fact it may have happened already. Stories about eccentric billionaires who had themselves cloned in some secret clinic in South Korea or the Middle East crop up from time to time. The cost is supposed to be $80,000. Not exactly a bargain, but well within the reach of many people around the world.[36] So far all appear to be fraudulent. But the day will come when one of them turns out to be genuine.

The point is, in this day and age, people believe they have the right to be equal. Not only legally and politically, as liberals used to demand; nor simply socioeconomically, as the socialists did; but in many other ways as well. If the rich and the powerful can have something, shouldn't the poor and the powerless have it too? Doesn't the doctrine of equal opportunity entitle them to have their offspring or, in case of cloning, themselves, made immune to AIDS even before they are born? Or to have blond hair and blue eyes and a height of over six feet tall? Or to be equipped with the highest IQ that medical science can give them? What future genetic engineer will resist the pleas of a mother who, although she has a tin ear and no money, is desperate to have a child as musical as Mozart? Filling in the necessary forms to obtain authorization and payment, surely the engineer will say that having such a child is essential to the mother's welfare. Left without, she might die ("languish," is the old term for this). If he can claim a nice fee for effort made, so much the better.

As so often, the "final" outcome will depend in large part on the cost. The treatments in question are unlikely to become as cheap as Ritalin. However, they may well come to carry a price-tag comparable to that of some kinds of plastic surgery. If so, then they may indeed lead to a world of the kind described by the English science-fiction writer H. G. Wells in his 1923 novel, *Men Like Gods*.[37] In the novel, a few Englishmen accidentally land in a different world populated by utopians. Following a series of discoveries in "physiological and psychological science," they have acquired "extraordinary possibilities of control" over their own bodies as well as social life. Science having learnt "to discriminate among births," almost everybody is energetic, sanguine, creative, receptive and good-tempered. Those who are not have died out or are dying out. As Wells specifically says, utopians know neither kindness nor mercy. In a world where everybody is perfectly equal such qualities are not required.

All children are born to perfectly healthy mothers. They grow up under perfectly healthy conditions, receive a perfectly good education, and form a perfect race of "stark Apollos."

The utopians have no private property and no classes—everybody helps everybody else with everything. The desire to dominate others "has been bred out of [them] by long centuries of equality and free cooperation." They have no politics, no government, and no special class of people in whose hands authority is concentrated. All they have is "a number of intelligences directed to the general psychology of the race and to the interaction of one collective function upon another." Yet these intelligences "rank no higher, and have no more precedence, than anybody else." Authority, based exclusively on expertise, "has been diffused back into the general body of the community." Political activity has "melted into the general body of criticism and discussion." And how about those who do not conform to the community's rules? They had better give their reasons and the reasons had better be good. If not, their mental state will be examined; the doctor has taken the place of the policeman.

Returning to our own world, perhaps the benefits of advances, past, present and future, of "physiological and psychological science" will be capable of being shared by all. However, in the more likely event they are limited to a few, the very idea of equality will be blown sky high. After all, most of humanity has lived without it for thousands of years before its modern conception was invented less than four hundred years ago. Since the middle of the nineteenth century to the middle of the twentieth, equality was narrowly confined to the members of the white races. Only since about 1900 on did it begin to be extended to women, and only since 1965 on was it interpreted in the sense of equality of opportunity. For most of human history, it was neither self-evident nor universally held to be true. Is it too fanciful to suggest that, in view of continuing advances in medical science, some new kind of hierarchy in which a race of genetically modified supermen and superwomen will lord it over the cattle-like majority may one day emerge?

*

Partly because minorities have turned into majorities and vice versa, partly because of advances in medical science, the world in which we live is a brave and new one indeed. The game of musical chairs being played by minorities and majorities is rooted in politics, including reverse discrimination, affirmative action, the idea of equal opportunity, and ultimately modern democracy itself. It may last, causing all societies to look somewhat like present-day Sweden and, to cite Francis Fukuyama, bringing about the End of History. However, other possibilities also exist. One is that the societies in question will be undermined from within by groups who have different ideas concerning women's equality in particular and whose birth rate is much higher than that of the rest. Already immigrants from poor countries pose a huge challenge to every single advanced country in which they have settled. Those challenges will only increase in the future. Another possibility is that ongoing developments will give rise to so much discontent, especially among men, as to result in armed rebellion and blow democracy itself sky-high. The two scenarios may be combined. Historically speaking, rare is the ruling class that has given up its privileges without a bloody fight.

Advances in genetic science raise all kinds of possibilities so dazzling, and so terrifying, as to make one's head reel. And we have yet to mention the possibility of creating cyborgs. Cyborgs are creatures, if that is the correct word, which are part human, part machine. Experiments in this direction are being made all the time, and they are bearing fruit. If eyes, ears, arms and legs can be repaired or enhanced, why not brains? The question is where such developments are leading. Will some people, who are genetically modified or have computer chips implanted in their brains, become more godlike than others? If so, what will be the fate of the less godlike? Will they share the fate of the Neanderthals who, many believe, were exterminated by the Cro-Magnons? Or will everyone become equally godlike? If so, will the godlike live peacefully together with "authority diffused among all" as Wells, and long before him, Rousseau, believed they would? Or will everybody live equally under the control of a vast computer that will trace not just his or her location and credit, as Wells suggests, but every thought and every feeling as well? Or will equality recreate a Hobbesian state of nature, causing civilization to collapse around its members' ears? The future alone will tell.

Chapter 10

Death and Beyond

Spectacular as recent advances in genetic science are, the time when some of us are granted eternal life does not appear to be around the corner. Even if it is, death will not really be eliminated. Rather, a person who undergoes cloning will have his or her DNA taken and implanted in an egg. The egg will then be implanted in some womb other than that of the person's original mother, enabling him, or rather a perfect copy of him, to be borne and born for the second time. Yet it is only the body that will be replicated. Whatever the mind has learnt and experienced from the moment of birth on will be irretrievably lost. The day may come when, to overcome this problem, all learnt material can be stored in a computer while the person in question is still alive. Later it will be transferred to his or her clone. The two techniques combined may well give us physical and spiritual immortality, or rather the chance of being resurrected as often as we want. If not enough women agree to lend their wombs for the purpose, perhaps we can use incubators instead. At that point Huxley's vision will really have become true. Even so, we shall not be saved from undergoing physical and spiritual death.

Suppose the necessary techniques are perfected, will they be equally available to everybody? Or will they be limited to those who can pay? If not, will there be committees which, on the basis of the appropriate guidelines, will determine who is going to be cloned and who will have to suffer his or her DNA being eradicated forever? These are questions we cannot yet answer. Many of us will not even want to see them answered. Yet insofar as decisions must be made concerning who is to be put on life support, for how long, and at the expense of whom, they are already being made on an everyday basis.

Speculation aside, in any kind of society at all times and places death, along with birth, was considered the most important event in the life of every individual. Here it is necessary to distinguish between those who died unexpectedly and those who were aware, perhaps for quite some time, of death's approach. For the former the moment they knew they were dying was the same in which they ceased to know. For the latter, their relatives and perhaps others as well, there was time to make preparations.

Nowadays most people die in hospital or in some kind of similar public institution. That means that differences between individuals can only be so great. Some get a private room, others just a bed that is separated from the rest by no more than a curtain. To quote the late filmmaker Peter Sellers, often the only ones present are a variety of "ping-making machines." Until not so long ago things were very different. Only the very poor went to the hospital to die. The rest remained in their homes. Normally, the wealthier and the more powerful an individual, the more people would attend his deathbed and the more prolonged and the more elaborate the preparations made. Some died in a palace, others in a hovel. However rich or modest the surroundings, death was a public occasion, Then, as now, prominent persons often prepared their obituaries long before they were needed. Inequality in front of death continued just as it had previously prevailed in life.

Yet there is another sense in which death is, and always has been, the great equalizer. In the words of the Old Testament: "For that which befalleth the sons of men befalleth beasts; even one thing befalleth them; as the one dieth, so dieth the other; yea, they have all one breath; so that a man hath no preeminence above a beast; for all is vanity. All go unto one place; all are of the dust, and all turn to dust."[1] During the late middle ages and the early modern period the *danse macabre* was a favorite subject for artists.[2] It is found in murals, stained-glass windows, illuminated manuscripts, early printed books, and sculptures. Though forms changed, the theme continued to provide inspiration right down into the nineteenth century. Some of the best known Romantic composers, such as Franz Schubert, Franz Liszt and Camille Saint Saëns put it to music.

Typically those who created the images and wrote the music tried to show the entire hierarchy of life. It started with pope and emperor and led through cardinal, king, baron, merchant and peasant all the way down to beggar. Both men and women, both the old and the young, were included. Neither the rich nor the poor, neither the beautiful nor the ugly, were spared as they were swept away by a skeleton or skeletons armed with scythes. However, here and there death is represented by an archer who unerringly hits his targets. Some skeletons lead their victims away on a leash, and some are mounted. Yet the point the artists wish to make is always the same: however high the position of some, and low that of others, before death they are all equal.

That being the case, preparations for death were often specifically designed to place the dying on an equal basis. This was done by reducing them to the lowest common denominator. Prior to dying, people lost all their functions, posts and possessions. Either they surrendered them out of their own free will or else, if they were facing execution, they had them taken away. In Paris near the Cathedral of Notre Dame tourists can visit the Conciergerie, the prison where those sentenced to be guillotined during the Great Terror were kept.[3] Among those who spent time there was Queen Marie-Antoinette. On display is a sad collection of some of the prisoners' last belongings; family souvenirs, letters, small items of dress, and the like. Having left everything but the clothes on their backs behind, they were loaded on a cart and driven to the Place de la Concorde. At that point they were equal indeed, the only remaining distinction being the one between those at the head of the queue and those awaiting their turn. To speak with Job, "naked I came from my mother's womb, and naked shall I return."[4]

Nor was this kind of thing always limited to material possessions alone. In some of the Christian traditions those who were about to die were supposed to confess their sins, ask forgiveness, and repent. They might also receive the Eucharist and be anointed with Holy Oil. No doubt some ceremonies were more elaborate, others much less so. Some had an archbishop to help them pass away, others just a simple parish priest. Yet the objective was always the same. However high or low the position a person had occupied during his life, he had to be stripped free of sin. People were supposed to die with their souls wiped clean. Though there were some exceptions, normally this benefit was awarded even to criminals. Once again, equality reigned.

In the case of both ordinary death and executions, this kind of equality only prevails for a relatively short time before life comes to an end. However, there do exist two kinds of organizations whose *raison d'etre* is precisely to prepare people to die if necessary; namely, monasteries on one hand and armed forces on the other. In the former the symbols, designed to remind the inmates that death will spare neither the highest nor the lowest, are everywhere. In some Buddhist monasteries they include the bones of large animals such as tigers, lions and elephants.[5] In Christian ones they may include somber colors, coffins, human skulls, graphic representations of the afterlife, and much else. Many Christian monasteries also display slogans such as *tempus fugit* (time flies) or *memento mori* (remember death). The objective may be to remind the monks that, since death is universal, inevitable and not very far away, they should regulate their conduct accordingly and overcome their fear of it.

Even less than monks, who after all lead an orderly life, are soldiers, especially those on campaign, in a position to know exactly when death may be coming at them. Not knowing when their time will come, it is necessary to ensure, as far as possible, they will be ready to face it at all times. The methods used for the purpose could easily fill a separate book.[6]

When focusing on the question of equality, we are facing a paradox. Since ancient times, no organizations have been more hierarchical, more disciplined, more unequal, than armies. Some men are field marshals, far more are mere privates. Napoleon's claim that every soldier carried a marshal's baton in his knapsack very seldom turned out to be true. In general, the stronger the military hierarchy is, the better the army. Thucydides says that the Spartan army was exceptional because the large number of officers made it possible to transmit orders quickly from the top to the bottom.[7] The Roman army was famous for its discipline. When a unit had shown cowardice in battle the troops were lined up. Lots were used to select one man out of every ten. Those who drew the wrong number were stoned or bludgeoned to death by their comrades.[8] All this is done to ensure that there should be no confusion as to who issues orders and who obeys them and carries them out. When danger threatens and death is harvesting people on every side, equality and democracy are the last things we want.

However, as the common use of lots shows, there is another aspect to the matter. If men are to put their life in jeopardy, it is essential that they be treated fairly. Fair treatment implies equality, at least of a certain kind. To repeat, no army can do without a strong hierarchy, discipline, and a strict division of labor that itself makes a command system necessary. Yet at the same time there can be no favoritism, no preference given to one man over another. Good times and bad, hardship and danger, must be equally shared by all. Rewards and punishments must be distributed equitably, or else the army will fall apart. Men must forget their individuality, respond to the same orders in the same predictable way, and become interchangeable. They must be prepared to take each other's place at a moment's notice. As German soldiers used to say at the time their country still had an army: "today it's you, tomorrow it's me."

All these forms of equality are easy to prescribe but very hard to practice. The larger and more sophisticated the army, and the greater and more imminent the danger, the more difficult the problem. Some will be at the front, others hundreds or even thousands of kilometers away. Some can see the whites in the enemy's eyes, others never set their eyes on an enemy at all. At certain times it is insoluble. How to decide who is to go on the suicidal mission that will open the way to the rest of the army? Who will stay behind in order to cover its retreat? That is why, as far back as Leonidas at Thermopylae in 480 BC, commanders have often asked for volunteers to step forward and undertake the most dangerous missions of all.

Without equality, cohesion is inconceivable. Cohesion, the ability to stick together and stay together through thick and thin, is the most important quality any military formation must have. Without it such a formation is but a loose gathering of men, incapable of coordinated action and easily scattered, and of little or no military use.[9] In all well-organized armies at all times and places, the first step towards cohesion has always been to put everyone on an equal basis. Often the process starts when all new recruits are given the same haircut. Beards may have to be taken off, moustaches trimmed, piercings and jewelry discarded. The U.S. Army will not take personnel whose bodies are marked by "any type of tattoo or brand that is visible while wearing a Class A [the military equivalent of the business suit] uniform."[10] Women are forbidden to wear colored nail-polish and must trim their nails to the prescribed length.

Next, recruits are put into uniform and prohibited from wearing anything else. The U.S. Marine Corps insists that, during basic training, everybody wear the same kind of government-issue glasses. They are old-fashioned, unbreakable, thick, provided with heavy rims, and quite ugly. Most private possessions are taken away and the rest reduced to the indispensable minimum. The underlying objective is to make everybody look and behave alike. At the same time they must be sufficiently different from everyone else as to make them instantly identifiable as soldiers. So different, and so identical, that their families, coming to witness the graduation parade, cannot make them out. As far as practical they are similarly fed, similarly lodged, and similarly treated. Everyone has the same rights and the same duties.

The basics having been instituted, the men, nowadays women too (but normally in separate groups, so as to take into account the different physical abilities of people of both sexes), are put through their paces. They rise together, wash together, eat together, and go to sleep together. Female recruits often find themselves menstruating together.[11] Beds are made to a uniform pattern. Everybody's shoes are lined up at exactly so and so many centimeters from their beds. Everybody is expected to use the same specialized military terms, phrases, and greetings. They are made to march about, roar out cadences in unison, drilled. What all of them cannot do together they do by turns. That includes kitchen duty, fatigue duty, guard duty, and the like. Nobody is overlooked, nobody has any special privileges. Those who do not do sufficiently well in exercises are made to repeat them as often as necessary until they draw level with everybody else. Those who try to show off by ostentatiously doing better than anybody else will be taught not to do so by the instructors or by their comrades. Rewards and punishments are meted out not to individuals but to entire units. This helps to create not only cohesion but fierce competition among them.

To maintain equality, everybody is obliged to share everything with everybody else. That is why, during the first weeks, neither letters nor phone calls are permitted. Even later, food packages reaching the men from outside are scrutinized. There must be enough for everybody to go around; otherwise they will be confiscated by the base personnel. The duty, and the right, to share include not just material possessions but joy, hardship, suffering, pain, and sorrow too. Commanders have always known it. None more so than Shakespeare's Henry V: "We few, we happy few, we band of brothers; for he to-day that sheds his blood with me shall be my brother."[12] Three hundred eighty-three years later, Nelson used the same phrase at the

Battle of the Nile. The men of some ancient Greek armies may even have shared their bodies. Mythological or real, the Sacred Band of Thebes was made up of a hundred and fifty pairs of homosexual lovers.[13] Entering battle, the Spartans sacrificed to the god Eros, the divine incarnation of sexual desire. Though details are scarce, some ancient and modern authors believe that this "sacrifice" may well have been a euphemism for homosexual sex between soldiers and young camp followers.[14]

Equality can also be based on shared heterosexual sex. After all, people's physiological needs are more or less similar. When death is decimating the ranks, who cares how they are met and with whom? A famous Israeli song, written shortly after the 1973 Yom Kippur War with its heavy losses, speaks of two soldiers, one alive, one dead. They were born in the same village, fought in the same battles, sown the same fields, and loved the same girls. Those who have been through the hell commonly called combat will know what I am describing here. Does all this sound utopian? That is because it is. No military organization however tight, not even the Spartan *agoge* or the U.S. Marine Corps at Paris Island, has ever succeeded in establishing equality to the point of making every soldier look and act and think and feel exactly alike. None has been able to erase the ordinary differences between human beings, certainly not completely, and certainly not for any length of time. But that has not stopped them from trying as best they could.

Long after the war has ended and they themselves have retired, soldiers look back in nostalgia to the time when they were all equal. They meet, they reminiscence, they drink, and they visit the places where they fought. They salute their fallen comrades in an attempt to resurrect the bond that held them together. They set up organizations of veterans so as to relive those infinitely terrible, infinitely precious, moments. Voluntarily or involuntarily, death causes everything inessential to be discarded and thrown away. Inside the storm of steel nobody is more, or less, equal than anybody else. Conversely, if soldiers are to do their duty, look death in the eye, and defy it then equality is absolutely necessary. It is when equality merges into brotherhood that the words of Paul the Apostle in his letter to the Corinthians apply: "Oh death, where is thy sting? Oh grave, where is thy victory?"

The fact that death is the great equalizer does not mean that everyone is treated equally after he dies. As far back into history as we can look, disposing of the bodies of the dead was accompanied by some kind of ceremony. The first stage might well consist of cleansing and purifying. There would be wailing, sometimes carried out by professional mourners; a practice mentioned in the Old Testament and still quite common today.[15] People would strew ashes on their heads, tear out their hair or let it grow unkempt, lacerate their faces and bodies, and wear the kind of clothing prescribed for such occasions. They might however, also hold a banquet in honor of the dead. In some cultures bodies were embalmed so as to preserve them. The more prominent the dead person, the more expensive the means used for the purpose. The ancient Egyptians had three kinds of embalmment graduated by their cost and obviously intended for different classes of people.[16] Equally obviously, though, most people were not embalmed at all. The method was known to many other civilizations including Han China and pre-Columbian Peru. It is still quite widely practiced.

On the whole, those who had been more equal during their lives tended to remain so after they had died, and the other way around.

As long as thirty thousand years ago, some were buried or cremated with great ceremony, others with little or none at all.[1] Some were accompanied by women, horses, lackeys, and any number of precious objects to serve them in the next world as they had done in the present one. Some had huge pyramids built to prevent their bodies and the objects with which they were surrounded from being violated. Others owned so little that nobody bothered. As anybody who has visited Jerusalem's Lion Gate knows, the adherents of some religions, monotheistic ones in particular, insisted on being buried as closely as possible to their holy places. They hope that, when the Messiah comes, they will be among the first to be resurrected. (One sect of self-made Jews even believes that the appointed place is my home town, Mevasseret Zion, west of Jerusalem! Mevasseret means "Herald".) Prominent Venetians were buried on the Isola di San Michele and elaborate monuments were erected over their graves. Commoners were dumped into the sea where their bones have formed a reef, visible as a dark stain under the water.

Not every community had a sea so close at hand. Still, at all times and places, mass graves have often been the final destination of the nameless and the poor. The same applies to the victims of the Nazi Einsatzgruppen and extermination camps. In this respect communist leaders, despite claiming to preside over societies in which everybody was equal, were no different from the rest. Lenin had his own mausoleum, which from 1953 to 1961 he was obliged to share with Stalin. When his nose and ears rotted away they had to be recreated in wax. Other Soviet Communist leaders were buried in the Kremlin Wall or else in a special cemetery for the more equal located not far away. Following Mao's death in 1976 the Politburo unexpectedly ordered his body to be embalmed. The doctors did not know how to do it, and they botched the job. After much effort they succeeded in making his face look normal, more or less. However, the rest of his body was so bloated with formaldehyde that his clothes had to be cut open in the back so that they would fit him.[18] It was placed inside a crystal coffin illuminated by specially-designed xenon lamps. Decades later, it still remained on display in the huge mausoleum located on Beijing's central square.

The Christian West was exceptional in that some prominent men and women did not have monuments appropriate to their status erected in their honor. Instead they had their remains interred under the floors of churches. Special crypts were constructed, often not for individuals but for entire families. The crypts and the dead they contained were then covered with stone slabs so that everybody would step on them. The custom, which originated in the middle ages, is still being practiced. The humility may have been real or fake, but in neither case was it the same as equality. In any case, lack of room meant that only a selected few could prove their humility in this way.

In the whole of history only two groups seem to have bucked the trend: namely, monks on the one hand and members of some armed forces on the other. Buddhist monks in China were sometimes given no burial at all. Instead the corpse of a dead monk would be taken to some field or valley. There it would feed the birds and wild animals, dogs included. Later the disciples of the dead, or else his fellow monks, would return to collect the remains of the skeleton and inter them.[19] However, not all Buddhists followed the system. In ancient India the bodies of deceased monks were cleansed, dressed in proper robes, placed on a bier, and cremated. Sometimes a monument, or *stupa*, that reflected the occupant's spiritual merit was built. A stupa looked much like an umbrella or a woman's breast turned upward. The place of the nipple was taken by a square structure containing the monk's ashes. Many were not built in the open but inside special structures or caves. Not only were some stupas much larger than others, but they were strategically placed in order of rank. The Buddha himself was credited with having issued instructions to that effect. Some stupas seem to have attracted worshippers, so that there could be no question of equality. In any case it is clear that only a small minority could be commemorated in this way, as most monks had to make do with smaller, more humble structures that did not last long.[20]

The bones of deceased Christian monks are sometimes made to serve a similar purpose. Bits and pieces taken from many different skeletons are either thrown together in a single heap, or placed next to each other on shelves, or used to create decorative patterns on walls. Capuchin Monasteries in Catholic countries such as Italy, Spain, and Portugal are especially likely to have bone rooms. The Church of All Saints at Sedlec, Bohemia, contains bones taken from the skeletons of between forty and seventy thousand individuals. They have been used to create all kinds of decorations, including coats of arms and chandeliers. Monasteries on Mount Athos in Greece, on the Sinai Peninsula, and in Ethiopia also have bone rooms. Normally there is no attempt to identify the remains, but here and there skulls have their owners' names painted on them or re provided with tags.[21] The emphasis on post-mortem equality is unmistakable. In Alsace many years ago, I came across a storeroom full of dusty bones that carried the words, in German and in French: "What you are, we have been; what we are, you will be."

The medieval Knights Templar in some ways linked the world of monasticism with that of chivalry. Very little has been written about the way the Knights were buried. However, the system seems to have been relatively egalitarian. The Knights did not erect stately

monuments for their dignitaries. Perhaps that was because they were
unable to do so. Out of twenty-two (some say twenty-three) Grand
Masters, four died in battle in the Holy land. Two died in a Sara-
cen prison. Six died in the Holy Land of disease, old age or other
reasons, four died in Cistercian abbeys where their bones were probably mixed with those of everybody else. One died in Italy, one in
Cyprus, and one was burnt at the stake. The remaining three died
in unknown locations and of unknown causes. Chapels, all of them
rather modest, holding the remains of lesser members of the Order
are found in various countries. The Knights were interred next to
each other in simple graves. Only the different clothes the effigies
wear show that those who rest there were men of different ranks.[22]
Visitors to Temple Church, London, often believe that the beautiful
stone effigies they see are those of the Knights Templar who built
the Church back in the twelfth century. In fact, though, it is not
the Knights but their rich and aristocratic supporters who are buried
there.

From ancient Egypt comes a mother's lament that, when her
son reaches manhood and joins the Pharaoh's army, his bones will
be scattered in the desert.[23] The bodies of slain enemy commanders
were often mutilated and/or put on display. That, for example, was
what happened to King Saul and his son Jonathan after their defeat
at the hands of the Philistines.[24] The higher-ranking a casualty, the
more likely he was to suffer such a fate. The bodies of the opposing rank and file were thrown into mass graves or simply left for
birds and animals to feed on. Among the Vikings, so self-evident
was the latter treatment that, in the sagas, it became almost synonymous with defeat.[25] In case one had won a victory and was left in
possession of the field, as the saying went, the normal practice was
likewise to bury one's own casualties in mass graves. The remains of

dead commanders stood a much better chance of being gathered and given a proper funeral. On the whole, distinctions between military personnel probably paralleled those that existed in civilian society. The more prominent a commander the more likely he was to receive special treatment, either negative or positive, after his death.

In view of the close links that have always existed between the military and the societies they served, it is not surprising that the first to think of a different way of doing things were the ancient Greeks. Judging by Athens, about which far more is known than about any other city-state, the bodies of the friendly slain were gathered and cremated. Greek custom also demanded that the defeated enemy be allowed to gather *his* dead. Only once, after Marathon, were the remains buried on the spot. Thucydides, who is our authority on this matter, says it was done as a special tribute to the men's courage.[26] The normal procedure was to take the bones or ashes back to the city where they were divided among the various tribes. Spartan soldiers even carried dog tags for the purpose. They were displayed in a public tent to enable friends and relatives to pay their respects.[27] Three days later the caskets, plus an empty one to mark the Greek version of the Unknown Soldier, made their way to the cemetery in a procession attended by male and female family members as well as professional mourners. An appropriate speech was held after which, Thucydides dryly informs us, people went home. Victorious commanders might have their statues made at the city's expense and erected at the appropriate places. That apart, everybody was treated equally and with a certain respect that was often missing at other times and places.

The Romans, like the Greeks, put great emphasis on giving every fallen soldier, regardless of rank, a proper burial.[28] With the decline of the Empire and the spread of Christianity, things changed. Nobody doubted that emperors, kings and barons were entitled to more elaborate funerals than ordinary soldiers. Only the spread of democratic ideas during the last years of the eighteenth century brought the beginnings of change. It caused practices originally devised for a few outstanding heroes to spread and be diluted, so to speak, until they embraced, or were supposed to embrace, every dead soldier. Already during the French Revolution several proposals were made to gather the remains of the fallen and give them a proper burial. At the time, there was no question of setting up special cemeteries for them. Instead soldiers were to be interred in ordinary ones where their ashes would be mixed with those of great men, thus enabling the "Braves," as Napoleon called them, to enter the Pantheon.[29] Little came of it, however. The *Grande Armée* carefully registered its dead. It did not alter the practice of disposing of most of them on the spot.

Another factor was the spread of mechanized transport, first via railways and then using motor vehicles. For the first time, military transportation provided for a practical method for moving the remains of dead soldiers to the places selected for disposing of them. During the nineteenth century, the country in which both democracy and transport were the most advanced was the United States. In 1862 it became the first one to establish, by an Act of Congress no less, dedicated military cemeteries. Partly because of their more pronounced class character, partly because many of them had remote colonies which made sending soldiers' remains home prohibitively expensive, European countries only followed much later.[30]

By the end of World War I every major country had established a special organization in charge of looking after the remains of those who had given their lives for it. Extraordinary heroes continued to be buried amidst great pomp and circumstance and might very well have statues erected to commemorate their deeds. Ordinary ones were either disposed of *en masse* amidst similar ceremonies or else received pale imitations of the treatment meted out to their betters. Reflecting ancient Greek practices, those whose remains could not be identified or even found were put on an equal basis with the rest, as far as possible, by being commemorated with the aid of eternal flames and tombs of the anonymous soldier.

Those responsible for shaping the graves of civilians may be bound by some kind of tradition. That apart, they are usually permitted to do more or less as they please. By contrast, modern military cemeteries are characterized above all by their uniformity. Everybody gets the same small plot and the same gravestone. The symbols and the epitaphs on each stone are dictated by the authorities. Only names, ranks, and dates of birth and death are different. Some armies also note the military occupation specialty and the religion of the dead. In Israel the outcome is occasional conflicts with the soldier's relatives who want to add this or delete that. Most countries have extended the way they treated their own soldiers to include enemy dead. They may not, it is true, expect any great ceremony. Still, the 1929 Geneva Convention requires that they be respectfully treated, i.e. not defaced or mutilated or subjected to procedures contrary to their own religion. It also requires that they be identified if possible. Their graves must be marked for future reference, and their names and personal effects handed over to representatives of the Red Cross. The latter is supposed to send them to the enemy government, which in turn will inform the families.

Both in the civilian world and the military one, it is hardly surprising that the treatment of the dead reflected that of the living. If only because of the expense involved, most societies gave far more elaborate funerals to the rich and the powerful than to the poor and the insignificant. That seems to have been as true in Paleolithic times as it is today. To this rule there have only been two exceptions: monks on one hand, and soldiers on the other. Dead monks of various times and places were more likely to receive equal treatment than the rest, but the custom was by no means universal. Dead soldiers received equal treatment when they gave their lives for their democracies or for countries such as Nazi Germany and the Soviet Union which claimed to be based on widespread popular support. Ancient Greece apart, such treatment of the dead really only began emerging during the second half of the nineteenth century.

Neither in the civilian nor in the military world is the funeral necessarily the end of the story. The vast majority of the dead are quickly forgotten almost as if they had never been. A few, however, being more equal than others, have monuments, streets, neighborhoods, and even entire towns built for them or named after them. Fewer still enter the collective memory in the sense that most people know, more or less, who they were. As time passes some reputations go up, others down. Heroes are transformed into villains, villains into heroes. Equilibrium, meaning a situation in which all are equal, is never achieved in death any more than it is in life.

The physiological and psychological state of death may perhaps be presumed to be the same for people of all cultures, times and places. However, when it comes to imagining the afterlife the situation is very different. Some archaeologists think that Neanderthals who lived fifty thousand years ago may have believed in it, but it is hard to be sure.[31] In the Mesopotamian Epic of Gilgamesh, which dates to about 2500 BC, the underworld is described as a rather dreary place. No light penetrates the dark and those who dwell there eat dust and feed on clay. They are "clad like birds with garments of wings." There is neither a hint of class distinctions nor of some being given preference over others.

In a different way, the same applies to Buddhism. For Buddhists Heaven and Hell are located not in the non-existent afterlife but here on earth. However, as long as people live they are graded on a kind of point system. Those whose karma, best translated as the sum total of actions of body, speech and mind, is good will be reborn into a higher station than the one they left behind. Those whose karma is bad will experience downward biological mobility, so to speak. They may well return to life in the form of lizards, flies, or similar loathsome creatures. A wise person will therefore do well to invest in *punya*, or merit, so as to become more, not less, than he is. In ascending order, there are three ways to do this: giving, virtue, and mental development. What distinctions there are, in other words, apply not to the afterlife but to the next incarnation. They are rooted in merit rather than in status, riches, or anything else.

Many other cultures likewise imagined afterlives with few distinctions between various kinds of dead. Consider the example of the Greeks. In the Odyssey the eponymous hero visits the underworld where he meets many famous men and women. They were, however, empty ghosts without substance. They do not eat, they do not drink, and they have no sense of touch. Whatever hierarchy may have existed among them during their lives seems to have faded away. A few individuals such as Tantalus and Sisyphus suffered dire punishment for sins they had committed against the gods during their lives. That apart, however, the inhabitants are undifferentiated.

Here it is worth adding two points. First, some Greeks, notably Plato in the *Republic* where he is speaking through Socrates' mouth, did indeed imagine a world in which the virtuous would be rewarded and the wicked, punished, each according to his deeds. Second, some people became gods after their death. A few Greeks, such as the above-mentioned Euhemerus, even believed that all the gods had originally been human.[32] After Alexander, many Hellenistic kings were deified. So, later on, were Julius Caesar, Augustus, and Claudius. Suetonius says that, when the Emperor Vespasian felt his end was near, he joked that, alas, he was turning into a god.[33] Considered from this point of view, there could be no question of equality after death.

The pre-Islamic Arabic afterworld was also inhabited by pale shadows. At the time the Arabs were a tribal society with no central government and no police force to maintain law and order. Disputes were waged by means of feuding that might go on for generations. The prevalent distinction was not between the equal and the more equal but between those who rested in peace and those whose death had not been avenged. The souls of the latter turned into owls. Each owl left the deceased through the top of his (there seems to be no reference to her) head. It circled the grave, screeching loudly and calling on his kin to do what had to be done.[34]

Some other societies had similar ideas.[35] Dead North American Indians famously went to the eternal hunting grounds. Presumably over there braves were as equal, or as unequal, as they had been on earth. Women and children may also have gone there, but I have been unable to find any categorical statements to that effect. There must have been animals, too, or else there would be nothing to hunt. In Scandinavian myth the souls of dead warriors, but not those of anybody else, went to Valhalla. Once they had passed the gates of "The Hall of the Slain" everybody seems to have been equal to everybody else. The heroes spent their time eating, drinking, making merry, and preparing to assist Odin in the coming fight against the wolf Fenrir that would mark the end of the world. It would therefore seem that, the presence of the semi-divine Valkyries apart, Valhalla was a purely masculine affair.[36]

In all these societies there was little question of the dead receiving unequal treatment, or occupying unequal status, in the world to come. In ancient Egypt the situation was entirely different. The earliest known versions of the Book of the Dead, consisting of long lists of spells meant to enable the dead to make his way into the afterlife, date from the time of the Fifth Dynasty, around 2400 BC. They were written on the walls of the Pharaohs' burial chambers inside the pyramids, the intention being to help the dead monarch reunite with his father, the god Ra. Towards the end of the second millennium BC similar texts also start making their appearance inside the graves of regional governors and other high-ranking officials. Later still they were often written on the inner walls of coffins, leading to a vast increase in their number. The process, which took several centuries, has been called "the democratization of the afterlife."[37]

The spirit of the deceased was known as *ba*. Often it was depicted in the form of a bird with a human head. Leaving the body behind, it used the spells to negotiate its way past all kinds of obstacles and fearsome guards that killed the unrighteous. A *ba* that had safely overcome all these hurdles would be met by the jackalheaded god Anubis and led into the presence of Osiris, the god of the underworld, himself. At this point the dead person was made to swear that he had not committed any out of a list of forty-two sins. Chief among them were theft, robbery, adultery, murder, and various forms of sacrilege. He had to be careful, for if he lied his heart might speak up and testify against him. Next the heart itself was weighed. On the other side of the scales was a feather. If the

scales balanced the journey of the deceased ended and he would find
a place in the afterlife. If not then it also ended, this time inside the
belly of another fearsome monster called Ammit, the Devourer, that
Osiris kept handy for the purpose.[38]

Much later, the most important religion that picked up the idea
of using the afterworld in order to distinguish between the good and
the bad, reward the former and punish the latter, was Christianity.
Just how it came to do so is an open question; Judaism, the parent
form which Christianity sprang, originally had little to say about
the matter. The Old Testament does use the term Gan Eden, the
Hebrew equivalent of Paradise. However, *gan* simply means a garden or park. Not a word is lost about the righteous going there after
their death and the sinners being excluded from it. The Prophet
Ezekiel had the vision of the Valley of Dry Bones. Yet the Lord
specifically told him that the bones represented "the whole house
of Israel." Nothing is said concerning any distinctions between the
various people, or groups, to whom they had belonged.[39]

In the Jewish Literature of Wisdom death is seen as the great
leveler and the afterworld as a dark place where the soul forgets
its troubles and rests.[40] Apparently no distinctions were drawn between different classes of people. The idea that, after death, some
would be rewarded and others punished only started entering Judaism during Hellenistic times by way of what is sometimes called
"proto-Apocalyptic" literature such as the book of Enoch. It is there
that we first hear of some going to Heaven and others to Hell.[41] In
68 AD, Josephus Flavius attempted to convince his companions to
surrender to the Romans during the siege of the city of Jodphat, by
telling them that the souls of the righteous would go to holiest of
holies and reminding them that those who committed suicide were
condemned to eternal darkness.[42]

The Talmud, following the book of *Job*, has a sentence or two about the righteous feasting on the flesh of Leviathan while seated in a tabernacle made of its hide. This led to some debate as to whether or not that flesh was kosher. Here and there a rabbi claimed that, in the afterlife, the humble would be elevated and the proud humiliated. But such notions never became part of mainstream Judaism. Some present-day rabbis have wondered why the Old Testament has so little to teach about the subject. At least one answered by saying that Jews, unlike the Egyptians from whose land they escaped, prefer to emphasize life, not death.[43]

By contrast, Christianity has always been riddled with ideas about the different fates that the righteous and the sinners would meet in the afterlife. Responding to the Sadducees, Jesus said the dead would indeed rise. But He did not mention any distinction between different classes of people.[44] Christians belonging to subsequent generations never tired of speculating about this subject. Many of them continue to do so today. The basic distinction has always been between Christians and everybody else. Provided they behaved themselves, the former could enter heaven. The latter were excluded from it even if they did. Those who, for one reason or another, were not allowed to enter Heaven would go to Hell. The latter was a place of fearful and eternal torture often described in literature as well as art. To Heaven and Hell, Catholics added Purgatory, the place where Christian penitents go.

Much the best-known description of the system is found in Dante's Divine Comedy. Clearly Dante was a man of immense learning familiar with all the sciences of his day. His poem, written between 1308 and 1321, presents a grand panorama of the afterlife never equaled before or since. Accompanied by the ancient Roman poet Virgil, who acts as a guide, Dante starts his voyage in Hell, a "deep place" where "the sun is silent." It is cold, it is windy, and it is always wet with sleet. It is divided into nine sections, or circles, in each of which a different class of sinners is lodged. For example, the fourth circle contains the greedy, the avaricious, and the miserly. Like Sisyphus they are doomed to roll heavy bags full of money upwards, forever. The fifth holds those guilty of anger, the sixth is the dwelling place of heretics, the seventh of men of violence, the eighth of fraudsters, and the ninth of traitors. Within each circle, the sinners undergo torments appropriate to their transgressions.

Purgatory is arranged on similar principles. Virgil, being a pagan (though a righteous one), cannot enter paradise, so here Dante's guide is Beatrice, modelled on a Florentine girl he knew and admired from afar. Unlike Hell, Paradise is a place of sunlight and temperate weather. There are located those who exercised the four cardinal virtues, i.e. prudence, justice, restraint, and courage; also, of those who practiced the three theological virtues of faith, hope and charity. Here Dante meets some of the Church's most important dignitaries including Thomas Aquinas, Saint Peter, and Saint John. They seem to spend their time conversing with each other and praising God. The entire enormous structure is capped by the Empyrean which contains the essence of God. Dante gets a glimpse of it, but says it is too magnificent for his powers of description.

The total number of circles listed by Dante is twenty-seven. As everybody gets his or her just desserts, of equality there can be no question. Most other Christian denominations also believe in resurrection, the afterlife, Heaven and Hell.[45] Indeed it is true to say that, wherever Christianity reigns, it has created or imagined elaborate hierarchies. At the top is Jesus who is or is not identical with the Lord. At his side is Mary who plays a sort of ancillary role; if a technological analogy may be permitted, she is like a scandisk device stuck into a USB port. Next in line come the Evangelists and the Apostles some of whom are much more important than others. Catholics, Greek Orthodox, and Slavic-Orthodox also have whole hosts of Saints, some important, some less so. At the other end of the scale are the various categories of sinners.

Given the role of religion in encouraging suicide-bombers to offer their lives, the Moslem heaven is of particular interest. As with Christianity, beliefs vary enormously. Reading the *Rubayait* (Verses) of Omar Khayyam, an eleventh-century Persian text, one gets the impression that the author did not believe one word of whatever others might say about the afterlife. Of clay you have been fashioned, he keeps saying, and to clay you will return. Make sure that, in the brief life you have been granted, you get as much enjoyment out of wine and tulip-cheeked girls as you can.[46]

A more orthodox view is that on the last day, also known as the Day of Standing Up, the Day of Separation, the Day of Reckoning, and the Encompassing Day, Allah will raise all people from the dead to be judged. It is physical, not merely spiritual, resurrection we are talking about here. Like their Christian colleagues, the righteous of both sexes, will experience eternal spiritual and physical joy in paradise. One Quran verse says that, over there, they will be even more unequal than they have been on earth.[47]

Conversely, sinners are destined for the Fire and will suffer eternal torment.

To this system there are two important exceptions. One is formed by the *shahids*, or martyrs, who have given up their lives for God. The other consists of "enemies of God," meaning apostates or those belonging to other religions who persecuted Moslems. They differ from the rest in that there is no waiting time. The former go straight to Heaven, the latter to the Fire. Some claim that not

only enemies of God but all sinners start suffering torments immediately after death. Heaven and Hell each contain seven sections
earmarked to receive different categories of the blessed and of sinners. In all this, the impact of Christianity is both evident and very
powerful.

In summary, it is not quite true that death is the great equalizer.
First, today's genetic science enables us to envisage a future in which
some people may be able to escape death, at least in some senses of
that term. Second, throughout history the treatment of the dead at
the hands of the survivors has varied enormously. Very often it was
a question of rich versus poor. Confronting death, the former have
their privileges just as they do in respect to almost everything else.
However, it is not solely a matter of means. In both east and west,
some monastic institutions have gone out of their way to make their
members meet death on equal terms. The armed forces of polities
claiming to be based on the popular will, both ancient and modern,
have also tried to ensure that fallen soldiers would be as equal in
death as they supposedly were during their lives.

Not all cultures believe in the afterlife, but many do. Generally
the ideas that different ones hold about the subject may be divided
into two groups. On one hand are religions that neither put any
particular value on what happens in the next world nor are terribly
interested in describing that world. In most cases it is a cold, dark,
eerie place inhabited by ghosts. Valhalla, being nice and festive,
forms an exception in this respect. However, it is only those who
died in battle who enter it and enjoy their existences in it in the first
place. On the other hand we have the monotheistic religions, Christianity and Islam in particular. Priests, Mullahs and Ayatollahs all

keep explaining that what happens to the souls of the deceased after death depends on whether they believed in the religion in question and also on whether or not they have sinned. Strangely enough, it is precisely the religions which never cease claiming that, as far as they are concerned, everybody is equal in the sight of God which have imagined the least egalitarian afterlives of all. One cannot help wondering whether there is a lesson there.

Chapter 11

The Promise and the Threat

Contrary to what some have claimed and are still claiming, the fundamental building block of nature is not equality but inequality. Long before mankind appeared on the scene, mammals, our primate cousins specifically included, formed elaborate hierarchies. Some animals, being strong and aggressive and intelligent and possessed of the gift of leadership, occupied the top positions and dominated the groups of which they were members. Others, being weaker and less aggressive and less intelligent and less able to lead, found themselves at the bottom of the social ladder and were dominated. Sir Zuckerman's methods may be outdated. However, his claim that, inside any given group of monkeys or apes, no two individuals have ever occupied exactly the same rank or enjoyed exactly the same status, retains its validity. Even if this did occasionally happen, it did not last for very long. To the contrary, it is hierarchy that makes the social life of these animals, and by no means only these animals, possible. Had every individual been equal to all the rest, inevitably disputes over access to resources, be they food or resting places or sexual partners, would have to be freshly fought out day by day and hour by hour. As it is, politics form a never-ending process. However, at least their more violent forms are to some extent restrained.

It is true that some human societies have been much more egalitarian than others. However, it is also true that no known human society has consisted of people all of whom were equal. Hobbes' state of nature is pure fiction, as he himself admitted it probably was.[1] The earliest inequalities were those that prevailed within the family: old and young, senior and junior, male and female. Furthermore, even the simplest known band-societies, so simple that their members did not even know how to make fire, were not quite egalitarian. In them some persons, usually owing to their closeness to the spirits and their presumed powers over physical nature, enjoyed a higher status than others. It is probably in these beginnings that all power, political and economic and military, originated. Compared with more sophisticated societies, bands and tribes without rulers are egalitarian. The way their own members see it, though, they are usually anything but. Instead they divide both individuals and groups into superiors and inferiors.

With the transition to chiefdoms inequality becomes even more pronounced. That was as true in Africa as in New Zealand, in the Middle East as in much of both Americas. Politically, socially and economically all these societies formed pyramids, some steep, others less so. None would have understood the idea of equality even if it had been thrust under their very noses. Only in the small, poor, unimportant country known as ancient Greece were some, but by no means all, chiefdoms able to come together and establish city-states. In spite of the rivers of ink that have been spilled about the subject, we have not the slightest idea how it was done. Over time the outcome was certain kinds of civic and political equality, however limited and however exclusive. In Sparta it also included the economic equality of some at the expense of all the rest. Yet even this experiment in equality was geographically constrained and only lasted for three centuries at most. In itself it was not very important. However, as an example on which others were to draw, the role it played in history cannot be overestimated.

Greece (and Rome) apart, the vast majority of chiefdoms never merged into city-states. Many remained as they were; in Asia and Africa they survived into the nineteenth and twentieth centuries when most were decapitated or wiped out by modern imperialist expansion. Others went on to set up kingdoms and empires, including some of the most powerful and longest-lasting the world has ever seen. Kingdoms and empires whose center did not hold, and which allowed their leading members to pass their privileges to their offspring, readily degenerated into feudal systems. Here and there centralized and decentralized periods alternated. Both monarchies and feudal regimes saw equality, be it political, or economic, or social, as the last thing they wanted. To the contrary, in every case inequality was precisely the basis on which they were built. What social justice existed was established and maintained by entirely different means. To wit, the ruler's promise to try cases fairly on one hand and the duty of handing out charity on the other. That was as true in ancient Iran and pre-Islamic Islam as it was in the Christian Middle Ages.[2]

These "Proud Towers," as, following a book by the late historian Barbara Tuchman, I have called them, were often confronted by revolts. However, most of those revolts aimed simply at getting rid of the people at the top and putting others in their place. Except in ancient Greece, rarely was there any attempt to establish equality. Among the revolts that did have that objective, the vast majority were suppressed fairly quickly. Even successful ones were normally only able to maintain themselves for a limited period before they too were destroyed. Often they destroyed themselves. No sooner had the leaders attained some kind of victory then they raised themselves as far above their followers as they could.

Such revolts apart, equality could only be found inside the social islands known as monasteries. The driving force of monasteries was religion. In both east and west, many monasteries incorporated some sort of relative, though hardly ever absolute, form of equality. Yet monasteries were utterly dependent on the protection and support of the unequal societies around them. But for that protection and that support, including not least the supply of new blood to replace that which the monks and nuns could not generate, they could not have existed.

From Plato on, many writers have imagined communities in which equality among all the members would be the norm. To maintain it some of them, Plato himself included, did not hesitate to resort to deception and/or the most drastic intervention in people's lives. That even included the times they were allowed to mate, the ways in which they could do so, with whom, and whether or not the offspring should be allowed to live. Others, with Rabelais at their head, simply positioned unlimited means and expected everybody to be perfect in everything, thereby making it unnecessary to have not only controls of this kind but any controls at all. Following this logic, quite a number of egalitarian utopias stood beyond place and time. That was because, as the authors in question well understood, they could not be realized even in principle.

The first political scientist to start from the idea that everybody—at any rate all adult males—has been born equal was Thomas Hobbes. At the time, so novel was the idea that he had to flee for his life. Since then, so self-evident has it become that I have been unable to find even one scholarly article dealing with the question as to where he took it from. Intimately familiar with ancient Greek historical writing though he was, we know that he did not derive it from them.[3] It was Hobbes who lit the fuse and set off the dynamite that is still shaking our world every day; it was his work that formed the starting point of all late-seventeenth and eighteenth-century writers who followed him.

The idea having been born, more and more people went on to envisage communities that would be based on it and incorporate it. Often using ancient Greece as their example, most of them thought in terms of civic and political equality. Substituting representation for direct democracy, they were able to extend it over areas and populations far larger than those of any Greek *polis*. Most of them also recognized the importance of socio-economic equality. However, except for Rousseau they did not go very far in analyzing it. Rousseau himself argued that, for an egalitarian community to be established, a return to direct democracy was necessary. To that extent, so far was he behind the times that it is impossible to take him seriously.

Liberal equality of the kind Locke, Montesquieu, and Jefferson had advocated finally found itself in the saddle after 1776 and 1789. Not that the struggle ended at that point. Opposition had to be overcome, bloody wars fought, repeated reverses suffered. In the United States, the first to adopt it, it was only in 1868 that the XIVth Amendment explicitly entitled all citizens to "the equal protection of the law." In Europe things developed more slowly still; as the German saying went, the one way to counter *Demokraten* was to use *Soldaten*. The British Dominions apart, outside Europe it only became an issue after World War I.

Even as equality slowly spread, not everybody was happy with it. Acting on the belief, which also goes back to ancient Greece, that civic and political equality is meaningless unless it is based on socio-economic equality, socialists and communists tried to abolish the more important forms of private property. The outcome was a series of polities that were democratic and egalitarian in theory. In practice, though, inside each one the unheard-of privileges of the ruling few contrasted with the impoverishment of the many. As the Cold War came to an end the system collapsed with astonishing suddenness, leaving little but ruin. Yet this fact has not prevented some people from advocating a return to it, proving how short human memory is.

The Nazis attacked liberal equality from a different angle. On one hand, building on earlier doctrines, they set up a racial hierarchy in which their own *Volk* occupied the top rungs and everybody else was further down. Yet at the same time they also tried to create a certain kind of equality *within* the community or *Volksgemeinschaft*. As the Nazis' opponents have never ceased pointing out, to some extent it was a sham. Property remained in private hands. Socio-economic gaps between the classes only decreased moderately if at all. The great industrialists, or chimney barons as they were known, remained in place. Nevertheless, especially during the early years of the regime, the promise of this kind of equality exercised a strong appeal. But for it, the Third Reich would have been inconceivable.

To turn their vision into reality the Nazis did two other things. First, like the Spartans whom they admired so much, they increasingly based their economy on Helot-like labor imported from the occupied countries and forcibly kept in place. Second and much worse still, they set out to exterminate those who did not measure up to a certain standard, whether medical or racial. Their crimes were among the worst in history and are likely to be forever remembered as a terrible example of what the quest for certain kinds of equality can do. Furthermore, similar to many socialist and all communist ones, the ship the Nazis ran was highly centralized and highly authoritarian. What equality was achieved, in other words, had to be paid for by liberty.

Nazi crimes have pulled the rug from under the feet of anyone who thought of "race" in terms similar to theirs, or so we hope. They also turned "discrimination" into the worst of all bad things, thus providing the proponents of equality with a black flag to rally against. The first important group to benefit from this were America's blacks. Others, including women, homosexuals and the disabled, soon followed. Putting in place affirmative action and reverse discrimination programs, many countries consciously started sacrificing present-day equality for the kind they hoped would one day prevail in the future. The result was to turn some previously-dominant groups, able-bodied heterosexual white males above all, into minorities. Certainly as far as opportunity is concerned, they have been rendered rather less than equal. Another danger, which in some countries is well on its way to being realized, is tribalization. By this is meant not just pork barrel politics—in any democracy, that is the norm. Rather, it means splitting society into so many more or less fixed groups, all ceaselessly seeking privileges at the expense of all the rest, as to make equality both meaningless and impossible.

Meanwhile, new questions are being raised by recent advances in medical science. Is everybody entitled to benefit from them, or are they going to be reserved for the rich and the powerful as has happened so often in the past? Seeking to lift everybody to certain standards of behavior, are we going to compel those who are perceived as falling short to take drugs and/or undergo hormonal treatment? Are we, perhaps, going to kill the biologically unfit, but instead of doing so after birth, as the Nazis did, end the life of babies asking to be born before they have had a chance to see the light of day? Many questions, few answers. Meanwhile, though, things are happening of themselves. Legions of fetuses are being aborted because tests have determined that they suffer from this or that congenital "defect," some very grave, some much less so. Already now, in quite some countries, the demand for equal access to all kinds of elective treatments is undermining the financial foundations of public health systems.

In so far as nobody has been able to escape it, death still remains the greatest equalizer of all. Great or small, our spirit will depart and our flesh will rot. Specifically, there exist two kinds of institutions whose primary mission is to prepare people for death, monasteries and the military. Each in its own way put a heavy emphasis on equality. But suppose we can one day do away with death, at least in some ways and to a certain extent; who is going to benefit? Shall all of us have the *right* to eternal life? That might make the earth even more overcrowded than it is. Or will it be necessary to choose? If so, who will make the relevant decisions, and on the basis of what criteria? Will serial murderers have the same claim to immortality as Mother Teresa? Certainly it is not too early to start thinking about these questions. Meanwhile, funeral rites continue to be as unequal as they have always been. Some go to the grave attended by all of the world's heads of state. Others are dumped into holes in the ground without so much as a prayer to bid them farewell or signs with their names on it.

Even that is not always the end of the matter. According to one Israeli poem, in the place where dead soldiers go "men will shake the hands of their commanders and commanders will slap the backs of their men." Thus some forms of hierarchy will be maintained beyond the grave. At least two major religions, Christianity and Islam, which together account for some two fifths of the world's entire population, still adhere to the idea of reward and punishment in the world to come. In doing so their implicit, and very often explicit, objective is to justify inequality in the present one.

Not surprisingly, the global economic crisis that began in 2008 provided a new impetus to the public debate about the alleged demise of equality. From early in the morning to late at night, we are flooded by learned explanations of the terrible things that will happen if "the Revolution of the Rich" is not contained and reversed.[4] However, the fact that such claims have often been postulated before should make us take them with a grain of salt. For example, the existence, in America, of "a ruling class, an omnipotent elite"[5] well on the way to perpetuating itself while excluding everybody else was postulated in 1956, at the height of the Eisenhower consensus. The author, C. Wright Mills has been called "the most inspiring sociologist of the second half of the twentieth century."[6] And how about the claim that Americans either must "establish a more equitable division of property and income" or prepare for "the fatal end of democracy" in the form of "despotism and decadence"?[7] Alas for the doomsayers, it was made not in 2015, but in 1879, amidst hordes of robber barons who populated the Gilded Age. Taking a wider perspective, how large a role has equality really played in human history? Can it be instituted and maintained for any length of time? What are the advantages? What are the costs? How large a role has equality really played in human history?

The longest-lived example of human equality, monasteries have long existed and still exist today. Often their cultural impact was considerable; especially in early medieval Europe where they were almost the sole depositories of knowledge for centuries. However, even at best they have only ever formed small islands of relative equality in a vast sea of inequality. The same is also true of utopian communities, whether religious ones in the USA or socialist ones such as the Israeli kibbutzim. The vast majority of societies did not even believe equality to be an ideal, let alone a possible reality. Outside of ancient Greece, where certain polities were able to maintain certain kinds of equality for a period of about three hundred years, its role in human affairs has been limited. Countless chiefdoms and kingdoms were born, rose, prospered, declined, died, and were replaced by others while equality was given hardly a thought. From Egypt to Persia and China to imperial Rome, some of the most powerful empires ever paid no respect to the concept.

These empires developed ideologies that were anything but egalitarian. One of the most important of those, Confucianism, has outlasted all the rest. Its emphasis on hierarchy, the deference of inferiors to superiors, and social harmony still plays a paramount role in large parts of today's world and will almost certainly continue to do so for a long time to come. Singapore, by common assent one of the most successful modern polities, attributes its achievements to Confucian principles. It has even erected a statue in the master's honor. Many other empires used religion in their attempts to justify inequality, institutionalize it, and maintain it. Feudal systems, decentralized and lacking a well-developed bureaucracy, tended to be as different from empires as different as they could be. However, they were just as hierarchical, just as inegalitarian and, in some cases, nearly as long-lived.

Both in Hobbes' own time and later, there must have been many who wished he had never been born. But for good or ill, there is no undoing his work or putting the equality genii back in its bottle. For close to four centuries now, the banners under which men and women mobilized and mounted the barricades were inscribed with equality. The word has acquired wings, crossed every ocean, and echoed across every continent and throughout every country. Hundreds of millions of people, who before they were conquered by modern imperialism had never heard about it, turned it against their masters and appealed to it to justify their own liberation. The quest for it has been the source both of great progress and of countless wars, some of them very bloody. If anything it seems to become more powerful, not less. Like everything else it is unlikely to last forever; but at present practically any movement seeking any kind of social change is compelled to adopt it. No substitute is in sight.

The greatest advantage of equality is that, in some ways, it appears just and is just. To call up the ghost of John Ball for the second time, "When Adam delved and Eve span, who was then the gentleman?" This question was formulated at the end of the fourteenth century. But it had been heard before and is still being heard today. In so far as it is just, equality can make a decisive contribution to peace and political stability without which the good life is inconceivable. The greatest disadvantage is that, to maintain it, certain kinds of justice, liberty and truth may very well have to be sacrificed.

First, justice. In most societies during most of history, people who were regarded as unequal received unequal justice as a matter of course. In Hellenistic Alexandria Greeks were administered less severe floggings than native Egyptians. In Rome slaves testifying in a court of law *had* to be tortured in order to get the truth out of them. During the Middle Ages, and in most countries until the time of the American and French Revolutions, no one in his right mind would have thought that aristocrats should be judged by anyone except their peers, nor that they should be subject to the degrading punishments to which their inferiors had to bear. Simply putting forward the idea of equality in this regard was to ask for trouble. Those days are gone and one hopes they will not return.

However, what has come later is no less problematic. Equality before the law is welcome, but without a certain economic equality it is a sham. And yet, enforcing economic equality is plainly unjust. Furthermore, by making everyone equal before the law we are riding roughshod over the fact that people are different and that these differences can be significant. Indeed no system that tries to force people into a common mold can be just. What is sauce for the goose is *not* always sauce for the gander. Is there really any reason why, in proportion to their income or property or any other distinctive characteristic, the rich should be made to pay more taxes than the poor? Should women really be made to work as hard, and to retire at the same age, as men? When it comes to entering a university or getting a job or being promoted, why should the able be punished and the less able rewarded? Doesn't imposing equality entail putting down excellence and promoting mediocrity? Isn't all this the very opposite of justice?

Second, liberty. Imposing equality entails the sacrifice of liberty because, as both history and biology prove, whenever people and animals are left alone it will not be long before some start becoming more equal, even much more equal, than others. It is probably true, as Hobbes wrote, that neither physical nor mental differences between different people can explain how some came to be elevated far beyond the rest. That, however, applies to the "state of nature." Once society was created, those who had what it takes to run faster started leaving the rest behind. And that is the way things should be in a free society. As the former British Prime Minister Margaret Thatcher said, shouldn't everyone be free to be as *unequal* as he or she wants?[8] If not, then what is left of liberty?

Third, truth. Here the problem is that, in many cases, the dogma of equality requires giving up the search for truth, even the idea of truth itself. Isn't treating all religions—or for that matter opinions—equally tantamount to saying that they simply do not matter? Conversely, are we going to prohibit those who still believe in the reality of race, as opposed to "ethnicity," from speaking freely like everyone else? What about women? What about homosexuals? Do we really want a situation, which in many places already exists, where in order to prevent "bias," only blacks are allowed to do research on blacks, women on women, and the like, thus making sure that the truth, assuming such a thing does in fact exist, will never be discovered?

From the beginning of history on, every single reformer who has ever wished to institute equality in one of its many forms has looked to education as the tool *par excellence* for achieving it. From the Cambodian dictator Pol Pot down, they have regularly targeted the young; the reason being that they are defenseless against their elders' attempts to brainwash them. But what if the quest for equality demands, as it has often done in the past and is very often doing even now, that the search for truth be abandoned and some dogma put in its place? In that case, what is the point of having any education at all? And suppose we conclude, as has happened countless times from the execution of Socrates on, that the search for truth is dangerous and cannot be tolerated. How long can censorship last before the bonds are broken and thought, bursting forth like an eagle out of its shell, demands the freedom that is its due?

The Second Law of Thermodynamics tells us that order at one spot can only be established by creating even greater disorder everywhere else. Similarly, the kind of equality that existed in ancient Sparta, or in monasteries, or which the Nazis tried to establish inside the *Volksgemeinschaft*, can only be established at the expense of other people who are not Spartiates, not monks, not Germans, and not equal. Monogamy, meaning the kind of legal equality that prevents any man from cornering and marrying more women than any other, is certain to lead to a sharp distinction between legitimate and illegitimate offspring and, in this way, give birth to its opposite. In many countries until well into the twentieth century, so long was the list of disabilities imposed on bastards that they were almost the converse of aristocratic privilege.[9] If that has ceased to be the case today, it is only because the prevalence of divorce is causing marriage itself to decline.

A handful of earlier experiments aside, the quest for equality has now lasted for a little under four centuries. During that period some forms of it have indeed been realized, to some extent. However, progress, if that is the correct term, has been held up by three factors. First, rarely if ever have the advocates of equality missed an opportunity to make themselves more equal than the rest, as many of them are still doing every day. Indeed it would be true to say that, to impose and maintain equality, some kind of hierarchy is absolutely necessary. Second, among the many different kinds of equality there are quite a few that stand in direct contradiction to each other. As soon as one kind is achieved, another one disappears. It is rather like trying to cover a big man with a small blanket. Some part of his body will always stick out. Third, the concept keeps being reinterpreted. No sooner has a semblance of equality been achieved in one way then it is upset in another. With science and technology racing ahead as they do, at no time has this been more true than precisely in ours. Even as the process unfolds, justice, liberty, and truth have all come under vicious attack.

That is why the modern fight against "bias" and "discrimination" is hopeless, indeed in many cases foolish. God guard us against the day when it is finally "won," the age-old human tendency to jockey for superiority ceases, and all of us are forced into the straitjacket of equality. On that day history, even human life itself, will have come to an inglorious end.

Equality, certainly equality of the kind Plato, Nabis, Caligula, Rousseau, Lenin, Stalin, Hitler, Mao Tze Dong, Pol Pot, and not a few present-day proponents of political correctness and diversity have envisaged, is a dream. When we keep in mind the costs that dream demands, the contradictions to which it inevitably leads, and the horrendous amounts of blood that are so often shed in its name, we would be wise to ensure that the quest for it does not become a nightmare.

Acknowledgements

The idea behind this book came to me like a dream—I do not know whence, I do not know why. But that does not mean I do not owe a debt of gratitude to a number of people. Chief among them is my friend of thirty years standing, Dr. Col. (res.) Moshe Ben David, a true intellectual who always takes an interest in what I am doing. Then there is Dr. Yuval Harari, my former student at the Hebrew University, who taught me that, when it comes to writing clearly and directly, I still had a lot to learn. Another friend, Dr. Major Lee Ting Ting of the People's Liberation Army, several times answered questions regarding the Chinese view of things that were beyond my competence.

Thanks to my agents and friends for over twenty years, Mr. Gabriele Pantucci and Ms. Leslie Gardner of Artellus Ltd, London, who have been their usual marvelous selves in keeping up my spirits and finding a publisher. Thanks also to my friend Michael Klonovsky has often inspired me with his pungent sayings about everything. My stepson Dr. Jonathan Lewy not only asked his habitual incisive questions but read the manuscript and commented on it. Finally, my wife Dvora put up with me as she always does. What is more, it was she who suggested the title. Thank you Benda, Yuval, Ting Ting, Gabriele, Leslie, Jonathan, and Dvora. Your friendship and love have been worth more to me that I can put into words.

Endnotes

Introduction

1. The best known work is Th. Piketty, *Capital in the Twenty-First Century*, Cambridge, Ma, Harvard University Press, 2014. See also R. Wilkinson and K. Pickett, *The Spirit Level; Why Greater Equality Makes Societies Stronger*, London, Bloomsbury Press, 2009.

2. Sun Yat Sen, *The Three Principles of the People*, Chunking, Ministry of Information of the Republic of China, 1943 [1925] pp. 218–221.

3. A. Huxley, *Brave New World*, Harmondsworth, Middlesex, Penguin, 1968 [1932], p. 66.

4. Letter to Bishop Mandell Creighton, 5 April 1887, in J. N. Figgis and R. V. Laurence, eds., *Historical Essays and Studies*, London, MacMillan, 1907.

1. Whence Inequality?

1. C. Packer and A. E. Pusey, I. "Cooperation and Competition among Groups of Male Lions," *Nature*, 296, 5859, April 1982, pp. 740–742; I. Teboekhorst and others, "Residential Status and Seasonal Movements of Wild Orang-Utans in the

Gunung Leuser Reserve (Sumatera, Indonesia)," *Animal Behavior*, 39, 6, 1990, pp. 1098–1109.

2. M. F. Bouissou, "Influence of Body Weight and Presence of Horns on Social Rank in Domestic Cattle," *Animal Behavior*, 20, 1972, pp. 474–477.

3. M. C. van Dierendornck and others, "An Analysis of Dominance ... in a Herd of Icelandic Horses in Captivity," *Netherlands Journal of Zoology*, 45, 3–4, 1995, pp. 362–385.

4. S. Zuckerman, *The Social Life of Monkeys and Apes*, London, Kegan Paul, 1932, pp. 233–238.

5. J. von Lavick-Goodall, *In the Shadow of Man*, Boston, MA, Houghton Mifflin, 1971, pp. 112–113. 173–179.

6. See the description in R. Wrangham and D. Peterson, *Demonic Males; Apes and the Origins of Human Violence*, Boston, MA, Mariner, 1996, pp. 1–27.

7. F. B.M. de Waal, *Our Inner Ape*, New York, NY, Riverhead, 2005, p. 88.

8. F. B. M. de Waal, *Chimpanzee Politics: Power and Sex among Apes*, Baltimore, Md, Johns Hopkins University Press, 2000 [1982], pp. 47, 49.

9. De Waal, *Our Inner Ape*, pp. 43–44.

10. De Waal, *Chimpanzee Politics*, p. 78.

11. See, for a short list of species where relations among individuals are based on dominance, E. Bonabeau and G. Therault, "Dominance Orders in Animal Species," *Bulletin of Mathematical Biology*, 61, 1999, p. 228.

12. S. F. Bronsman and F. B. M. De Waal, "Monkeys Reject Unequal Pay," *Nature*, 425, 18 September 2003, pp. 297–299.

13. *The Travels of Marco Polo*, Harmondsworth, Penguin, 1972, [1299], p. 258.

14. For a general account of the islands see A. Radcliffe-Brown, *The Andaman Islanders*, Glencoe, Il, Free Press, 1948 [1922]; also F. A. Dass, *The Andaman Islanders*, Nabu Press, 2011 [1922].

15. E. H. Man, "Of the Aboriginal Inhabitants of the Andaman Islands," *Journal of the Anthropological Institute of Great Britain*, 12, 1863, pp. 126–127.

16. Radcliffe-Brown, *The Andaman Islanders*, p. 43.

17. "In every age group, two to four times as many men as women engaged in hunting." M. J. Goodman and others, "The Compatibility of Hunting and Mothering among the Agta Hunters of the Philippines," *Sex Roles*, 12, 11, 1985, p. 1202.

18. Radcliffe-Brown, *The Andaman Islanders*, p. 157.

19. See, in general K. Maddock, *The Australian Aborigines*, London, Penguin, 1982.

20. J. Altman, *Hunter-Gatherers Today: An Aboriginal Economy of North Australia*, Canberra, ACT, Australian Institute of Aboriginal Studies, 1987, p. 147.

21. E. E. Evans-Pritchard, *The Nuer*, Oxford, Oxford University Press, 1969 [1940], p. 6.

22. *Judges*, 5.7.

23. Evans-Pritchard, *The Nuer*, pp. 220–225; A. I Richards, "African Kings and Their Royal Relatives," *Journal of the Royal Anthropological Institute*, 91, 2, July–December 1961, p. 135.

24. A. Fienup-Riordan, *The Nelson Island Eskimo: Social Structure and Ritual Distribution*. Anchorage, Ak, Alaska Pacific University Press, 1983, p. 10.

25. Aristotle, *Politics*, London, Heinemann, Loeb Classical Library, (LCL), 1932, 1.2.19–21.

26. E.g. B. A. Bettencourt and others, "Evaluations of Ingroup and Outgroup Members," *Journal of Experimental Social Psychology*, 33, 3, May 1997, pp. 244–275; J. M. Rabbie and M. Horowitz, "The Arousal of Ingroup-Outgroup Bias by a Chance of Win or Lose," *Journal of Personality and Social Psychology*, 69, 1969, pp. 223–228.

27. C. Storrs, ed., *The Fiscal-Military State in Eighteenth-Century Europe*, Burlington, Vt, Ashgate, 2009.

28. J. J. Rousseau, *The Social Contract*, Harmondsworth, Penguin, 1981 [1762], p. 49.

29. A. Earle, "A Narrative of Nine Months' Residence in New Zealand in 1827," *The National Standard*, 20.4.1833, p. 244; J. E. Alexander, *Incidents of the Maori War*, Christchurch, Capper, 1976, p. 36.

30. H. Rider Hagard, *The Treasury of Allan Quartermain*, Radford, Va, Wilder, 2007 [1887], 1, p. 175.

31. W. S. Churchill, *The River War*, New York, NY, Award, 1964 [1899], p. 286.

32. K. Marx, *The German Ideology*, Moscow, Progress, 1976 [1844], p. 53.

33. K. Marx, *Capital*, New York, NY, Cerf, 1956 [1867–1884], pp. 836–837; F. Engels, *Herr Eugen Duehring's Revolution in*

Science, London, Lawrence and Wishart, 1934 [1878], pp. 146–147.

34. *Judges* 21.25.

35. See, for the role played by metal, V. Lull, "A New Assessment of Agraric Society and Culture," in W. H. Waldern, ed., *The Deya Conference of Prehistory*, Oxford, BAR International Series, 229, 1984, 1, pp. 222–223.

36. J. Cook, *A Voyage to the Pacific Ocean*, London, Stockdale, 1784, 2, p. 188.

37. See J. Gottschall, *The Rape of Troy: Evolution, Violence and the World of Homer*, Cambridge, Cambridge University Press, 2008, pp. 69, 81, 86–7.

38. See, on the way these things worked among the Bashu of eastern Zaire, R. M. Packard, *Chiefship and Cosmology*, Bloomington, Id, Indiana University Press, 1981, pp. 2–3, 48.

39. See D. Bronwen, "Rank, Power, Authority: A Reassessment of Traditional Leadership in South Pacific Societies," *Journal of Pacific History*, 14, 1, 1979, pp. 2–27.

40. William J. Argyle, *The Fon of Dahomey: A History and Ethnography of the Old Kingdom*, Oxford, Clarendon, 1966, pp. 63, 87–8; Helene d'Almeida-Topor, *Les Amazones: une armée des femmes dans l'Afrique precoloniale*, Paris, Rochevignes, 1984), p. 43.

41. *Iliad*, LCL, 1925, 2, 211–277.

42. See, in addition to Zuckerman, de Waal, *Chimpanzee Politics*, [1983].

43. De Waal, *Our Inner Ape*, pp. 49–51. For reproductive success in general see R. Trivers, "Parental Investment and Sex-

ual Selection," in B. Campbell, ed., *Sexual Selection and the Descent of Man*, 1871–1971, Chicago, Il., Aldine, 1972, pp. 136–207.

44. E. Trinkaus and A. P. Buzhilova, "The Death and Burial of Sunghir 1," *International Journal of Osteoarchaeology*, 5 November 2010.

2. The Greek Miracle

1. *Iliad*, 1.185–187

2. See, for Homeric social organization, M. I. Finley, *The World of Odysseus*, London, Chatto & Windus, 1954, pp. 58–124.

3. Hesiod, *Works and Days*, LCL, 2006, 170, 202.

4. Thucydides, *The Peloponnesian* War, LCL, 1919, 3.94.

5. *New Cambridge Ancient History*, Cambridge, Cambridge University Press, 1965, 8, p. 538.

6. W. Donlan, "The Social Groups of Dark Age Greece" *Classical Philology*, 80, 4, October 1985, p. 297.

7. See W. Greenwalt, "Why Pella?," *Historia*, 48, 2, spring 1999, pp. 158–183; and C. H. Makaronas, "Pella; Capital of Ancient Macedonia," *Scientific American*, 6, 1966, pp. 98–105.

8. C. G. Starr, *The Origins of Greek Civilization, 1100–650 B.C.*, New York, NY, Norton, 1991, p. 301.

9. See e.g. L. J. Samsons, "Mass, Elite, and Hoplite-Farmer in Greek History," *Arion*, 5, 3, 1998, pp. 99–123.

10. See, for what commanders did in battle, M. van Creveld, *Command in War*, Cambridge, Ma, Harvard University Press, 1985, pp. 41–43.

11. D. Herlihy, "The Triumph of Monogamy," *The Journal of Interdisciplinary History*, 25, 4, spring 1995, pp. 577–579.

12. E. Stavrianopoulou, "Ensuring Ritual Competence in Ancient Greece," in U. Hüsken, ed., *When Rituals Go Wrong*, Leiden, Brill, 2007, pp. 183–196.

13. Plutarch, *Parallel Lives*, Lycurgus, LCL, 1919, 5.1.

14. Herotodus, *The Histories*, LCL, 1920, 1.65.

15. Thucydides, *The Peloponnesian War*, 4.80.3; Aristotle, *Politics*, 1269 a 37–39.

16. Plutrach, *Lycurgus*, LCL, 1932, 8.1–2.

17. Plutarch, *Parallel Lives*, Pelopidas, LCL, 1932, 23.3.

18. Plutarch, *Parallel Lives*, Lycurgus, 5.2.

19. Plutarch, *Parallel Lives*, Lycurgus, 19.3.

20. N. Mertyens, "The Perioikoi in the Classical Lakedaimonian Polis," in A. Powell and S. Hodkinson, eds., *Sparta; Beyond the Mirage*, London, Duckworth, 2002, p. 287.

21. Herodotus, *The Histories*, 7.234.

22. Plutarch, *Parallel Lives*, Lycurgus, 15.1.

23. Plutarch, *Parallel Lives*, Lycurgus, 30.1. I have slightly changed the Loeb translation.

24. Polybius, *The Histories*, LCL, 1922, 13.6.

25. See Aristotle, *The Constitution of the Athenians*, LCL, 1935, 6; Plutarch, *Parallel Lives*, Solon, LCL, 1932, 15.2; and Aristotle, The *Constitution of the Athenians*, 12.4 quoting Solon himself.

26. *Numbers*, 27.1–11.

27. Aristotle, *Politics*, 2.7.18.

28. J. Ober, *Mass and Elite in Democratic Athens*, Princeton, NJ, Princeton University Press, 1989, p. 64.

29. G. Herman, *Morality and Behavior in Democratic Athens*, Cambridge, Cambridge University Press, 2006, p. 34.

30. Athenaios, *The Learned Banqueters*, LCL, 1927, 695a–b.

31. G. Vlastos, "Isonomia," *American Journal of Philology*, 54, 4, 1953, pp. 337–366.

32. See on this R. Sinclair, *Democracy and Participation in Athens*, Cambridge, Cambridge University Press, 1988, pp. 8–9.

33. Herodotus, *The Histories*, ii.80.

34. Thucydides, *The Peloponnesian War*, 6.39.

35. Thucydides, *The Peloponnesian War*, 2.35–46. See also P. Debnar, *Speaking the Same Language: Speech and Audience in Thucydides' Spartan Debates*. Ann Arbor, Mi, University of Michigan Press, 2002, pp. 2–5.

36. Xenophon, *Constitution of the Lacedaemonians*, LCL, 1925, 1.2.

37. See on this E. Millender, "Herodotus and Spartan Despotism," in A Powell and S. Hodkinson, eds., *Sparta*, p. 30.

38. Polybius, *The Histories*, 13.6.

39. See on this H. C. Mansfield, *Machiavelli's Virtue*, Chicago, Il, University of Chicago Press, 1996, pp. 89–90.

40. V. Metha, "Sparta in the Enlightenment," Dissertation Submitted to George Washington University, 2009, available at http://gradworks.umi.com/3338792.pdf, p. 121

41. G. W. F. Hegel, "Vorlesungen ueber die Philosophie der Geschichte," in *Saemtliche Werke*, Stuttgart, 1928, I, p. 335.

42. C. de Montesquieu, *The Spirit of the Laws*, Cambridge, Cambridge University Press, 1989 [1748], 5.3.44, 5.7.50, 7.2.96; G. B. de Mably, *Collection complete de l'Abbé de Mably*, Paris, Desbriere, 1794–1795, 4.21.

43. J. J. Rousseau, *Emile*, New York, NY, Basic Books, 1979, p. 119; see also Metha, "Sparta in the Enlightenment," pp. 180–183.

44. See G. Dart, *Rousseau, Robespierre and English Romanticism*, New York, NY, Cambridge University Press, p. 199.

45. See "From Thermopylae to Stalingrad: The Myth of Leonidas in German Historiography," in Powell and Hodkinson, *Sparta*, pp. 331–32.

46. Aristotle, *Politics*, 1269b15–19.

47. Aristotle, *Politics*, 2.8.1.

48. Plutarch, *Parallel Lives*, Alexander, LCL, 1932, 14.

49. See D. Dawson, *Cities of the Gods: Communist Utopias in Greek Thought*, New York, NY, Oxford University Press, 1992, pp. 130–145.

50. Plato, *The Republic*, LCL, 1930, 414.c.

51. *Republic*, 556 E.

52. Plutarch, Solon, 1.3.2.

53. Plutarch, *Parallel Lives*, Pericles, LCL, 1932, 37.2–5; Xenophon, *Hellenica*, LCL, 1918, 2.4.25.

54. See, for an attempt to determine the nature and limits of that ancestry, S. C. Humphreys, "Family Tombs and Tomb Cult

in Ancient Athens," *Journal of Hellenic Studies*, 100, January 1980, pp. 96–126.

3. The Proud Tower

1. *Judges*, 15.5.

2. See R. Drews, "Phoenicians, Carthage and the Spartan *Eunomia*," *The American Journal of Philology*, 100, 1, spring 1979, p. 49.

3. *Aristotle, Politics*, 1272b–1273a and Polybius, *The Histories*, 10.18.1 and 36.4.6. For what little is known about the Carthaginian Constitution see U. Kahrstedt, *Geschichte der Karthager*, Berlin, Weidemann, 1913, 2, p. 37.

4. Livy, *Roman History*, 1.30.

5. See E. Hildinger, *Swords Against the Senate: The Rise of the Roman Army*, Rome, Da Capo, 2002, p. 59.

6. Velleius Paterculus, *Compendium of Roman History*, LCL, 1924, 2.29.113; Caesar, *African War*, LCL, 1955, 35.4.

7. J. Bleicken, *Geschichte der Roemischen Republik*, Munich, Oldenbourg, 2004, p. 40.

8. J. Carcopino, *Het Dagelijks Leven in Het Oude Rome*, Utrecht, Prisma, 1961, pp. 118–131.

9. For a translation of the text, done by Prof. Stan Samuel of Wesleyan University, Texas, see http://www.kchanson.com/ancdocs/meso/hammurabi.html.

10. Ulpian in *The Digest of Justinian*, Philadelphia, Pa, University of Pennsylvania Press, 2009, vol. 4, 50.17.32.

11. Seneca, *Epistles*, LCL, 1917, vol. 1, Moral Letters to Lucillius, 47, *On Master and Slave*, 10.

12. Suetonius, *The Lives of the Caesars, LCL, 1914,* Caligula, 29, 30, 32.

13. See e.g. E. A. Eldredge, *A South African Kingdom: The Pursuit of Security in Nineteenth-Century Lesotho*, Cambridge, Cambridge University Press, 1993; J. Nyakatura, *Anatomy of an African Kingdom: A History of Bunyoro Kitara*, Garden, City, NJ, Anchor, 1973; J. J. Maquet, *The Premise of Inequality in Ruanda: A Study of Political Relations in a Central African Kingdom*, Oxford, Oxford University Press, 1962; M. Herskovits, *Dahomey, an Ancient African Kingdom*, Oxford, Augustin, 1938.

14. See, for the Hyksos, C. Booth, *The Hyksos Period in Egypt*, Risborough, Shire, 2005; for China under the Mongols J. D. Langlois, ed., *China under Mongol Rule*, Princeton, NJ, Princeton University Press, 1981; for the position of Japan's emperor, Emiko Ohnuki-Tierny, "The Emperor of Japan as Deity (Kami)," *Ethnology*, 30, 3, July 1991, pp.199–215.

15. See most recently A. Schomp, *Ancient Mesopotamia*, New York, NY, Watts, 2005.

16. N. Davies, *The Ancient Kingdoms of Mexico*, London, Penguin, 1981, pp. 188–196.

17. See Th. C. Patterson, *The Inca Empire*, Oxford, Berg, 1997.

18. J. F. Richard, *The Mughal Empire*, Cambridge, Cambridge University Press, 1996, pp. 253–281.

19. C. N. Reeves, *Akhenaten: Egypt's False Prophet*, London, Thames & Hudson, 2005.

20. *Analects*, 12.11.

21. *Analects*, 15.24.

22. *Analects*, 10.1–5; see also Anping Ching, *Confucius: A Life of Thought and Politics*, New Haven, Ct, Yale University Press, 2008, p. 177.

23. *Analects*, 2.19 and 8.9–10.

24. I. Robinet, *Taoism: Growth of a Religion*, Stanford, Ca, Stanford University Press, 1997 [1992, French], pp. 3–4.

25. Inside China: J. A. Rapp, *Daoism and Anarchism*, n.p, Continuum, 2012, chapter 1. Outside China: F. L. Bender, "Taoism and Western Anarchism," *Journal of Chinese Philosophy*, 10, 1, 2008, pp. 5–26, at http://onlinelibrary. wiley.com/doi/10.1111/j.1540-6253.1983.tb00271.x/pdf.

26. See A. Vervoorn, "Taoism, Legalism, and the Quest for Order in the Warring States," *Journal of Chinese Philosophy*, 8, 3, September 1981, 303–324.

27. See, for him, G. Scholem, *Sabbatai Sevi: The Mystical Messiah: 1626–1676*, London, Routledge 1973.

28. See K. Mannheim, "The End of Time and the Rise of Community," in J. Gager, ed., *Kingdom and Community: The Social World of Early Christianity*, Englewood Cliffs, NJ, Prentice-Hall, 1975, pp. 32–35.

29. See F. Hoveyda, "Social Justice in Early Islamic Society," in K. D. Irani and M. Silver, eds., *Social Justice in the Ancient World*, Westport, Ct, Greenwood, 1993, p. 109.

30. See, on the Arab conquest and the establishment of empire, G. R. Hawting, *The First Dynasty of Islam: The Umayyad Caliphate, A.D. 661–750*, London, Routledge, 1986.

31. M. Hasshim Kamali, *Freedom, Equality and Justice in Islam*, Cambridge, Islamic Texts Society, 2002, pp. 47–102; L.

Marlow, *Hierarchy and Egalitarianism in Islamic Thought*, Cambridge, Cambridge University Press, 1997, pp. 48–49.

32. *Esther* 4.5–5.3.

33. The illustration, taken from the *Chroniques de France*, is available at http://www.agefotostock.com/en/Stock-Images/ Rights-Managed/HET-1276131.

34. See M. van Creveld, *The Rise and Decline of the State*, Cambridge, Cambridge University Press, 1999, p. 41.

35. See, for example, A. M. Ramsay, "The Speed of the Roman Imperial Post," *Journal of Roman Studies*, 15, 1929, pp. 60–74.

36. See, for the history of the term, S. Morillo, "A 'Feudal' Mutation? Conceptual Tools and Historical Patterns in World History," *Journal of World History*, 14, 4, December 2003, pp. 531–536; also E. A. R. Brown, "The Tyranny of a Concept; Feudalism and Historians of Medieval Europe," *American Historical Review*, 79, 4, October 1974, pp. 1063–1088.

37. For feudalism as a particular relationship between the public and the private see van Creveld, *The Rise and Decline of the State*, pp. 49–52.

38. M. Grant, *The Fall of the Roman Empire*, New York, NY, Collier, 1990, pp. 42, 62.

39. Tacitus, *Germania*, LCL, 1914, especially 11–12.

40. Einhard and Notker the Stammerer, *The Life of Charlemagne*, Harmondsworth, Penguin, 1989 [829–836], p. 75.

41. *Six Books of the Commonwealth*, book 1, chapter 10, in J. H. Franklin, ed., *Bodin on Sovereignty*, Cambridge, Cambridge University Press, 1992, pp. 70–72.

42. L. S. Marcus, "Shakespeare's Comic Heroines, Elizabeth I, and the Political Uses of Androgyny," in M. B. Rose, ed., *Women in the Middle Ages and the Renaissance*, Syracuse, N.Y, Syracuse University Press, 1986, pp. 113–134.

43. S. Reynolds, *Kingdoms and Communities in Western Europe, 900–1300*, Oxford, Clarendon Press, 1997, p. 259.

44. A. Fox and J. Guy, *Reassessing the Henrician Age: Humanism, Politics and Reform 1500–1550*, Oxford, Blackwell, 1989, p. 15.

45. *Dieu et mon droit*: H. Southern and N. Harris Nicolas, *Retrospective Review*, London, Baldwin & Cradock, 1828, 2, p. 531.

46. See, on the origins and development of heraldry, J. Foster, *The Dictionary of Heraldry: Feudal Coats of Arms and Pedigrees*, New York, NY, Arch Cape, 1989 [1902], pp. xiii–xv.

47. For a short list of noble privileges see A. de Tocqueville, *The Ancien Regime and the French Revolution*, New York, NY, Collier, 1966 [1856], pp. 56–61.

48. *The Wealth of Nations*, Chicago, Il, Chicago University Press, 1976 [1776], p. 253.

49. See, for the Middle Ages, Reynolds, *Kingdoms and Communities in Western Europe*, pp. 67–78.

50. See, on the way Europe became split between east and west, J. H. Elliott, *Europe Divided, 1559–1598*, Oxford, Blackwell, 2000 [1968].

51. See e.g. D. Herlihy, "Three Patterns of Social Mobility in the Middle Ages," *Journal of Interdisciplinary History*, 3, 3, spring 1973, pp. 623–647; and A. Everit, "Social Mobility in Early

Modern England," *Past and Present*, 33, April 1966, pp. 56–73. Chapter 4.

4. Islands in the Sea

1. See the excellent article by A. Fuks, "Patterns and Types of Social Economic Revolution," in A. Fuks, *Social Conflict in Ancient Greece*, Jerusalem, Magnes, 1984. pp. 9–39.

2. A. Fuks, "Social Revolution in Greece in the Hellenistic Age," in Fuks, *Social Conflict in Ancient Greece*, p. 45.

3. Pausanias, *Description of Greece*, LCL, 1918, 7.169.

4. A. Fuks, "The Bellum Achaicum and Its Social Aspect," in Fuks, *SociaConflictiAncient Gr* 270 "Social Revolution in Dyme in 116–114 B.C," in Fuks, *Social Conflict in Ancient Greece*, pp. 282–288.

5. Seeitchell, "The Definition of Patres and Plebs: An End to the Struggle of the Orders," in K. A. Raaflaub, ed., *Social Struggles in Ancient Rome*, Oxford, Blackwell, 1986, pp. 128–167.

6. See on this subject Th. Urbainczyk, *Slave Revolts in Antiquity*, Berkeley, Ca, University of Califoa ress, 2004, pp. 1–2, 32–33; also K. Bradley, *Slavery and Rebellion in the Roman World*, London, Batsford, 1989, p. 81.

7. Very short lists of "Revolutions and Rebellions" as well as "Coup d'etats and Coup Attempts" are available at http://en.wikipedia.org/wiki/List_of_revolutions_and_rebellions as well as http://en.wikipedia.org/wiki/List_of_coups_d'etat_and_coup_attempts. See also M. van Creveld, ed., *The Encyclopedia of Revolutions and Revolutionaries*, Jerusalem, Jerusalem Publishing House, 1996.

8. There is a list of Caribbean slave-revolts in "Breaking-Free," Caribbean-Guide.info, at http://caribbean-guide.info/past.and.present/history/slave.rebellion/.

9. See E. P. Boardman, "Christian Influence upon the Ideology of the Taiping Rebellion," *Far Eastern Quarterly*, 10, 2, February 1951, pp. 115–124.

10. E.g. C. J. Mclain, *In Search of Equality: The Chinese Struggle Against Discrimination in Nineteenth-Century America*, Berkeley, Ca, University of California Press, 1994.

11. D. J. Treiman, "Equality and Inequality under Chinese Socialism," *American Journal of Sociology*, 113, 2, September 2007, pp. 415–445; C. Riskin and others, *China's Retreat from Equality*, New York, NY, Eastgate, 2001.

12. Matthew 19.24.

13. See on this J. Le Goff, *Medieval Civilization*, Oxford, Blackwell, 1988, pp. 299–304.

14. See R. H. Hilton, "Peasant Movements in England before 1381," *Economic History Review*, new series, 2, 2, 1949, pp. 117–136.

15. From Thomas Walsingham's *Historia Anglicana*, (ca. 1377–1392), quoted in P. H. Freedman, *Images of the Medieval Peasant*, Stanford, Ca, Stanford University Press, 1999, p. 60.

16. See the classic account by F. Engels, *The Peasant War in Germany*, International Publications, n.p. 2000 [1850].

17. A summary of the articles is available at http://en.wikipedia.org/wiki/Twelve_Articles.

18. M. Luther, "Secular Authorlty. To Whar Extent It Should be Obeyed," in *Martin Luther*, J. Dillenberger, ed., New York, NY, Anchor, 1961, 2, p. 328.

19. "Against the Robbing and Murdering Bands of Peasants" [German], in O. Clemens, ed., *Luthers Werke*, Berlin, de Gruyter, 1966, 3, p. 69.

20. There is a list (in German) of such revolts at http://de. wikipedia.org/wiki/Liste_von_Bauernaufst%C3%A4nden.

21. See H. J. Goertz, *The Anabaptists*, London, Routledge, 1996, pp. 114–116.

22. See, for this entire episode, L. H. Zuck, "Anabaptism; Abortive Counter-Revolt within the Reformation," *Church History*, 26, 3, September 1957, pp. 211–226.

23. *Letter to the Galileans*, 3.27.28.

24. M. R. Salzman, *The Making of a Christian Aristocracy*, Cambridge, Ma, Harvard University Press, 2002, especially pp. 218–219.

25. W. Klatt, "Caste, Class and Communism in Kerala," *Asian Affairs*, 3, 3, October 1972, pp. 275–287.

26. M. Wijayaratna, *Buddhist Monastic Life*, Cambridge, Cambridge University Press, 1990, pp. 143–152.

27. P. Van der Veer, "Taming the Ascetic: Devotionalism in a Hindu Monastic Order," *Man*, 22, 4, December 1987, pp. 680–695.

28. Wijayaratna, *Buddhist Monastic Life*, pp. 15–16.

29. H. Welch, "Dharma Scrolls and the Succession of Abbots in Chinese Monasteries," *T'oung Pao*, Second Series, Leiden, Brill, 1963, pp. 101–102, 109.

30. S. Dutt, *Early Buddhist Monasticism*, New Delhi, Mushiram Manoharlal, 1996 [1924], pp. 113–145.

31. H. D. Evers, "Monastic 'Landlordism' in Ceylon: A Traditional System in a Modern Setting," *The Journal of Asian Studies*, 28, 4, August 1969, pp. 685–692.

32. *Numbers* 6.1–21.

33. See, for a general account, J. Murphy-O'Connor, "The Essenes in Palestine," *The Biblical Archaeologist*, 40, 3, September 1977, pp. 100–124.

34. Ph. Rousseau, "Christian Asceticism and the Early Monks," in I. Hazlett, eds., *Early Christianity; Origins and Evolution to AD 600*, London, SPCK, 1991, p. 118.

35. Cannon 4, quoted in J. G. Davies, *The Early Christian Church*, London, Weidenfeld & Nicolson, 1966, p. 241.

36. "The Works of Monks," in R. J. Deferrari, ed., *Saint Augustine*, Washington DC, Catholic University Press, 1981, pp 331–396.

37. An English translation of the Rule is available at https://web.archive.org/web/*/http://rule.kansasmonks.org/.

38. *The Rule of the Master*, C. Philippi, trans., Kalamazoo, Mi, Cistercian Publications, 1977, pp. 122–123.

39. *The Rule of the Master*, p. 153.

40. *The Rule of the Master*, p. 251.

41. *The Rule of the Franciscan Order*, Article 5, at http://www.fordham.edu/halsall/source/stfran-rule.html.

42. "Private property is absolutely forbidden to regulars." H. J. Schroeder, ed., *The Doctrinal Decrees and Cannons of the Council of Trent*, n.p, 1842, chapter 2, pp. 218–219.

43. S. Evangelisti, "Monastic Poverty and Material Culture in Early Modern Italian Convents," *The Historical Journal*, 47, 1, 2004, p. 3.

44. W. R. Ward, *Christianity under the Ancien Régime, 1648–1789*, Cambridge, Cambridge University Press, 1999, pp. 38, 196.

45. Plato, *Republic*, 373e. See also H. Syse, "Plato: The Necessity of War, the Quest for Peace," *Journal of Military Ethics*, 1, 1, 2002, pp. 36–44.

46. Plato, *The Laws*, LCL, 1926, 1.629D.

47. English text of Euhemerus (much abbreviated from the original book) in Diodorus, *The Library of History*, LCL, 1939, 5.41–6.6.1; of Iamboulus, in *ibid*, 2.55–60.

48. Zhang Longxi, "Utopian Vision, East and West," *Utopian Studies*, 13, 1, 2002, pp. 1–20.

49. The English text is available at http://afe.easia.columbia. edu/ps/china/taoqian_peachblossom.pdf.

50. See, in general, F. Graus, "Social Utopias in the Middle Ages," *Past and Present*, 38, December 1969, pp. 3–19.

51. Ovid, *Metamorphoses*, 1.89–112, available at http://www. poetryintranslation.com/PITBR/Latin/Metamorph.htm#anchor_Toc64105456.

52. S. J. G. Hall, "Chillingham Cattle; Dominance and Affinities and Access to Supplementary Food," *Ethology*, 71, 3, January-December 1986, pp. 201–215.

53. E.g. *Die Chronik der Boehmen des Cosmas von Prague*, B. Berholtz, ed., Berlin, Weidemann, 1923, ii, pp. 7–9; Huon de Bordeaux, *Esclarmonde, Clarisse et Florent*, M. Schweigel, ed., Marburg, Universitäts-Druckbücherei, 1898, p. 151, verses 6054–6081.

54. From F. Rabelais, *Gargantua and Pantagruel* (1532). I have used the English translation in M. L. Berneri, *Journey through Utopia*, New York, NY, Schocken, 1950, p. 139.

55. Th. More, *Utopia*, Harmondsworth, Middlesex, Penguin, 1975 [1516], pp. 82, 128.

56. More, *Utopia*, p. 101.

57. For the English text, see http://www.gutenberg.org/files/ 2816/2816-h/2816-h.htm.

58. For the English text see http://www.archive.org/stream/ christianopolis00andr/christianopolis00andr_djvu.txt.

5. Liberal Equality

1. For a long list of such works see Erasmus, *The Education of a Christian Prince*, New York, NY, Norton, 1964, L. K. Born, trans, pp. 44–132.

2. Bodin, *Six Books of the Commonwealth*, pp. 26–51. See also van Creveld, *The Rise and Decline of the State*, pp. 176–177.

3. van Creveld, *The Rise and Decline of the State*, p. 86; J. A. Lynn, *The Wars of Louis XIV, 1667–1714*, London, Longman, 1999, pp. 105–159.

4. Th. Hobbes, *Leviathan*, J. Plamenatz. Ed., London, Collins, 1952 [1651], pp. 204–205.

5. J. Mitchell, "Hobbes and the Equality of All under One," *Political Theory*, 21, 1, February 1993, p. 3.

6. See on this P. King, *The Ideology of Order; A Comparative Analysis of Jean Bodin and Thomas Hobbes*, London, Routledge, 1999.

7. Hobbes, *Leviathan*, p. 141.

8. Hobbes, *Leviathan*, pp. 176–177.

9. J. Locke, *The Second Treatise on Government*, in *idem*, *Two Treatises on Government*, P. Laslett, ed., Cambridge, Cambridge University Press, 1968, pp. 301–348.

10. C. D. Clark, *English Society 1688–1832*, Cambridge University Press, 1985, pp 90, 409.

11. See R. Berthoff, "Peasants and Artisans, Puritans and Republicans: Personal Liberty and Communal Equality in American History," *American Historical Review*, 69, 3, December 1982, pp. 579–598.

12. C. Kintzler, "Le droit à l'instruction," in *Recherches sur Diderot et l'Encyclopédie*, 8, 1990, p. 96.C. Coutel, "Concordet et le question de l'égalite," *Dialogue*, 37, 1998, pp. 681–692; A. Adamovsky, "Aristotle, Diderot, Liberalism, and the Idea of 'Middle Class'," *History of Political Thought*, 26, 2, 2005, pp. 304–310.

13. G. Michaud, "Une nouvelle conception de la vie monastique en France dans la seconde moitié du dix-huitième siècle," in Voltaire Foundation, ed., *Studies on Voltaire and the Eighteenth Century*, 2000, 2, pp. 59–72.

14. De Waal, *Our Inner Ape*, pp.201–219.

15. J. J. Rousseau, *Discourse on the Origins of Inequality*, Oxford, Oxford University Press, 1994 [1750], part 1, pp. 45, 47, 53.

16. Rousseau, *Discourse on the Origins of Inequality*, part 2, pp 55, 78, 80.

17. Rousseau, *The Social Contract*, p. 61.

18. J. L. Talmon, *The Origins of Totalitarian Democracy*, London, Mercury, 1961, pp. 38–49.

19. See on this Locke, *Two Treatises of Government*, pp. 380–381; J. W. Gough, *John Locke's Political Philosophy*, Oxford, Clarendon, 1973, pp. 76–77.

20. Rousseau, *The Social Contract*, pp. 90–96.

21. Thucydides, *The Peloponnesian War*, 2,.40.2.

22. Rousseau, *The Social Contract*, p. 141.

23. See Reynolds, *Kingdoms and Communities*, pp. 22, 284–285.

24. See, on the English connection, P. T. Maniacs, "Montesquieu and the Eighteenth-Century Vision of the State," *History of Political Thought*, 2, 2, June 1981, pp. 313–347.

25. C. de Montesquieu, *The Spirit of the Laws*, London, Hafner, 1949 [1748], part 1 pp. 42–45, 111.

26. Montesquieu, *The Spirit of the Laws*, pp. 42–43.

27. Montesquieu, *The Spirit of the Laws*, pp. 42–43.

28. *1. Samuel* 12.18.

29. J. le Maistre, *Considerations on France*, Cambridge, Cambridge University Press, 1994 [1797], pp. 29–33.

30. C. Shammas, "A New Look at the Long Term Trends in Wealth Inequality," *American Historical Review*, 98, 2, April 1993, p. 427.

31. G. W. Domhoff, "Wealth, Income and Power," 2012(?), at http://www2.ucsc.edu/whorulesamerica/power/wealth.html.

32. Most famously by C. A. Beard, *An Economic Interpretation of the Constitution of the United States*, The Lawbook Exchange, 2011 [1913].

33. Letter to de Marbois, 1817, in S. K. Padover, ed., *Thomas Jefferson on Democracy*, New York, NY, Mentor, 1946, p. 29.

34. The English text is available at www2.warwick.ac.uk/fac/arts/history/undergraduate/modules/hi153new/timetable/wk2/declaration.

35. Rousseau quoted in S. Loomis, *Paris in the Terror: June 1793–July 1794*, Philadelphia, Pa, Lippincott, 1964, p. 276.

36. See A. De Dijn, "Balancing the Constitution; Bicameralism in Post-Revolutionary France, 1814–1830," *European Review of History*, 12, 2, 2005, pp. 249–268.

37. "Germany, a Winter's Tale," 1844.

38. See F. O. Ramirez and J. Boli, "The Political Construction of Mass Schooling: European Origins and Worldwide Institutionalization," Sociology of Education, 60, 1, January 1987, pp. 2–17.

39. See on this R. Liberles, "The Historical Content of Dohm's Treatise on the Jews," in Friedrich Naumann-Stiftung, ed., *Das deutsche Judentum und der Liberalismus—German Jewry and Liberalism*, Koenigswinter, Comdok, 1986, pp. 44–69; also G. L. Mosse, *Germans and Jews*, New York, NY, Grosset & Dunlap, 1970, pp. 39–42.

40. See C. W. Dohm, *Ueber die burgerliche Verbesserung der Juden*, Berlin, Nicolai, 1781, especially vol. 1, pp. 26–28, 39, 119, 130.

41. See on this K. Marx, "On the Jewish Question." [1843], at http://www.marxists.org/archive/marx/works/1844/jewi sh-question/index.htm; H. Bender, *Der Kampf um die Judenemanzipation in Deutschland in Spiegel der Flugschriften*, Jena, Frommann, 1939, p. 69; also P. Pulzer, *The Rise of Political Anti-Semitism* in *Germany and Austria*, London, Halban, 1988, pp. 221–222.

42. See F. Kobler, *Napoleon and the Jews*, New York, NY, Schocken, 1976.

43. L. Waldman, "Employment Discrimination against Jews in the United States—1955," *Jewish Social Studies*, 18, 3, July 1956, pp. 208–216.

44. N. Kareem Nittle, "Are U.S. Universities Discriminating Against Asian Students?," About.com, 25.4.1011, at http://racerelations.about.com/b/2011/04/25/are-u-s-universities-discriminating-against-asian-students.htm.

45. Text available at http://www.un.org/en/universal-declaration-human-rights/index.html.

6. Socialist Equality

1. Online etymology dictionary, at http://www.etymonline.com/index.php?search=Socialism.

2. See Berneri, *A Journey through Utopia*, pp. 143–173.

3. See C. Beecher, *Fourier: The Visionary and his World*, Berkeley, Ca, University of California, 1986.

4. See S. F. Delano, *Brook Farm*, Cambridge, Ma, Belknap, 2004.

5. See J. Harrison, *Owen and the Owenites in Britain and America*, London, Francis & Taylor, 2009.

6. See M. M. Cosgell, "The Family in Utopia," *Journal of Family Studies*, 25, 4, October 2000, pp. 491–503.

7. See S. Klaw, *Without Sin: The Life and Death of the Oneida Community*, London, Penguin, 1993.

8. See on him L. Foster, *John Humphrey Noyes and the Origins of the Oneida Community*, Urbana, Il, University of Illinois Press, 2001.

9. D. Young, *America's Spiritual Utopias*, Westport, Ct, Praeger, 2008, pp. 127–128.

10. See R. Fike, ed, *Voices from The Farm: Adventures in Community Living*, Tn, Book Publishing Company, 1998.

11. M. Altman, *Thanks for Coming*, New York, NY, Harper, 2009, pp. 253–262.

12. M. Kaffman, "Divorce in the Kibbutz," *Family Process*, 32, 1, March 1993, pp. 117–133.

13. See U. Leviathan and others, eds., *Crisis in the Kibbutz*, Westport, Ct, Greenwood, Praeger, 1998.

14. See G. Mars, "Hidden Hierarchies in Israeli Kibbutzim," in J. G. Flanagan, ed., *Rules, Decisions and Inequality in Egalitarian Societies*, London, Gower, 1989, pp. 100–105.

15. See E. Bernstein, *The Preconditions of Socialism*, Cambridge, Cambridge University Press, 1993 [1899]; and V. I. Lenin, "What Is to Be Done?", 1902.

16. The text is available at http://www.anu.edu.au/polsci/marx/classics/manifesto.html.

17. T. Clark and A. Dilnot, "Long-Term Trends in British Taxation and Spending," *IFS Briefing Notes*, 2002, p. 7.

18. See C. D Norma, *The Nationalization of British Industry, 1945–1951*, London, HMSO, 1975.

19. A. B. Atkinson, "The Distribution of Income in the UK and OECD Countries During the Twentieth Century," *Oxford Review of Economic Policy*, 15, 4, 1999, pp. 56–75.

20. N. Gilbert, *Capitalism and the Welfare State*, New Haven, Ct, Yale University Press, 1981, pp. 52–54; M. Wright, "Public Expenditure in Britain: The Crisis of Control," *Public Administration*, 55, 2, April 2007, table I p. 146.

21. See S. J. Pope, "Aquinas on Almsgiving, Justice and Charity," *The Heythrop Journal*, 32, 2, April 1991, pp. 167–191.

22. E. Bellamy, *Looking Backward*, Harmondsworth, Penguin, 1987 [1888].

23. See A. Lipow, *Authoritarian Socialism in America*, Berkeley, Ca, University of California Press, 1982, pp. 96–118.

24. See R. Conquest, *Harvest of Sorrow: Soviet Collectivization and the Terror-Famine*, Oxford, Oxford University Press, 1987.

25. P. Kennedy, *The Rise and Fall of the Great Powers*, New York, NY, Vintage, 1987, table 21 p. 243.

26. For some figures, see W. S. Dunn, *The Soviet Economy and the Red Army*, New York, NY, Praeger, 1995, p. 43.

27. See G. O'Leary and E Watson, "The Role of the People's Commune in Rural Development in China," *Pacific Affairs*, 55, 4, winter 1982, pp. 593–612.

28. On the way the system worked at the day-to-day level, see H. Smith, *The Russians*, London, Sphere, 1973, pp. 41–73; also, for an earlier period, S. Fitzpatrick, *Everyday Stalinism*, Oxford, Oxford University Press, 1999, pp. 95–105.

29. J. Niederhut, *Die Reisekader*, Leipzig, Evangelische Verlagsanstalt, 2005.

30. M. Voslenksy, *Nomenklatura: The Soviet Ruling Class*, New York, NY, Doubleday, 1984, pp. 189, 191.

31. Smith, *The Russians*, pp. 117–119.

32. See the graphic account in Yu Hua, *Chronicle of a Blood Merchant*, New York, NY, Anchor, 2004.

33. See on those vacations S. S. Montefiore, *Stalin*, New York, NY, Vintage, 2003, pp. 71–81.

34. F. W. Deakin, *The Embattled Mountain*, Oxford, Oxford University Press, 1971; and F. MacLean, "Tito," *Foreign, Affairs*, 28, 2, 1940, pp. 231–246.

35. M, Djilas, *Tito*, London, Weidenfeld & Nicolson, 1981, pp. 110.

36. R. Payne, *Mao Tse Tung*, New York, NY, Weybright & Talley, 1950, p. 167.

37. Li Ziushi, *The Private Life of Chairman Mao*, New York, NY, Random, 1994, pp. x, 18–29.

38. H. von Karasek, "Honecker's Nische," *Der Spiegel*, 14.8.1995.

39. See, for China, C. Riskin and A. Rahman Khan, *Inequality and Poverty in China in the Age of Globalization*, Oxford, Oxford University Press, 2001; for the West, M. Kaus, *The End of Equality*, New York, NY, Basic Books, 1995; and, more recently, W. W. Goldsmith and E. J. Blakely, *Separate Societies*, Philadelphia, Pa, Temple University press, 2010.

7. The Rise and Fall of Racism

1. Virgil, *Aeneid*, LCL, 1916, .852.

2. B. Lewis, *Race and Slavery in the Middle East*, New York, NY, Oxford University Press, 1990, pp. 44–45, 53.

3. D. Ayalon, "The Harem: A Major Source of Islam's Military Might," in B. Z. Kedar and R.J. Zwi Werblowsky, eds., *Sacred Space: Shrine, City, Land*, London, Macmillan, 1998, p 146.

4. H. Camen, "Una Crica della Conciencia en la Edad de Oro den España," *Bulletin Hispanique*, 88, 3–4, 1986, pp. 321–356.

5. See for the debate L. Hanke, *Aristotle and the American Indians*, Indianapolis, In, Indiana University Press, 1970 [1959].

6. W. D. Jordan, *The White Man's Burden*, New York, NY, Oxford University Press, 1974, pp. 50–54.

7. *Deuteronomy* 26.5.

8. See, in general, G. Schemann, *Gobineau*, New York, NY, Arno, 1979.

9. J. R. Llobera, *The Making of Totalitarian Thought*, New York, NY, Berg, 2003, p. 68.

10. Chu Y. Huang and others, "Genetic Relationship of Populations in China," *Protocol of the National Academy of Science*,

95, 1998, pp. 11763–11778; M. Scielstad and others, "A View of Modern Human Origins from Y Chromosome Microsatellite Variation," *Gene Research*, 9, 1999, pp. 558–567.

11. A. de Gobineau, *Essai sur l'inegalité des races humaines*, n.p, n.d [1853–1855], *passim*.

12. Th. Jefferson, *Notes on the State of Virginia*, 1781, Query 14, http://avalon.law.yale.edu/18th_century/jeffvir.asp.

13. G. Jahoda, *Images of Savages: Ancient Roots of Modern Prejudice in Western Culture*, London, Routledge, 1999, p. 83.

14. See on this G. L. Mosse, *Towards the Final Solution: A History of European Racism*, London, Dent, 1978, pp. 175–176.

15. See M. Cornwall, *The Undermining of Austria-Hungary: The Battle for Hearts and Minds*, Macmillan, Basingstoke, 2000.

16. Th. Herzl, *Old-New Land*, n.p. CreateSpace, 2011 [1902].

17. A. de Gobineau, *Essai sur l'inegalité des races humaines*, n.p, n.d., 1853–1855, i, 220–222, v, 16.

18. E. Haeckel, *Natürliche Schöpfungsgeschichte*, Berlin, Reimer, 1868, p. 519.

19. Quoted in H. Bahr, "Ernst Haeckel," *Der Antisemitismus*, Berlin, Fischer, 1894, p. 69.

20. Quoted in C. Koonz, *The Nazi Conscience*, Cambridge, Ma, Belknap, 2003, p. 2. I wish to thank Prof. Koonz for her book which provided the inspiration for the present section.

21. Quoted in Koonz, *The Nazi Conscience*, p. 163.

22. J. G., Herder, *Werke*, E. Kuehnemann, ed., Stuttgart, Union deutsche Verlagsgesellschafr, 1889, vol. 1 pp. 401–403.

23. See for the evolution of these concepts, R. Stackelberg, *Idealism Debased: From Volkisch Ideology to National Socialism*, Kent, OH, Kent University Press, 1981.

24. Quoted in Koonz, *The Nazi Conscience*, p. 138.

25. Quoted in Koonz, *The Nazi Conscience*, p. 69.

26. See J. Leeb, ed., *Wir waren Hitlers Elitschüler*, Hamburg, Rasch & Röhring, 1998.

27. See for Lebensborn G. Lilienthal, *Der "Lebensborn e.V": ein Instrument nationalsozialistischer Rassenpolitik*, Stuttgart, Fischer, 1985.

28. L. Wijler, *Herinneringen*, Herzliya, private edition, 1975, p. 105.

29. W. L. Shirer, *Berlin Diary*, Baltimore, Md, Johns Hopkins University Press, 2002 [1941], p. 327, entry for 27.6.1940.

30. Koonz, *The Nazi Conscience*, pp. 171, 185, 197.

31. J. Lewy, "A Biological Threat or a Social Disease? Alcoholism and Drug Addiction in Nazi Germany," *Journal of European Studies*, 39, 3, 2009, pp. 371–385.

32. See E. A. Carlson, *The Unfit; A History of a Bad Idea*, Cold Stream, NY, Cold Stream Harbor Laboratory Press, 2001.

33. See W. Darré, *Neuadel aus Blut und Boden*, Munich, Lehman, 1930, pp.130–132; and M. Burleigh, *Death and Deliverance: 'Euthansia' in Germany, 1900–1945*, London, Taylor & Francis, 1995.

34. Koonz, *The Nazi Conscience*, p. 46.

35. The Statement is available at http://unesdoc.unesco.org/images/0012/001269/126969eb.pdf.

36. Quoted in J Torpey, "Making Whole What Has Been Smashed," *Journal of Modern History*, 73, 2001, p. 344.

37. See D. Roediger, "Gook: The Short History of an American-ism," *Monthly Review*, March 1992, p. 1.

38. D. Schoetz, "Georgia High School to Celebrate First Ever Integrated Prom," ABC News, 10.4.2007, available at http://abcnews.go.com/US/story?id=3026519&page=1.

39. See on this H. Adam, "The Politics of Ethnic Identity: Com-paring South Africa," "Journal of Ethnic Studies", 18, 3, 1995. pp. 457–475.

40. J. Seekings, "The Continuing Salience of Race: Discrimina-tion and Diversity in South Africa," *Journal of Contemporary African Studies*, 26, 1, 2008, 1–25.

41. See on this K. Prewitt, "Race in the 2000 Census: A Turn-ing Point," in J. Perlmann and M. Walters, eds., *The New Race Question: How the Census Counts Multiracial Individu-als*, New York, NY, Russell Sage, 2002, pp. 354–361.

42. J. Hope, "Brits Believe Mixed-Race People Are 'The Most At-tractive and Successful'," Mail Online, 15.4.2010, http://www.dailymail.co.uk/sciencetech/article-1265949/Mixed-race-people-attractive-finds-British-study.html.

43. R. Lynn, "The Intelligence of American Jews," *Elsevier*, 36, 1, 2004, pp. 201–206. Zhang Ping, "Israel and the Jew-ish People in Chinese Cyberspace since 2002," in M. Avrum Ehrlich, ed., *The Jewish–Chinese Nexus: A Meeting of Civiliza-tions*. London, Routledge, 2008, pp. 103–115.

44. See E. Bleich, "Where Do Moslems Stand on Ethno-Racial Hierarchies in England and France?" *Patterns of Prejudice*,

43, 3–4, 2009, pp. 379–400; and F. A. Gerges, "Islam and Muslims in the Mind of America," *Annals of the American Academy of Political and Social Science*, 58, 1, July 2003, pp. 73–89.

45. M. Currat and M. Exofficier, "Modern Humans Did Not Mix with Neanderthals during Their Range Expansion into Europe," *PLOS Biology*, 2, 12, 2004, at `http://www.plosbio logy.org/article/info%3Adoi%2F10.1371%2Fjournal.pbio .0020421`.

46. R. J. Herrnstein and C. Murray, *The Bell Curve*, New York, NY, Basic Books, 1994, especially pp. 269–316.

8. Minorities Into Majorities

1. Radcliffe-Brown, *The Andaman Islanders*, p. 177.

2. See on this M. van Creveld, *The Privileged Sex*, Createspace.

3. Ph. Longman, "The Return of Patriarchy," *Foreign Policy*, 153, March–April 2006, pp. 56–60, 62–65.

4. Zuckerman, *The Social Life of Monkeys and Apes*, pp. 235–237; Goodall, *In the Shadow of Man*, pp. 112–113, 124, 127–128, 173–179.

5. de Waal, *Our Inner Ape*, pp. 10, 17, 113–114, 117.

6. See on this "'So We All Became Mothers:' New Roles for Men in Recent Utopian Fiction," *Science-Fiction Studies*, 12, 1985, pp. 156–183.

7. G. Slomp, "Hobbes and the Equality of Women," *Political Studies*, 42, 1992, pp. 441–452.

8. Quoted in Carroll and Noble, *The Free and the Unfree*, London, Penguin, 1992, p. 15.

9. See on him F. du Plessix Gray, *At Home with the Marquis de Sade: A Life*, New York, NY, Simon and Schuster, 1998.

10. *Analytical Review*, iii, February 1790, in *The Works*, New York, NY, New York University Press, 1989, 1, p. 92; iv, June 1789, ibid, 1, p. 119.

11. See on this S. Gutman, *The Kinder, Gentler Military; Can America's Gender-Neutral Armed Force Still Win Wars?* New York, N.Y., Scribner.

12. *A Vindication of the Rights of Men*, in *Works*, 5, pp. 41, 44, 45, 78.

13. L. Goldstein, "Early Feminist Themes in French Utopian Socialism: The St.-Simonians and Fourier," *Journal of the History of Ideas*, 43, 1982, 1, p. 1.

14. On women during the age of total war see M. van Creveld, *Men, Women and War*, London, Cassell, 2004, pp. 126–48.

15. V. I. Lenin, *Married Women in the Labor Force*, New York, N.Y., Harvester, 1966 [1921].

16. On Krupskaya see Alena Heitligner, *Women and State Socialism*, London, MacMillan, 1979, pp. 42, 108; on Kollontai B. R. Rosenthal, "Love on the Tractor: Women in the Russian Revolution and After," in R. Bridenthal and C. Koonz, eds., *Becoming Visible; Women in European History*, Boston, Ma, Houghton Mifflin, 1977, pp. 377, 388.

17. Goldman, *Women, the State and Revolution*, pp. 65, 119–122.

18. Joel C. Moses, *The Politics of Women and Work in the Soviet Union and the United States*, Berkeley, Ca., Institute of Inter-

national Studies, 1983, pp. 32–36; Heitinger, *Women and State Socialism*, p. 158.

19. B. Friedan, *The Feminine Mystique*, New York, NY, Dell, 1983 [1963], pp. 17–18, 194–195, 197, 266, 275–276, 298–299; S. de Beauvoir, *The Second Sex*, New York, NY, Knopf, 1971 [1959], p. 760.

20. L. F. Fitzgerald and others, "Why Didn't She Just Report Him?" *Social Issues*, 51, 1, spring 1995, pp. 117–138.

21. See O. Aviezer and A. Sagi, "Balancing the Family and the Collective in Raising Children: Why Communal Sleeping in the *Kibbutzim* Was Bound to End," *Family Process*, 41, 3, Sept. 2002, pp. 435–454.

22. See on this, in great detail, S. Gordon, *Prisoners of Men's Dreams: Striking out for a New Feminine Future*, Boston, Ma, Little Brown, 1991.

23. See on this van Creveld, *Men, Women and War*, pp. 149–160.

24. C. W. Hoge, "Mental Health Problems ... After Returning from Deployment to Iraq or Afghanistan," *Journal of the American Medical Association*, 295, 2006, pp. 1023–1032; R. Kimerling and others, "Military-Related Sexual Trauma Among Veterans Health Administration Patients Returning from Afghanistan and Iraq," *American Journal of Public Health*, 100, 8, August 2010, pp. 1409–1412.

25. F. Trovato and N. M. Lalu, "Narrowing Sex Differentials in Life-Expectancy in the Industrialized World: Early 1970s to Early 1990s," *Biodemography and Social Biology*, 43, 1–2, 1996, pp. 20–37; F. Meslé, "Differences in Life Expectancy

between the Sexes," *Symposium Proceedings*, Max Planck Insitute, ed., 2004.

26. Suetonius, *The Twelve Caesars*, Caesar, 22.

27. R. Lutmann, "The Pink Triangle: The Persecution of Homosexual Males in Concentration Camps in Nazi Germany," *Journal of Homosexuality*, 6, 1/2, fall/winter 1980/81, p. 141–160.

28. Th. Pastorello, "1981; la fin du délit d'homosexualite," Historie@suite101, 8.12.2010, at http://thierry-pastorello .suite101.fr/1981--la-fin-du-delit-dhomosexualite-a22036.

29. C. Gane-McCalla, "Sesame Street Announces Bert and Ernie Are Not Gay," *NewsOne*, 12.8.2011, at http://newsone.com/ entertainment/casey-gane-mccalla/sesame-street-ernie -and-bert-gay/.

30. See M. E. Kabay, "A Security Analysis of' 'Don't Ask, Don't Tell'," *Network World*, 3.11.2010, http://www.networkworld. com/newsletters/sec/2010/110110sec2.html.

31. The relevant passages are available at http://www.spaceandm otion.com/kama-sutra-homosexuality.htm.

32. *The Times of India*, 2.7.2009, http://timesofindia.india times.com/photo.cms?msid=4728348.

33. J. W. Coleman, *The New Buddhism*, Oxford, Oxford University Press 2002, p. 146.

34. M. O. Lao and M. L. Ng, "Homosexuality in Chinese Culture," *Culture, Medicine and Psychiatry*, 13, 4, 1989, pp. 465–488.

35. T. B. Neilands and others, "Assessment of Stigma towards Homosexuality in China," *Archives of Sexual Behavior*, 37, 5, 2008, pp. 838–844.

36. Ayalon, "The Harem," pp. 145–146.

37. Mission Islam, Islam and Homosexuality, at http://www.missionislam.com/knowledge/homosexuality.htm.

38. See e.g. G.E. Hekma, "Queers and Muslims: The Dutch Case," 2008 (?), at http://digitalcommons.macalester.edu/cgi/viewcontent.cgi?article=1490&context=macintl.

39. "Facts about Gay Rights", Dosomething.org, at http://www.dosomething.org/tipsandtools/11-facts-about-gay-rights.

40. P.A.P Blog, "Statistics on the Discrimination of Homosexuals," 2010 (?), at https://web.archive.org/web/*/http://filipspagnoli.wordpress.com/stats-on-human-rights/statistics-on-discrimination/statistics-on-discrimination-of-homosexuals.

41. D. Sadeh, "Tel Aviv Leads Best Gay City Contest," Yenetnews.com, 8.1.2020, at http://www.ynetnews.com/articles/0,7340,L-4172501,00.html.

42. *Leviticus* 21.16–22.

43. See M. Foucault, *Madness and Civilization: A History of Insanity in the Age of Reason*, New York, N.Y, New American Library, 1965; also the same author's *Discipline and Punish: The Birth of the Prison*, London Penguin, 1979.

44. See on this, in great detail, N. Kittrie, *The Right to be Different: Deviance and Enforced Therapy*, Harmondsworth, Penguin, 1974.

45. See on these treatments E. Shorter, *A History of Psychiatry*, New York, NY, J. Wiley, 1997, pp. 209–215, 210–219, 220–224, 225–229.

46. U.S. Department of Labor, "Bureau of Labor Statistics-Social Workers," 2003, available at www.bls.gov/oco/ocos060/htm; and Psychiatric News, 36, 5, 2.3.2001, available at http://pn.psychiatryonline.org/cgi/content/full/36/5/3.

47. See J. Hechinger and D. Golden, "When Special Education Schools Go Easy on Students," *Wall Street Journal*, 25.6.2006.

48. Aspen Education Group, *Your Child and ADHD*, n.p, n.d, p. 14, at https://web.archive.org/web/*/http://www.4-adhd.com/youchildandadhd.pdf.

49. Figure from G. E. Zuriff, "Extra Examination Time for Students with Learning Disabilities," *Applied Measurement in Education*, 13, 1, 2000, p. 99.

50. L. E. Booren and B. K. Hood, "Learning Disabilities in Graduate School," *Observer*, March 2007, at https://web.archive.org/web/*/http://www.psychologicalscience.org/observer/getArticle.cfm?id=2146.

51. See Ichisada Miyazaki and C. Schirokauer, *China's Examination Hell*, New Haven, Ct, Yale University Press, 1981.

52. "Does a Restaurant Have the Unrestricted Right to Refuse Service to Specific Patrons?" LegalMatch, at http://www.legalmatch.com/law-library/article/restaurants-right-to-refuse-service.html.

53. See E. Schuman, "El Al's Legendary Security Measures Set Industry Standards," *Israel Insider*, 3.10.2001, at https://web.

archive.org/web/*/http://www.israelinsider.com/channels/security/articles/sec_0108.htm.

54. "Will Profiling Make a Difference?" *New York Times*, 4.1.2010.

55. Quoted in "Airport Security Measures Draw Accusations of 'Profiling'," 6.1.2010, FoxNews.com, at http://www.foxnews.com/politics/2010/01/06/airport-security-measures-draw-accusations-profiling/.

56. See on the Eta H. H. Smythe, "The Eta: A Marginal Japanese Caste," *American Journal of Sociology*, 58, 2, September 1952, pp. 194–196.

57. R J. Foley, "Denied Jobs, Blacks in Iowa Test a New Bias Theory," Yahoo! News, 17.2.20102, at http://news.yahoo.com/denied-jobs-blacks-iowa-test-bias-theory-080416196.html.

58. There is an excellent article on the Human Sex Ratio at http://en.wikipedia.org/wiki/Human_sex_ratio.

59. See J. Blake, "Are Whites Racially Oppressed?" Cnn.Com, 4.3.2011, at http://edition.cnn.com/2010/US/12/21/white.persecution/.

9. Brave New World

1. See, for what has happened to some of the researchers in question See S. Pinker, *The Blank Slate: The Modern Denial of Human Nature*, New York, NY, Penguin, 2003, Kindle ed., locs. 2422–2771.

2. Available at http://www.merriam-webster.com/dictionary /affirmative%20action and at http://dictionary.refere nce.com/browse/reverse+discrimination.

3. The text, dated 4 June 1965, is available at http://www.lbjlib.utexas.edu/johnson/archives.hom/speeches.hom/650604.asp.

4. The speech is available at http://www.h-net.org/~hst306/documents/great.html.

5. H. von Borch, *The Unfinished Society*, London, Sidgwick and Jackson, 1963, p. 14.

6. See, for the elderly and blue collar: A. Sum and others, "The Great Recession of 2008–2009 and the Accompanying Blue Collar Depression," Boston, Ma, Northwestern University, 2010, at http://www.massworkforce.com/documents/TheGreatRecessionof2008-2009andtheAccompanyingBlueCollarDepression.pdf. For males: D. Cauchon, "Women Gain as Men Lose," *USA Today*, 2.9.2009.

7. "Sweden Set to Scrap University Gender Quotas," *The Local*, 12.10.2012, at https://web.archive.org/web/*/http://www.thelocal.se/24330/20100112/

8. See M. Kintz, "German Members of the Bundestag—Recruitment and Legislative Career," 2008, at http://homepages.wmich.edu/~m0kintz/IASGPPaper2008-2.pdf.

9. "Affirming a Divide," *The Economist*, 28.1.2012, pp. 39–41.

10. C. Gradin, "Race and Income Distribution: Evidence from the U.S., Brazil and South Africa," 2010. 7 table 1, at http://www.ecineq.org/milano/WP/ECINEQ2010-179.pdf.

11. C. Hoff Sommers, *The War Against Boys*, New York, NY, Simon & Schuster, 2001.

12. See, for a brief summary, K. Lovett, "Bleeding Sweden: The Fall into Ideological Depravity," *Voice for Men*, 27.11.2007, at http://www.avoiceformen.com/feminism/feminist-govern ance-feminism/bleeding-sweden-the-fall-into-ideolog ical-depravity/.

13. See on this H. Smith, *Men on Strike: Why Men Are Boycotting Marriage, Fatherhood and the American Dream*, New York, NY, Encounter, 2013.

14. C. Donnelly, "'Fundamental Inequality' at the Heart of Domestic Violence, Say Experts," *NewEurope*, 2.3.2012, at http://www.neurope.eu/article/fundamental-inequality-heart-domestic-violence-say-experts.

15. "Pregnant Women Risk Murder in U.S., Report Finds," 23.2.2005, at http://www.jrrobertssecurity.com/securit y-news/security-crime-news0043.htm; J. Levine, "No. 1 Cause of Death in Pregnant Women: Murder," WeBMD Medical News, 21.12.2004, at http://www. webmd.com/baby/news/20010320/number-1-cause-of-death -in-pregnant-women-murder; "Domestic Violence Homicides," *Domestic Violence Resources*, at https://web.archive.org/web/*/http://www.dvrc-or. org/domestic/violence/resources/C61/.

16. "Bestiality and Sweden," *Conservapedia*, at http://www.conse rvapedia.com/Bestiality_and_Sweden; M. Blake, "Sweden Set to Ban Bestiality," Mailonline, 31.10.2014, at http:// www.dailymail.co.uk/news/article-2341789/Sweden-set-

ENDNOTES: CHAPTER 9   351

ban-bestiality-scrapping-legal-loophole-legal-animal
-did-suffer.html.

17. Suetonius, *The Twelve Caesars*, Nero, 35.

18. *Historia Naturalis*, LCL, 1971, 12.84.

19. See e.g. Join Together Staff, "Nida Reports Good Results from Computer Counseling," *National Drug Abuse Summit*, 29.4.2008, at http://www.drugfree.org/join-together/ad diction/nida-reports-good-results.

20. C. Chung, "'Westernizing' Surgery on the Rise," *Sunday Morning Herald*, 3.2.20102.

21. C. Hakim, *Erotic Capital*, New York NY, Basic Books, 2011.

22. A. C. Little and B. C. Jones, "Attraction Independent of Detection Suggests Special Mechanisms for Symmetry Preferences in Human Face Perception," *Proceedings of the Royal Society of Biological Sciences*, 366, 12, June 2011, pp. 943–947.

23. T. Blackwell, "Demand for Plastic Surgery Growing among Canada's Youth," *National Post*, 10.9.2011.

24. "Cosmetic Surgery, Denmark," at http://www.arslanbeyosb .org/711-cosmetic-surgery-denmark-cosmetic-surgery-o ptions-denmark-cosmetic-surgery-india.html.

25. I. Oakeshott, "Plastic Surgery on the NHS?" *MailOnline*, 3.2.2012, at http://www.dailymail.co.uk/health/article-189310/Plastic-surgery-NHS.html.

26. C. Begley, "Parents May Face Jail over Compulsory Drug Orders," National Alliance against Mandated Mental Health Screening and Psychiatric Drugging of Children, 2002, at http://www.ritalindeath.com/begley.htm.

27. "Gay Party Guests Face Hormonal Treatment," *The Guardian*, 30.11.2005.

28. See "Chemical Castration," at http://en.wikipedia.org/wiki/Chemical_castration.

29. "What is Prenatal Screening?", Lucille Packard Children's Hospital at Stanford, 2012, at http://www.lpch.org/Diseas eHealthInfo/HealthLibrary/pregnant/tests.html.

30. See A. Goetz, *Die Aktion T4*, Berlin, Hentrich, 1987, p. 14.

31. Bloomberg, "Ritalin Use Rise Concerns Conservative Leader Cameron," 30.7.2007, at http://psychwatch.blogspot.com/2007/07/ritalin-use-in-uk-concerns-conservative.html.

32. *Republic* 460c.

33. Huxley, *Brave New World*, pp. 174–175.

34. S. Tomasula, "Genetic Art and the Aesthetics of Biology," *Leonardo*, 35, 2, April 2002, pp. 137–144.

35. M. Adams, "Dead Cows Carcasses 'Resurrected' to Produce Beef," *Natural News.com*, 16.8.2010, at http://www.naturalnews.com/029487_cloned_beef_DNA.html.

36. I. Sample, "What's Wrong with Cloning Humans?" *The Guardian*, 22.4.2009.

37. Available at http://gutenberg.net.au/ebooks02/0200221.txt.

10. Death and Beyond

1. *Ecclesiastics*, 19–20.

2. See, in General, S. Oosterwijk, "Of Corpses, Constables, and Kings: The Danse Macabre in Late Medieval and Renaissance

Culture," *Journal of the British Archaeological Association*, 157, 2004, pp. 61–90.

3. See, for its history, "The Conciergerie," at http://www.ca-paris.justice.fr/index.php?rubrique=11018&ssrubrique=11076&article=15446.

4. 21.1.

5. N. Yalman, "The Ascetic Buddhist Monks of Ceylon," *Ethnology*, 1, 3, July 1962, pp. 315–328.

6. See M. van Creveld, *The Culture of War*, New York, NY, Ballantine, 2008.

7. Thucydides, *The Peloponnesian War*, 5.66.3–4.

8. Polybius, *The Histories*, 6, 38, 2.

9. See, for the way it is created, M. van Creveld, *Fighting Power*, Westport, Ct, Greenwood, 1983.

10. Message 051601Z, 5.6.1998.

11. See, for this phenomenon, "menstrual synchrony," at http://www.menstruation.com.au/periodpages/menstrualsynchrony.html.

12. Act 4 Scene 3.

13. See on them G. DeVoto, "The Theban Sacred Band," *Ancient World*, 23, 2, 1992, pp. 3–19.

14. See B. Bertosa, "Sacrifice and Homosexuality in the Spartan Army," *War and Society*, 28, 2, October 2009, especially p. 10.

15. 1. *Samuel* 18.7.

16. A. Tchapla, "Characterization of Embalming Materials of a Mummy of the Ptolemaic Era," *Journal of Separation Science*, 27, 3, February 2004, pp. 217–234.

17. Ibid.

18. Li Zhisui, *The Private Life of Chairman Mao*, pp. 19–20.

19. Cui Yan, "Comment Again on Religious Nature of Burial Custom 'Huang Keng' in Taiyuan in the Tang Dynasty," *Journal of Luoyang University*, 3, 2003, article abstract.

20. R. Decaroli, *Haunting the Buddha*, Oxford, Oxford University Press, 2004, pp. 136–140; G. Schopen, "Ritual Rights and Bones of Contention," *Journal of Indian Philosophy*, 22, 1, 1994, pp. 39–41.

21. "The Dead on Display," n.p, n.d, at http://www.templiers.net/etudes/index.php?page=chapelle-du-creach.

22. "Pierres tombales de la chapelle du Creac'h," n.p, n.d. at http://www.templiers.net/etudes/index.php?page=chapelle-du-creach.

23. J. Janssen, *Growing Up in Ancient Egypt*, n.p, Golden House, 2007, pp. 103.

24. *1. Samuel* 31.11.

25. See sagas quoted in S. Strualson, *Heimskringla: The Lives of the Norse Kings*, New York, NY, Dover, 1990, pp. 229, 236.

26. Thucydides, *The Peloponnesian War*, 2.34.1–7.

27. Diodorus, *The Library of History*, 8.27.2.

28. Tacitus, *Annales*, LCL, 1914, 7.

29. J. Cambry, *Rapports sur les scupltures, presenté a l'Administration Centrale du Department de la Seine*, Paris, Quimper, 1799, p. 66.

30. See, for these developments, G. L. Mosse, *Fallen Soldiers*, New York, NY, Oxford University Press, 1991, pp. 44–46.

31. J. Viegas, "Did Neanderthals Believe in an Afterlife?" Discovery.com, 20.4.2011, at http://news.discovery.com/history/neanderthal-burial-ground-afterlife-110420.html.

32. *Odyssey*, Book 11.

33. S. Spyridakis "Zeus Is Dead: Euhemerus and Crete," *The Classical Journal*, 63, 8, May 1968, pp. 338–339.

34. Suetonius, *The Twelve Caesars*, Vespasian, 23.

35. T. Emil Homerin, "Echoes of a Thirsty Owl: Death and Afterlife in Pre-Islamic Arabic Poetry," *Journal of Near Eastern Studies*, 44, 3, July 1985, pp. 168–169.

36. See F. Norbeck, *Religion in Primitive Society*, New York, NY, Harper & Row, 1961, p. 76.

37. See H. Donoghue, *From Asgard to Valhalla*, London, Tauris, 2009, pp. 68–62.

38. S. D'Auria and others, *Mummies and Magic: The Funerary Arts of Ancient Egypt.* Museum of Fine Arts, Boston, Ma, 1989, p. 6.

39. See, for the journey through the afterlife, J. H. Taylor, ed., *Ancient Egyptian Book of the Dead*, British Museum Press, London, 2010, pp. 209–212.

40. *Ezekiel* 37.1–14.

41. *Job*, 13–19; R. E. Murphy, "Death and the Afterlife in the Wisdom Literature," in J. Neusner and others, eds., *Judaism in Late Antiquity*, Leiden, Brill, 1995, 3, p. 105.

42. J. J. Collins, "The Afterlife in Apocalyptic Literature," in Neusner and others, eds., *Judaism in Late Antiquity*, p. 121–122.

43. *The Jewish War*, LCL, 1930, 3.8.5.

44. C. B. Kastner, *Understanding the Afterlife*, Jerusalem, Devora, 2007, p. 49; J. Bin Nun, "Why Isn't the Afterlife Mentioned in the Old Testament?"at http://tora.us.fm/tnk1/tora/ohb.html.

45. *Mark* 12.24–27; *Mat.* 22.29–32; *Luke* 20.34–38.

46. See, for a short summary, "Christian Beliefs about the Afterlife," at http://www.religionfacts.com/christianity/beliefs/afterlife.htm.

47. P. Avery, trans., *The Rubbaiyat of Omar Khayyam*, Harmondsworth, Penguin, 1984.

48. 2.21.

49. 2.21.

11. The Promise and the Threat

1. Hobbes, *Leviathan*, p. 144.

2. Ancient Iran: F. Mehr, "Social Justice in Ancient Iran," in Irani and Silver, eds., *Social Justice*, p. 80. Pre-Islamic Society: Hoveyda, "Social Justice in Early Islamic Society," p. 117.

3. See J. Laird, "Hobbes on Aristotle's 'Politics,'" *Proceedings of the Aristotelian Society*, 43, 1942, pp. 1–20.

4. See M. Lind, *The Next American Nation: The New National-ism and the Fourth American Revolution*, New York, N.Y, Free Press, 1995, pp. 181–216.

5. C. Wright Mills, *The Power Elite*, Oxford, Oxford University Press, 1956, p. 20.

6. T. Gitlin, "C. Wright Mills, Free Radical," at http://www.uni-muenster.de/PeaCon/dgs-mills/mills-texte/GitlinMills.htm.

7. Henry Carter Adams: quoted in D. Ross, *The Origins of American Social Science*, Cambridge, Cambridge University Press, p. 152.

8. Speech to the Conservative Party Conference, 10.10.1975, at http://www.margaretthatcher.org/document/102777.

9. See H. H. Robbins and F. Deak, "The Family Property Rights of Illegitimate Children: A Comparative Study," *Columbia Law Review*, 30, 3, March 1930, pp. 308–329.